Chinese DeMYSTiFieD

Hard stuff made easy

Claudia Ross, Ph.D.

New York Chicago San Francisco Lisbon London Madrid Mexico City
Milan New Delhi San Juan Seoul Singapore Sydney Toronto

CONTENTS

PREFACE

Welcome to *Chinese Demystified*!

You are probably reading this book because you are studying Mandarin Chinese or are planning to do so. One look at a page in a Chinese textbook or grammar is enough to let you know that Chinese is very different from English. Chinese is written with Chinese characters, not with an alphabet, and even when a romanization system is used to indicate the pronunciation of Mandarin Chinese, it includes features that do not occur in English, such as the consonant cluster zh and tone marks over vowels (for example, ā, á, ǎ, à). But Mandarin Chinese is also easier to learn in some ways than languages that are more familiar to English speakers, such as Spanish and French. Its grammar is very regular, and it does not use inflections or declensions to vary the form of nouns, pronouns, verbs, adjectives, and so on. This book will help you take the mystery out of Mandarin and make it easier for you to learn.

Chinese Demystified is intended to supplement the regular textbook in your first few years of Mandarin Chinese language study, and to help you review the basic structures and functions of Mandarin before you move on to more advanced language study. Its examples and exercises are presented in Simplified characters, Traditional characters, and pinyin (the most widely used romanization system), so they will be accessible to you no matter what textbook you are using. This book draws from a relatively small number of basic Chinese words commonly introduced in textbooks for beginners. But if you haven't yet learned a word that is used in an example here, don't worry. English translations are provided for all examples, so you will always be able to follow along.

The goal of *Chinese Demystified* is to help you understand the basic structure of Mandarin and perform common language functions, such as asking questions, making comparisons, and describing people, places, and things. The exercises and quizzes in each chapter will help you practice Mandarin structure and functions and verify your understanding and mastery.

How to Use This Book

Each chapter in *Chinese Demystified* contains simple explanations of grammatical constructions, illustrated with many examples and practice opportunities. When you approach a new construction, first read the explanation and then study the examples until you understand the grammatical pattern that they illustrate. Once you see how the pattern works, complete the Oral and Written Practice exercises. These exercises are the heart of the chapter, and they will help you learn the language. Don't be shy about using the Oral Practice exercises to rehearse saying phrases and sentences aloud. If you have the chance to travel to China for study, work, or pleasure, you will need to be able to speak Chinese—and you can't speak without practice. You can also find excellent pronunciation guides on the Internet, including pronunciation practice activities. Of course, if you're studying Chinese in a classroom setting, you can follow your instructor's pronunciation or use the audio materials that accompany your textbook.

At the end of each chapter is a ten-question quiz that reviews the concepts you learned in the chapter. This is an "open book" quiz. You should try to achieve

A NOTE ON THE PRESENTATION OF CHINESE IN THIS BOOK

Mandarin words, phrases, and sentences are presented in this order: Simplified characters, Traditional characters, pinyin. When both Simplified and Traditional characters are shown on the same line, a centerline dot separates them.

老师的书 · 老師的書　lǎoshī de shū　*the teacher's book*

你写字写得很好看。· 你寫字寫得很好看。
Nǐ xiě zì xiě de hěn hǎokàn.
You write characters nicely.

Traditional sentences often follow their Simplified counterparts on a separate line.

我学中文。
我學中文。
Wǒ xué Zhōngwén.
I am studying Chinese.

a score of 80 percent on the quiz before moving on to the next chapter. The book ends with a final exam, which consists of 100 questions that cover all the language concepts in the book. The final exam is a "closed book" test. A good score is 75 percent or higher.

If you are just beginning your study of Mandarin, read Chapter 1 for an overview of the language, then work through the chapters in the order in which each topic is covered in your language textbook. For example, when you begin to study numbers, read Chapter 4 of *Chinese Demystified* and do all of the practice exercises and the quiz. You can check your answers in the Answer Key at the back of the book, but don't check until you have completed an entire exercise or quiz. Circle your mistakes, then read the chapter again so that you understand what you did wrong, and work through the exercises again.

If you are using this book to review what you have already learned, you can start in any chapter. The material in each chapter is presented in order of complexity, but the chapters are relatively independent of each other.

Chinese takes longer for English speakers to learn than most other languages, in large part because Chinese has a character-based writing system, but also because English and Chinese share almost no vocabulary in common. Studying Chinese is an adventure, and great discoveries await you along the way. Don't be discouraged by the time it takes to reach familiar milestones, such as reading a map, a menu, or a newspaper printed in Chinese characters. Just keep the following Chinese proverb in mind, and enjoy your journey.

不怕慢，就怕站！
Bù pà màn, jiù pà zhàn!
Don't be afraid of going slow. Just be afraid of standing still.

Good luck in your studies!

ACKNOWLEDGMENTS

三人行，必有我师焉。
When three people walk together, one of them will always be my teacher.
　—THE ANALECTS OF CONFUCIUS

I wish to thank the many people who have helped me in the preparation of this book.

I thank my first Chinese language teachers at the University of Michigan, James Dew, Jing-heng Ma, and Hilda Tao.

I thank my colleagues in Chinese at the College of the Holy Cross, from whom I am always learning new things about Chinese.

I thank the students in the Chinese program at the College of the Holy Cross for reading and providing feedback on chapters of this manuscript.

Finally, I thank my family for their suggestions, feedback, and patience.

PART ONE

THE BASICS OF MANDARIN CHINESE

CHAPTER 1

Mandarin Chinese Pronunciation and Characters

In this chapter, you will learn about:

Chinese Around the World
Spoken Mandarin
The Structure of the Mandarin Syllable
Tones
Consonants
Vowels
Traditional and Simplified Chinese Characters
Strokes

Chinese Around the World

Mandarin Chinese is the official language of mainland China (the People's Republic of China) and Taiwan (the Republic of China). In mainland China, it is called 普通话·普通話 pǔtōnghuà *the common language.* In Taiwan, it is called 国语·國語 guóyǔ *the national language.* Mandarin is the most widely spoken of all the Chinese dialects, which include Shanghainese (a Wu dialect), Cantonese (a Yue dialect), Taiwanese (a Min dialect), Hakka (a Kejia dialect), and several others. The combined population of mainland China and Taiwan is over 1.3 billion, or one-fifth of the world's population; that is, one-fifth of the world's people speak some dialect of Chinese as their native language.

In addition to mainland China and Taiwan, Chinese is spoken in Singapore (whose official languages are English, Mandarin Chinese, Malay, and Tamil), as well as in Hong Kong and Macau (former foreign colonies now officially reunited with mainland China).

Spoken Mandarin

Mandarin is spoken over a wide area of China, and the pronunciation of Mandarin varies by region. Even the pronunciation of standard Mandarin varies, depending on whether the standard is Putonghua or Guoyu. In standard Putonghua, the pronunciation is based on that in modern-day Beijing, though without some of the features that characterize the local Beijing dialect. In standard Guoyu, the pronunciation is based on that in modern-day Taipei. Putonghua and Guoyu differ in a number of features that you can explore as you continue your study of Mandarin in your home country and in the Chinese-speaking world.

The Structure of the Mandarin Syllable

Mandarin is written with Chinese characters, but the characters do not indicate pronunciation. When it is necessary to indicate pronunciation (for example, in textbooks and dictionaries), a transcription system is used. The most widely used transcription system is pinyin (formally known as "Hanyu Pinyin"), whose literal meaning is *piece together the sounds.* Although pinyin is written with the same alphabet used in English, some of the letters in the pinyin system are pronounced differently than they are in English. We will discuss these differences later in this chapter.

Mandarin pronunciation is traditionally described in terms of a syllable divided into two parts, an *initial consonant* and a *final.* A syllable need not have an initial consonant, but it always has a final. The final always has at least one vowel—and it may have two or three vowels in a row, or one or two vowels and a final consonant. If a syllable does not have an initial consonant and the first vowel of the final is i, i is written as y in pinyin. If a syllable does not have an initial consonant and the first vowel of the final is u, u is written as w.

A syllable has a contour tone, or it may have a neutral tone. This chapter will help you learn to read pinyin and correctly pronounce the consonants, vowels, and tones of the Mandarin syllable.

Tones

Mandarin tones are typically referred to as first tone, second tone, third tone, fourth tone, and neutral tone. The various tones may be indicated with a number after the syllable (1, 2, 3, 4, or—for neutral tone—5), or with a tone mark written above the vowel. A difference in tone is as significant as a difference in a consonant or vowel in determining meaning. In the following chart, note how the meaning of the syllable *ma* changes in Mandarin, depending on the tone.

	Tone Indicated with a Number	Tone Indicated with a Tone Mark	Meaning
1st tone	ma1	mā	*mom*
2nd tone	ma2	má	*hemp*
3rd tone	ma3	mǎ	*horse*
4th tone	ma4	mà	*to scold*
Neutral tone	ma5	ma (no tone mark)	marker of yes-no questions

The 1st, 2nd, 3rd, and 4th tones are contour tones. Contour tones are characterized by a *pitch contour*—a specific shape or direction of the pitch of the voice—across an entire syllable. The contours of the Mandarin tones are illustrated in the following chart. The vertical gray bar on the left is a reference for how high your pitch is when you begin the tone. The horizontal or slanted line shows the direction that your voice moves as you pronounce the syllable.

1st tone   mā   The pitch starts high and stays high → over the course of the syllable.

2nd tone   má   The pitch starts low and rises ↗ over the course of the syllable.

3rd tone   mǎ   3rd tone has three different contours:

   • Falling-rising contour. If a syllable with 3rd tone occurs at the end of a phrase, sentence, or clause, the tone is pronounced as a falling-rising tone ↘↗.

   • Rising contour. If a syllable with 3rd tone occurs before another syllable with 3rd tone, it is pronounced as if it were 2nd tone (a rising tone) ↗.

   • Low and level. If a syllable with 3rd tone occurs before any other syllable, it is pronounced as a level tone with low pitch.

4th tone   mà   The pitch starts high and falls ↘ over the course of the syllable.

A syllable in neutral tone does not have a pitch contour. Instead, its pitch is determined by the preceding tone. If it follows a syllable with 1st or 2nd tone, it is slightly lower than the ending pitch of the 1st or 2nd tone. If it follows a syllable with 3rd tone, it is slightly higher than the ending pitch of the 3rd tone. If it follows a syllable with 4th tone, it is slightly lower than the ending pitch of the 4th tone.

Although English is not a tone language, it uses pitch contour, called *intonation*, to indicate certain types of meaning. Some of the common intonation patterns in English are identical to the tone contours of Mandarin.

1st tone   The "singing" intonation: When you hold a note steady (try singing *la*), you are using the contour of 1st tone →.

2nd tone | The "surprise" intonation: When you ask a question or express surprise in English, you are using the contour of 2nd tone: *What!?* ↗ In English, we also use rising intonation when reciting a list. All items in the list except the last one are recited using rising intonation: *red* ↗, *yellow* ↗, *green* ↗, *blue* ↗, *and white* ↘. The last item in a list is recited with falling intonation ↘, comparable to 4th tone in Mandarin—see below.

3rd tone | The low version of the 3rd tone is a level tone in low pitch. In English, we often use low pitch to express impatience or give a bored response to a question.

4th tone | The "angry" intonation: In English, we use this intonation to express anger, as in the forceful use of the word *No!* ↘ We also use falling intonation for the last item of a recited list—see 2nd tone, above.

Oral Practice

Read the following syllables aloud, focusing on the contour of the tone.

1. pēn
2. sū
3. lái
4. tóu
5. dú

6. mǎ
7. hǎo
8. fàng
9. mò
10. bìng

Written Practice 1-1

Rewrite the following syllables, placing tone marks above the vowel in each.

1. bu4 _____
2. qing3 _____
3. mang2 _____
4. shi4 _____
5. chu1 _____

Consonants

Mandarin has 21 consonants that can occur at the beginning of a syllable. They are written in pinyin as follows.

b p m f d t n l g k h j q x zh ch sh r z c s

Mandarin consonants are traditionally recited in this order, each followed by a specific vowel.

bo po mo fo de te ne le ge ke he ji qi xi
zhi chi shi ri zi ci si

For pronunciation of Mandarin vowels, see the next section.

Only three consonants can occur at the end of a syllable: the consonants n and ng (as in English *sing* and *rang*) and—in Beijing—the suffix r.

The r suffix is an optional sound. In written form, it occurs at the end of a syllable, but in speech, it replaces the vowel or consonant that would otherwise follow the main vowel of the syllable. For example, kǒudài *pocket* is pronounced kǒudàr, fèn *a portion/share of something* is pronounced fèr, xiǎohái *child* is pronounced xiǎohár, and diànyǐng *movie* is pronounced diànyǐr.

Most consonant letters in pinyin are pronounced the way they are in English. Following are the consonants that are pronounced differently.

h   Pronounced farther back in the throat than it is in English, and often with more friction than English *h*.

zh   Pronounced like the *j* in *jam* or the name *Joe*. It is always pronounced with the lips "pursed," that is, rounded and pushed forward as if you were blowing out a candle.

r   In English, *r* is pronounced with lips that are rounded and moving. Say the words *reed, red, roll,* and *rule* and feel how your lips move as you say the *r*.

    In Mandarin, the lips do not move when pronouncing *r*. To say *r* correctly, position your lips to say the English word *red*, then say the word *red* without moving your lips. Try it again without adding the *d*. If you are doing it correctly, you will be pronouncing the consonant *r* in the syllable *re*. Note that your lips are "pursed" the way they are when you say *zh*.

z   Pronounced as *d* + *z*, like the *ds* in *fads.* This combination occurs only at the end of a syllable or word in English; it occurs at the beginning of a syllable in Mandarin.

c   Pronounced as *t* + *s*, like the *ts* in *cats,* This combination occurs only at the end of a syllable or word in English; it occurs at the beginning of a syllable in Mandarin.

j   Pronounced like the *j* in *jeep,* but with your tongue close to the roof of your mouth and with your lips in a broad smile.

q   Pronounced like the *ch* in **cheese,** but with your tongue close to the roof of your mouth and with your lips in a broad smile.

x   Pronounced like the *sh* in **sheep,** but with your tongue close to the roof of your mouth and with your lips in a broad smile.

Vowels

The Mandarin syllable final consists of a single vowel, a combination of vowels, or a combination of one or more vowels and a final consonant (either *n* or *ng*). These finals are represented in pinyin as follows.

6 simple finals	a e i o u ü
13 compound finals	ai ao ei ia iao ie iou (iu) ou ua uai üe uei (ui) uo
16 nasal finals	
8 front nasals	an en ian in uan üan uen (un) ün
8 back nasals	ang eng iang ing iong ong uang ueng
1 retroflex final	er

    Pinyin uses the letters a, e, i, o, u, and ü to represent all of the vowel sounds of Mandarin. The letters a and ü are pronounced the same wherever they occur in a syllable, but the pronunciation of e, i, o, and u depends on the other consonants and vowels in the syllable. A pronunciation guide for Mandarin vowels follows.

GENERAL RULES FOR WRITING VOWEL COMBINATIONS IN PINYIN

If a syllable begins with i, i is written in pinyin as yi.

i → yi	ie → ye	iang → yang
ia → ya	iou → you	ing → ying
iao → yao	in → yin	iong → yong

If a syllable begins with u, u is written in pinyin as w.

u → wu	uei → wei	uang → wang
ua → wa	uo → wo	ueng → weng
uai → wai	uen → wen	

If a syllable begins with ü, ü is written in pinyin as yu.

ü → yu	üan → yuan
üe → yue	ün → yun

If the vowel combination uei is preceded by a consonant, it is written ui.

guei → gui
duei → dui

If the vowel combination iou is preceded by a consonant, it is written iu.

jiou → jiu	niou → niu
liou → liu	

GUIDE TO PRONOUNCING MANDARIN VOWELS

a   Pronounced like the vowels in *hot*, *ma*, and *shop*.

ü   A high, front, rounded vowel—"high" and "front" because your tongue is high and forward in your mouth, and "rounded" because your lips are rounded. The sound *ü* does not occur in English, but it does occur in French and other languages. To pronounce it, say *ee* as in *cheese* and note the position of your lips. They should be relatively close together and form a smile. Your tongue should be high and flat against the roof of your mouth. Now, say *ee* again and, without moving your tongue, slowly round your lips as if to say *oo* as in *fool*. If you succeeded in keeping your tongue high and flat against the roof of your mouth while you round your lips, then you have succeeded in pronouncing ü.

e, ye, yue	(e alone, or after ü, y, yu, ju, qu, or xu) Pronounced like the *e* in *get*.
e	(after any consonant except y, without a following consonant or vowel) Pronounced low and back in the mouth, similar to *ou* in *could*.
en	Pronounced like the *en* in *chicken*.
eng	Pronounced like the *ung* in *lung* and *sung*.
ei	Pronounced like the *ay* in *way*.
i	(after j, q, or x) Pronounced like the *ee* in *cheese*. Your lips should be spread as in a smile, and your tongue should be high and flat against the roof of your mouth.
	(after z, c, or s) Not actually a vowel sound at all. To pronounce it correctly, simply continue the *s* or *z* sound from the preceding consonant. For the pronunciation of z and c, see above.
	(after zh, ch, sh, or r) Pronounced like r. In Mandarin, *r* is pronounced with no movement of the lips.
ian	Pronounced *yen*.
o	(in the syllables bo, po, mo, fo, uo, and wo) Pronounced *awe*. In this syllable, o is a spelling variant of uo, which is spelled o if it follows b, p, m, or f. It is spelled wo if it is not preceded by a consonant.
ou	Pronounced *owe*, like the vowel in *go* and *row*.
ong	Pronounced like the *oon* in *soon*, but with *ng* at the end instead of *n*.
u	(after j, q, or x) Pronounced like ü.
	(after any other consonant) Pronounced like the *oo* in *too*.
ui, wei	Pronounced like the *ay* in *way*. If the vowel combination uei is preceded by a consonant, it is written ui. If it is not preceded by a consonant, it is written wei.
uo, wo	Pronounced like the *wa* in *war*. When *uo* is not preceded by a consonant, it is written as wo.

Oral Practice

Read the following syllables aloud.

wán	wǎng	wèn
wǒ	wài	wéi
zǔ	zàng	zuò
zǒu	yìng	yòng
yī	yuàn	yùn
bǎ	bèi	bó
bái	pái	péi
zhuō	zhǔn	jūn
chú	qù	qī
jué	chī	zì

Traditional and Simplified Chinese Characters

Chinese characters are the basic units of reading and writing Chinese and have a history of more than 3,000 years. Some Chinese dictionaries include more than 40,000 Chinese characters, though most of these characters are not commonly used in contemporary writing. In mainland China, basic literacy is defined as the mastery of 1,500 to 2,000 characters. You need to know about 3,000 characters to read a newspaper, and college-educated adults in China can generally read and write 5,000 or more characters.

Some characters occur in a traditional, complex form, as well as in a simplified form. For example, the traditional form of the character for *country* is written 國, and the simplified form is written 国. Mainland China has officially adopted the simplified form of characters; in Taiwan, the traditional form of characters is the official form. Hence, mainland China is generally described as using simplified characters and Taiwan is generally described as using traditional characters. However, most characters have only one form, so most of the characters used in mainland China and in Taiwan are the same.

In this book, where simplified and traditional characters are given together, they are separated by a dot, with the simplified form first, for example, 国 · 國 guó *country.*

Strokes

Chinese characters are composed of *strokes.* The simplest character, 一 *one,* is written with a single stroke. The character for *ten,* 十, is written with two strokes. A small number of characters have more than 30 strokes each, although most have 14 or fewer. Simplified characters, as the name suggests, have fewer strokes than the corresponding traditional characters. For example, the character for *dragon* is written with five strokes in its simplified form (龙) and 16 strokes in its traditional form (龍).

STROKE ORDER

Strokes are written in a specific order and in a specific direction. Most beginning textbooks provide information about the number of strokes and the order and direction of strokes for each new character. There are several important reasons to pay attention to this information about strokes and stroke order.

- The most efficient way to learn a character is to write it exactly the same way every time. There is evidence that *stroke order* is stored in your brain as part of your knowledge of a character. If you write the same character in different ways, you make it harder for your brain to memorize the character.

- Characters are organized in Chinese dictionaries by their number of strokes. If you do not know how to count the strokes of a character according to Chinese conventions, you will not be able to use a dictionary to look up unfamiliar characters.

- Characters are organized in electronic dictionaries by stroke *and* stroke order. Some electronic dictionaries enable you to look up a character by writing the character on the computer screen with your mouse or other input device. To use this kind of electronic dictionary, you must be able to identify the strokes of a new character and write them in the correct order.

- In Chinese culture, characters are not only a tool for expressing information—they are a form of art. If they are written incorrectly, they are not pleasing to the eye. The appearance of one's handwriting is not an important issue for most Americans, but for Chinese, handwriting is very important and reflects one's education, intelligence, and skill. You should make a good impression by writing your characters according to the rules.

THE RADICAL

Strokes are the basic building blocks of Chinese characters. Strokes are organized into units, and recognizing these units will help you learn and remember Chinese characters.

The first unit of a character to identify is the *radical*. A radical is the part of the character that is used to categorize it in a Chinese dictionary. For traditional characters, there are 214 radicals. For simplified characters, there are 189 radicals. You should consult the radical index of a Chinese dictionary to become familiar with the radicals of Chinese characters.

Radicals sometimes provide information about the meaning of the character. For example, the *mouth* radical (口) usually indicates that the character has something to do with speaking. It is a part of the characters 问·問 *to ask a question* and 吗·嗎 (sentence-final marker of yes-no questions). A variation of the water radical 水 (氵) is part of the characters for 海 *ocean* and 湖 *lake.*

Most radicals are located in a predictable position within the character. The variation of the water radical that occurs in the characters for *ocean* and *lake* is always located on the left side of the character. As you can see, the mouth radical occurs on the left when a character has a left-to-right orientation, but it may occur on the bottom when a character has a top-to-bottom orientation. Sometimes, the character is a radical all by itself. For example, 口 *mouth* and 水 *water* are distinct characters.

A few common radicals occur on the right. Examples include 阝, which comprises the right side of the character 都 dōu *all,* and 寸 cùn, which comprises the right side of the character 对·對 duì *correct.*

RECURRING PARTS IN CHARACTERS

Once you have identified the radical in a Chinese character, you should look for other recurring parts. Many characters consist of sequences of strokes that recur in many other characters. Identifying the recurring parts makes it much simpler to memorize new characters. Note the recurring parts in the following groups of characters: 很 腿 跟, 是 提, 早 掉 朝. Recurring parts sometimes provide cues to pronunciation. For example, in simplified characters, 让 ràng and 上 shàng rhyme with each other, and 很 hěn and 跟 gēn rhyme in both character sets. However, 腿 tuǐ does not rhyme with 很 hěn and 跟 gēn, even though it shares a recurring part with them.

THE BASIC RULES OF STROKES AND STROKE ORDER

When writing characters, observe the following basic rules.

1. All characters in a block of text are written as if they are filling the space of equal-sized squares. No matter how many strokes a character has, each character is written so that it fills the space of one of the squares. Even punctuation takes up a square. When Chinese children are learning to write, they use paper with printed squares in order to help them write well-proportioned characters.

她	是	学	生	。

2. A horizontal stroke is written before a vertical stroke.

一	十

3. Characters are generally written from top to bottom and from left to right.

`	亠	二	丰	主

4. Boxes have three strokes. The first stroke is a downward vertical stroke. The second stroke is the upper righthand corner. (The top and right side of a box are always written as a single corner stroke.) The third stroke is the bottom stroke and closes the box.

丨	冂	口

5. If a character includes a box with an element inside the box, the box is filled in first and then the box is closed.

 國 → 國

6. If a character consists of a center with symmetrical sides, the center
   is written first and then the sides are written, left to right.

   亅 → 小

7. Falling strokes are distinguished from rising strokes. A stroke to
   the left of a vertical line may be a falling stroke or a rising stroke.
   　　A falling stroke "falls" down and to the left of the vertical stroke.
   In the character 小 above, the stroke on the left is a left falling stroke.

   ↙ 小

   　　A rising stroke begins at the left of the vertical stroke and rises
   to intersect the stroke.

   ↗ 扌

8. Some radicals occur on the left but are written last. Usually, if
   a radical is written on the left side of a character, it is written first,
   but the radical 辶 occurs on the left and is always written last.

   文 → 这

9. Little differences can be critical.
   　　Note the difference in the length of the middle and bottom horizontal
   lines in these characters: 土 tǔ and 士 shì.
   　　Note that the only difference between 王 wáng and 主 zhǔ is the dot
   at the top of the latter. When you write 王 wáng, be careful not to draw
   the vertical line through the top horizontal stroke; otherwise, it could
   be confused with 主 zhǔ.
   　　The characters 主 zhǔ and 圭 guī look very similar, but they are written
   very differently. 主 zhǔ is written with a dot on top and 王 wáng below it.
   圭 guī is the character 土 tǔ written twice, once above and once below.
   　　Note that 圭 guī is written differently than the right side of 推 tuī,
   whose right side is written as a dot, three horizontal lines, a vertical line,
   and a horizontal line at the bottom, as follows.

丶	亠	亖	亖	丯	丰

When you first begin to study characters, do not assume that you know how
to write each new character. Instead, carefully follow the stroke order guide for
each character provided in your textbook.

Written Practice 1-2

Rewrite each character and indicate the number of strokes used in writing it.

1. 人 ＿＿＿ ＿＿＿
2. 十 ＿＿＿ ＿＿＿
3. 五 ＿＿＿ ＿＿＿
4. 女 ＿＿＿ ＿＿＿
5. 好 ＿＿＿ ＿＿＿

6. 看 ＿＿＿ ＿＿＿
7. 四 ＿＿＿ ＿＿＿
8. 西 ＿＿＿ ＿＿＿
9. 姓 ＿＿＿ ＿＿＿
10. 先 ＿＿＿ ＿＿＿

QUIZ

Using a Mandarin Chinese dictionary, look up the pronunciation and meaning of each of the following important radicals. The 10 radicals can be found in either a traditional character dictionary or a simplified character dictionary.

	Character	Pronunciation	Meaning
1.	用	＿＿＿＿＿	＿＿＿＿＿＿＿＿＿
2.	豆	＿＿＿＿＿	＿＿＿＿＿＿＿＿＿
3.	小	＿＿＿＿＿	＿＿＿＿＿＿＿＿＿
4.	水	＿＿＿＿＿	＿＿＿＿＿＿＿＿＿
5.	日	＿＿＿＿＿	＿＿＿＿＿＿＿＿＿
6.	月	＿＿＿＿＿	＿＿＿＿＿＿＿＿＿
7.	土	＿＿＿＿＿	＿＿＿＿＿＿＿＿＿
8.	大	＿＿＿＿＿	＿＿＿＿＿＿＿＿＿
9.	火	＿＿＿＿＿	＿＿＿＿＿＿＿＿＿
10.	方	＿＿＿＿＿	＿＿＿＿＿＿＿＿＿

CHAPTER 2

An Overview of Mandarin Grammar

In this chapter, you will learn about:

Parts of Speech
The Building Blocks of a Mandarin Sentence
The Order of Information in a Mandarin Sentence

Parts of Speech

Following is a list of the parts of speech found in Mandarin, along with short descriptions and examples.

Noun (N) A word that can be counted or that can be described by an adjectival verb.

EXAMPLES 一个人·一個人 yī gè **rén** *one person*
一个思想·一個思想 yī gè **sīxiǎng** *one thought*
很大的国家·很大的國家 hěn dà de **guójiā** *a very big country*

Noun Phrase (NP) A noun plus any description of it.

Pronoun (Pro) A word that replaces a noun.

EXAMPLES 我 wǒ *I/me*
你 nǐ *you*

Verb (V) A word that can be negated, or that can be preceded by a prepositional phrase. Mandarin has action verbs, adjectival verbs, modal verbs, and stative verbs, each of which has distinct properties; they are described below.

Action Verb (Action V) A word that refers to an action. Action verbs can be preceded by modal verbs, followed by the aspect suffixes 了 le or 过·過 guò, and suffixed with resultative verb endings. See Chapter 8 for a detailed discussion of action verbs.

EXAMPLES 吃 chī *to eat*
跑 pǎo *to run*
学·學 xué *to study*

Adjectival Verb (AV) A word that can be preceded by 很 hěn *very* and that can be used when comparing nouns (*I am **faster** than you*). Words that are adjectives in English are adjectival verbs in Mandarin. Many textbooks and grammars label these words as adjectives, but they function differently from adjectives in languages like English. See Chapter 7 for a detailed discussion of adjectival verbs.

EXAMPLES   好 hǎo *good*
           快 kuài *fast*
           漂亮 piàoliang *pretty*

Modal Verb (MV)   A word that expresses ability, possibility, permission, or future time. Modal verbs can be negated and can be followed by action verbs or prepositional phrases + action verbs. See Chapter 10 for a detailed discussion of modal verbs.

EXAMPLES   会·會 huì *can, will*
           能 néng *can*
           可以 kéyǐ *can*

Stative Verb (SV)   A word that refers to states such as *like, fear,* and *want.*
     Mandarin stative verbs, like adjectival verbs, can be preceded by 很 hěn *very* and other intensifiers. Unlike adjectival verbs, they cannot be used to make comparisons. See Chapter 7 for a detailed discussion of stative verbs.

EXAMPLES   喜欢·喜歡 xǐhuan *to like*
           希望 xīwàng *to hope*

Verb Phrase (VP)   A verb, its object(s), and any associated prepositional phrase(s) and adverb(s).

Intensifier (Int)   A word that describes the intensity of adjectival verbs and stative verbs.

EXAMPLES   很 hěn *very*
           非常 fēicháng *extremely*

Adverb (Adv)   A word that occurs at the beginning of a verb phrase and describes the action or situation in some way. See Chapters 16–18 and 20 for detailed discussions of adverbs.

EXAMPLES   只 zhǐ *only*
           已经·已經 yǐjing *already*
           也 yě *also*
           忽然 hūrán *suddenly*

Negation (Neg)   A type of adverb that goes at the beginning of a verb phrase. Mandarin has two words that are commonly used for negation, 不 bù and 没 méi. Negation is discussed in detail in all of the chapters that focus on verbs.

Preposition (Prep)   A word that precedes a noun phrase and indicates direction, location, or other relationship. Prepositions are discussed in Chapter 18 and in many of the chapters that focus on actions and action verbs.

EXAMPLES   在 zài *at, on*
到 dào *to*
从·從 cóng *from*
往 wǎng *toward*
给·給 gěi *to, for*
跟 gēn *with*
对·對 duì *toward*
替 tì *for, on behalf of*

Prepositional Phrase (PP)   A preposition and the noun phrase that follows it.

Conjunction (Conj)   A word that links two identical grammatical categories. Conjunctions are discussed in Chapter 5.

EXAMPLES   和 hé *and*
跟 gēn *and*

Connecting Word (CW)   A word that joins phrases or clauses and indicates a relationship between them.

EXAMPLES   因为·因為 yīnwei *because*
所以 suóyǐ *therefore*
虽然·雖然 suīrán *although*
可是 kěshì *but*
如果 rúguǒ *if*

Particle (Part)   A syllable that indicates a grammatical function.

EXAMPLES   的 de
了 le

Final Particle (FPart)   A syllable that occurs at the end of a sentence and conveys grammatical meaning or speaker perspective.

EXAMPLES 吗·嗎 ma
呢 ne
吧 ba

Number (Num) Numbers are discussed in Chapter 4.

EXAMPLES 一 yī *one*
二 èr *two*
三 sān *three*

Specifier (Sp) and Demonstrative (Dem) A word that describes a noun and means *this, that, which*, etc.

A specifier occurs with a classifier (or a number + classifier) and noun.

EXAMPLE 那三本书·那三本書 **nà** sān běn shū ***those*** three books

A demonstrative identifies or "points" to a noun, but without a noun immediately following it.

EXAMPLE 那是书。·那是書。**Nà** shì shū. ***That*** is a book.

Specifiers and demonstratives are discussed in Chapter 5.

Classifier (Cl) A word that follows the specifier and/or number in a noun phrase. Sometimes called *measure words,* classifiers are discussed in Chapter 4.

EXAMPLES 一个人·一個人 yī **gè** rén *one person*
一杯水 yī **bēi** shuǐ *one **cup of** water*
那本书·那本書 nà **běn** shū *that book*

Oral Practice

Read each of the following Mandarin noun phrases and identify the noun.

1. 那个学生·那個學生 nàge xuésheng *that student* →
学生·學生 xuésheng *student*

2. 两本书·兩本書 liǎng běn shū *two books* → 书·書 shū *book*

3. 很大的房子 hěn dà de fángzi *a very big house* → 房子 fángzi *house*

4. 一张飞机票·一張飛機票 yī zhāng fēijī piào *one airplane ticket* →
飞机票·飛機票 fēijī piào *airplane ticket* OR 票 piào *ticket*

Written Practice 2-1

Read each of the following Mandarin sentences and write the Chinese and pinyin forms of the verb.

1. 我买了一本字典。· 我買了一本字典。
   Wǒ mǎi le yī běn zìdiǎn.
   I bought a dictionary.

   _____

2. 他喜欢中国饭。· 他喜歡中國飯。
   Tā xǐhuan Zhōngguó fàn.
   He likes Chinese food.

   _____

3. 那本书很贵。· 那本書很貴。
   Nà běn shū hěn guì.
   That book is very expensive.

   _____

4. 他们都学中文。· 他們都學中文。
   Tāmen dōu xué Zhōngwén.
   They all study Chinese.

   _____

The Building Blocks of a Mandarin Sentence

Following is a list of elements in a Mandarin sentence.

Subject   The noun phrase that refers to the actor of an action verb (*I ate the food*), that has the quality described by the predicate (*I am hungry*), or that experiences the state of a stative verb (*I like you*).

Predicate   Everything in the sentence that pertains to the verb, including the verb, its object(s), and any time phrases, location phrases, prepositional phrases, adverbs, etc. (*I **watched a movie yesterday***).

Object   The *direct object* is the noun phrase toward which the action of the verb is directed or the noun phrase that is affected by the action of the verb.

我吃了**晚饭**。 · 我吃了**晚飯**。
Wǒ chī le **wǎnfàn**.
*I ate **dinner**.*

The *indirect object* is the noun phrase that receives the direct object. Very few Mandarin verbs take an indirect object.

我给**他**钱。 · 我給**他**錢。
Wǒ gěi **tā** qián.
*I gave **him** money.*

Topic   The phrase that indicates what a conversation or text is about. Topics ordinarily occur at the beginning of the sentence, before the subject.

中国电影，我觉得很有意思。 · **中國電影**，我覺得很有意思。
Zhōngguó diànyǐng, wǒ juéde hěn yǒu yìsi.
***Chinese movies**, I think they are very interesting.*

Clause   A clause may be an independent sentence or a dependent clause. A dependent clause is part of a larger sentence; it includes a verb, and may include the subject or object of the verb. Following is an example of a noun described by a dependent clause.

我昨天看的电影 · **我昨天看**的電影
wǒ zuótiān kàn de diànyǐng
*the movie that **I saw yesterday***

This type of dependent clause is discussed in Chapter 13.

Oral Practice

Read each of the following sentences aloud and identify the subject.

1. 他们都会说中国话。　　　　　→　他们
   他們都會說中國話。　　　　　　　他們
   Tāmen dōu huì shuō Zhōngguó huà.　tāmen
   They can all speak Chinese.　　　*they*

2. 那两本书都很贵。
   那兩本書都很貴。
   Nà liǎng běn shū dōu hěn guì.
   Those two books are both very expensive.

   → 那两本书
   那兩本書
   nà liǎng běn shū
   those two books

3. 今天的考试很难。
   今天的考試很難。
   Jīntiān de kǎoshì hěn nán.
   Today's test was very difficult.

   → 今天的考试
   今天的考試
   jīntiān de kǎoshì
   today's test

4. 我的朋友都会开车。
   我的朋友都會開車。
   Wǒ de péngyou dōu huì kāi chē.
   My friends can all drive.

   → 我的朋友

   wǒ de péngyou
   my friends

Written Practice 2-2

Read each of the following Mandarin sentences, then write the Chinese and pinyin forms of the direct object.

1. 我昨天看了一个电影。· 我昨天看了一個電影。
   Wǒ zuótiān kàn le yī gè diànyǐng.
   I saw a movie yesterday.

   _____

2. 他们在家吃晚饭。· 他們在家吃晚飯。
   Tāmen zài jiā chī wǎnfàn.
   They eat dinner at home.

   _____

3. 请给我那本书。· 請給我那本書。
   Qǐng gěi wǒ nà běn shū.
   Please give me that book.

   _____

4. 他不会用筷子。· 他不會用筷子。
   Tā bù huì yòng kuàizi.
   He can't use chopsticks.

The Order of Information in a Mandarin Sentence

Mandarin has a relatively fixed word order. That is, there is usually only one acceptable way that phrases can be ordered in a sentence, and a phrase that conveys a specific type of information can only occur in one location in a sentence.

SIMPLE DECLARATIVE SENTENCES

The order of information in a simple declarative sentence in Mandarin is as follows.

Subject + Predicate

我	懂。
Wǒ	dǒng.
I	*understand.*

THE POSITION OF THE OBJECT

If the verb takes an object, the order of information in the sentence is as follows.

Subject + Verb + Object

我	学	中文。
我	學	中文。
Wǒ	xué	Zhōngwén.
I	*study*	*Chinese.*

THE POSITION OF *TIME WHEN* PHRASES

Time when phrases indicate the time at which a situation happens. If the time of a situation is not being emphasized, the *time when* phrase comes after the subject and before the predicate.

Subject + *Time when* + Predicate

我	昨天	看了一个电影。
我	昨天	看了一個電影。
Wǒ	zuótiān	kàn le yī gè diànyǐng.
I	*yesterday*	*saw a movie.* (*I saw a movie yesterday.*)

To emphasize the *time when* a situation takes place, the *time when* phrase comes before the subject.

***Time when* + Subject + Predicate**

昨天	我	看了一个电影。
昨天	我	看了一個電影。
Zuótiān	wǒ	kàn le yī gè diànyǐng.
Yesterday	*I*	*saw a movie.*

Time when phrases are discussed in more detail in Chapter 19, in the context of clock and calendar time.

Written Practice 2-3

Rewrite each of the following sentences in Chinese and pinyin, adding the *time when* phrase in parentheses. Then translate the sentence into English.

1. 他们在饭馆吃饭。(每天晚上) · 他們在飯館吃飯。(每天晚上)
   Tāmen zài fànguǎn chī fàn. (měitiān wǎnshang)
   They eat at a restaurant. (*every evening*)

   _____

2. 他在宿舍睡觉。(现在) · 他在宿舍睡覺。(現在)
   Tā zài sùshè shuì jiào. (xiànzài)
   He is sleeping at the dormitory. (*now*)

   _____

3. 我们在公园打球吧。(明天) · 我們在公園打球吧。(明天)
   Wǒmen zài gōngyuán dǎ qiú ba. (míngtiān)
   Let's play ball at the park. (*tomorrow*)

---

4. 他们喝了咖啡。(十点钟) · 他們喝了咖啡。(十點鐘)
   Tāmen hē le kāfēi. (shídiǎn zhōng)
   They drank coffee. (*10 o'clock*)

THE POSITION OF PREPOSITIONAL PHRASES

In Mandarin, a prepositional phrase generally comes *before* the verb and its object. Note that in English, the prepositional phrase always comes *after* the verb and its object.

Subject +	**PP**	+ **Verb Phrase**
他	跟朋友	聊天。
Tā	gēn péngyou	liáo tiān.
He	*with friends*	*chats.* (*He chats with friends.*)

THE POSITION OF LOCATION PHRASES

A phrase that indicates the *location where a situation takes place* comes before the verb phrase. A location phrase is a type of prepositional phrase. The preposition in a location phrase is 在 zài *at, in, on.*

Subject +	*Location*	+ **Verb Phrase**
我	在图书馆	念书。
我	在圖書館	念書。
Wǒ	zài túshūguǎn	niàn shū.
I	*at the library*	*study.* (*I study at the library.*)

If the location phrase refers to a *destination* (the place where the object ends up as a result of the action), it generally comes after the verb.

Subject	+ Verb Phrase	+ *Destination*
他	跑	到公园去了。
他	跑	到公園去了。
Tā	pǎo	dào gōngyuán qù le.
He	*ran*	*to the park.*

Location is discussed in more detail in Chapter 18.

THE RELATIVE ORDER OF A *TIME WHEN* PHRASE AND A *LOCATION* PHRASE

If a sentence contains a *time when* phrase and a *location* phrase, the *time when* phrase comes before the *location* phrase.

Subject	+ *Time When*	+ *Location*	+ Verb Phrase
我们	每天	在图书馆	念书。
我們	每天	在圖書館	念書。
Wǒmen	měitiān	zài túshūguǎn	niàn shū。
We	*every day*	*at the library*	*study.*

(*We study at the library every day.*)

THE POSITION OF ADVERBS

Adverbs come before the verb phrase. If a sentence contains a prepositional phrase before the verb, the adverb comes before the prepositional phrase.

Subject	+ Adverb	+ Verb Phrase
我	已经	看了那个电影。
我	已經	看了那個電影。
Wǒ	yǐjing	kàn le nàge diànyǐng.
I	*have already*	*seen that movie.*

Subject + Adverb + Verb Phrase

她	也	喜欢学中文。
她	也	喜歡學中文。
Tā	yě	xǐhuan xué Zhōngwén.
She	*also*	*likes to study Chinese.*

Adverbs are discussed in more detail in Chapters 16–18 and 20.

THE POSITION OF DURATION PHRASES

Expressions that indicate the duration of an activity come after the verb.

Subject + Verb + Duration

他	睡了	六个小时。
他	睡了	六個小時。
Tā	shuì le	liù gè xiǎoshí.
He	*slept*	*for six hours.*

Duration is discussed in more detail in Chapter 21.

THE ORDER OF INFORMATION IN QUESTIONS

In Mandarin, the order of information in questions and in declarative sentences is identical. Compare the following question-and-answer pairs.

Question	**Answer**
她是学生吗？· 她是學生嗎？	她是学生。· 她是學生。
Tā shì xuésheng ma?	Tā shì xuésheng.
Is she a student?	*She is a student.*
你学什么？· 你學甚麼？	我学中文。· 我學中文。
Nǐ xué shénme?	Wǒ xué Zhōngwén.
What do you study?	*I study Chinese.*
他们在哪儿打球？· 他們在哪兒打球？	他们在公园打球。· 他們在公園打球。
Tāmen zài nǎr dǎ qiú?	Tāmen zài gōngyuán dǎ qiú.
Where do they play ball?	*They play ball in the park.*

Content questions are discussed in detail in Chapter 15.

TOPICS AND TOPIC-COMMENT CONSTRUCTION

Word order is very important in Mandarin, and as you have seen, most phrases have a fixed location in the sentence. However, certain types of phrases may come at the beginning of a sentence for emphasis. When a phrase comes at the beginning of a sentence in this way, it is often referred to as a *topic*.

Time when phrases may come at the beginning of the sentence for emphasis.

Normal Order	***Time when* Is Topicalized**
Subject + *Time when* + VP	***Time when* + Subject + VP**
我昨天没睡觉。· 我昨天没睡覺。	昨天我没睡觉。· 昨天我没睡覺。
Wǒ **zuótiān** méi shuì jiào.	**Zuótiān** wǒ méi shuì jiào.
*I **yesterday** didn't sleep.*	***Yesterday** I didn't sleep.*

The object of the verb may come at the beginning of the sentence for emphasis.

Normal Order	**Object Is Topicalized**
Subject + Verb + Object	**Object + Subject + Verb**
我不想吃那个菜。· 我不想吃那個菜。	那个菜我不想吃。· 那個菜我不想吃。
Wǒ bù xiǎng chī **nàge cài**.	**Nàge cài** wǒ bù xiǎng chī.
*I don't want to eat **that dish**.*	***That dish** I don't want to eat.*

QUIZ

Read each of the following sentences, then write the Chinese and pinyin forms of the subject.

1. 我很喜欢红颜色的衣服。· 我很喜歡紅顏色的衣服。
   Wǒ hěn xǐhuan hóng yánsè de yīfu.
   I really like red clothing.

   _____

2. 那个书店也有一个饭馆。· 那個書店也有一個飯館。
   Nàge shūdiàn yě yǒu yī gè fànguǎn.
   That bookstore also has a restaurant.

   _____

3. 那个电脑非常贵。· 那個電腦非常貴。
Nàge diànnǎo fēicháng guì.
That computer is extremely expensive.

Rewrite each of the following sentences, adding the *time when* phrase and the prepositional phrase in parentheses in the correct order and position.

4. (每天下午) (在公园) 我的奶奶走路。·
(每天下午) (在公園) 我的奶奶走路。
(měitiān xiàwǔ) (zài gōngyuán) Wǒ de nǎinai zǒu lù.
My grandmother walks in the park every afternoon.

---

5. 我们吃饭。(在饭馆) (明天晚上) ·
我們吃飯。(在飯館) (明天晚上)
Wǒmen chī fàn. (zài fànguǎn) (míngtiān wǎnshang)
Tomorrow night, we are eating at a restaurant.

---

6. (在图书馆) 我妹妹做了作业。(昨天晚上九点钟) ·
(在圖書館) 我妹妹做了作業。(昨天晚上九點鐘)
(zài túshūguǎn) Wǒ mèimei zuò le zuòyè. (zuótiān wǎnshang jiǔdiǎn zhōng)
My younger sister did homework in the library at 9 o'clock last night.

---

7. (在家) (今天晚上) 她看电视。· (在家) (今天晚上) 她看電視。
(zài jiā) (jīntiān wǎnshang) Tā kàn diànshì.
She is watching television at home tonight.

Read each of the following sentences, then write the Chinese and pinyin forms of the object of the verb.

8. 我喜欢看外国电影。· 我喜歡看外國電影。
Wǒ xǐhuan kàn wàiguó diànyǐng.
I like to watch foreign movies.

---

9. 他看了两本书。· 他看了兩本書。
   Tā kàn le liǎng běn shū.
   He read two books.

   _____

10. 我的朋友喝了三瓶可乐。· 我的朋友喝了三瓶可樂。
    Wǒ de péngyou hē le sān píng kělè.
    My friends drank three bottles of cola.

    _____

CHAPTER 3

Chinese Names and Titles

In this chapter, you will learn about:

Chinese Names
Titles and Terms of Address
Addressing Others

Chinese Names

A Chinese name consists of a family name and a given name, in the following order.

Family name + Given name

Almost all Chinese family names are one syllable long. Given names are one or two syllables long. Following are some Chinese names, with their English equivalents. Do you see why we cannot call a Chinese family name the *last name*?

	Family Name	**Given Name**
王明德 Wáng Míngdé	王 Wáng	明德 Míngdé
陈美玲·陳美玲 Chén Měilíng	陈·陳 Chén	美玲 Měilíng
刘春·劉春 Liú Chūn	刘·劉 Liú	春 Chūn

Following are the names of several famous Chinese people. The family name is in bold type.

孙中山·孫中山 **Sūn** Zhōngshān (Sun Yatsen, first president of the Republic of China)
巩俐·鞏俐 **Gǒng** Lì (contemporary actress)
张艺谋·張藝謀 **Zhāng** Yìmóu (contemporary movie director)
李白 **Lǐ** Bái (8th-century poet)
鲁迅·魯迅 **Lǔ** Xùn (20th-century author)

There are about 100 common family names in Chinese. Among those, the most common are 白 Bái, 陈·陳 Chén, 高 Gāo, 何 Hé, 李 Lǐ, 林 Lín, 刘·劉 Liú, 马·馬 Mǎ, 王 Wáng, 张·張 Zhāng, 周 Zhōu, and 朱 Zhū.

Chinese given names always have a meaning, and families often select names for their children that convey positive qualities. For example, the given name 明德 Míngdé means *understand righteousness*. The given name 美玲 Měilíng means *beautiful sound of jade*. Given names may also have literary or social significance.

Written Practice 3-1

The following Chinese people have Americanized their names so that the family name occurs at the end, in bold type. Rewrite each of the names in the order in which they occur in Chinese, with the family name first.

1. Péngfēi **Wáng** _____
2. Xīnhuā **Táng** _____
3. Huìkāng **Xú** _____
4. Píng **Zhāng** _____
5. Dàoyú **Lín** _____
6. Lì **Zhōu** _____
7. Xìngróng **Ráo** _____
8. Wēiqīng **Mǎ** _____

Titles and Terms of Address

Titles may be used alone or along with a name, when addressing or referring to other people. Using a title is generally more formal and more respectful than using a person's name alone. Titles come after a person's name.

MR., MRS., AND MISS

In Taiwan, the following titles are regularly used for *Mr., Mrs.,* and *Miss.*

Mr.	先生 xiānsheng	陈先生·陳先生 Chén xiānsheng	
		陈爱平先生·陳愛平先生 Chén Ài Píng xiānsheng	
Mrs.	太太 tàitai	王太太 Wáng tàitai	
		王惠娜太太 Wáng Huìnà tàitai	
Miss	小姐 xiǎojie	李小姐 Lǐ xiǎojie	
		李丽小姐·李麗小姐 Lǐ Lì xiǎojie	

In Taiwan, the titles 先生 xiānsheng, 太太 tàitai, and 小姐 xiǎojie may be used to address other people, with or without using the person's name. For example, a man may be addressed as 先生 xiānsheng *Mr.* or as 白先生 Bái xiānsheng *Mr. Bai.* The terms 先生 xiānsheng and 太太 tàitai may also be used to refer to one's husband or wife. That is, a man may refer to his wife as 我的太太 wǒ de tàitai *my wife,* and a woman may refer to her husband as 我的先生 wǒ de xiānsheng *my husband.*

In mainland Chinese, the terms 先生 xiānsheng, 太太 tàitai, and 小姐 xiǎojie are rarely used, and for historical reasons, there is no single set of words that is used in their place.

On very formal occasions, a woman's husband may be referred to as 丈夫 zhàngfu and a man's wife may be referred to or addressed as 夫人 fūren *Mrs.* A woman may refer to her husband as 我的丈夫 wǒ de zhàngfu *my husband,* and someone may refer to another person's wife as 你的夫人 nǐ de fūren *your wife.* 夫人 fūren may also occur alone as a term of address, or after a person's name as a title or term of address.

夫人 fūren *Mrs.*   周夫人 Zhōu fūren *Mrs. Zhou*

In formal situations, a woman may also be referred to or addressed as 女士 nǚshì *Ms.,* which occurs with the woman's name, not alone.

王女士 Wáng nǚshì   王惠娜女士 Wáng Huìnà nǚshì

In very informal situations, a man may refer to his wife as 我的老婆 wǒ de lǎopo *my wife, my old lady;* similarly, a woman may refer to her husband as 我的老公 wǒ de lǎogōng *my husband, my old man.* The expressions 老婆 lǎopo and 老公 lǎogōng are very similar in tone and usage to the slang expressions *old lady* and *old man* in American English. As a student, you should never use them to either address or refer to someone's spouse; to do so would be considered disrespectful.

Probably because there are no truly neutral expressions in mainland China that are equivalent to *Mr., Mrs.,* and *Miss,* people usually address each other in other ways. The most common of these include using professional titles and kinship terms.

PROFESSIONAL TITLES

Following are several common professional titles.

老师·老師	lǎoshī	*teacher*	经理·經理	jīnglǐ	*manager*
校长·校長	xiàozhǎng	*principal*	司机·司機	sījī	*driver*
医生·醫生	yīshēng	*doctor*	服务员·服務員	fúwùyuán	*waiter*
护士·護士	hùshi	*nurse*			

All of these professional titles except 服务员·服務員 fúwùyuán *waiter* can be used with or without a person's name. As with all titles, the title follows the name.

医生·醫生	yīshēng	马医生·馬醫生	Mǎ yīshēng
司机·司機	sījī	张司机·張司機	Zhāng sījī
老师·老師	lǎoshī	谢老师·謝老師	Xiè lǎoshī

The title 服务员·服務員 fúwùyuán *waiter* does not occur with a person's name.

KINSHIP TERMS

Kinship terms are words that refer to family members. Chinese has many more kinship terms than English. This is because Chinese has separate words referring to older and younger siblings, as well as separate words referring to relatives on one's father's side and one's mother's side of the family.

Following are kinship terms that refer to one's immediate family.

爸爸	bàba	*dad*		女儿·女兒	nǚ'ér	*daughter*
父亲·父親	fùqin	*father*		哥哥	gēge	*older brother*
妈妈·媽媽	māma	*mom*		弟弟	dìdi	*younger brother*
母亲·母親	mǔqīn	*mother*		姐姐	jiějie	*older sister*
儿子·兒子	érzi	*son*		妹妹	mèimei	*younger sister*

Following are kinship terms that refer to one's extended family.

爷爷·爺爺	yéye	*grandfather (father's father)*
外公	wàigōng	*grandfather (mother's father)*
奶奶	nǎinai	*grandmother (father's mother)*
外婆	wàipó	*grandmother (mother's mother)*
叔叔	shūshu	*uncle (father's older or younger brother)*
舅舅	jiùjiu	*uncle (mother's older or younger brother)*
姑姑	gūgu	*aunt (father's sister)*
阿姨	āyí	*aunt (mother's sister)*

Kinship terms are usually used without a person's name. When used with a person's name, the kinship term always follows the name.

刘阿姨·劉阿姨 Liú āyí   *Aunt Liu*
朱爷爷·朱爺爺 Zhū yéye   *Grandpa Zhu*

Addressing Others

A term of address may include a person's family name, given name, and title, in that order. The way you address another person depends on his or her relationship to you. Generally speaking, the more formal your relationship, the more information you include in your term of address. The closer you are to someone, the less information you include in your term of address. Given names are more personal in China than in the United States, so you only address very close friends and family members with their given names alone.

ADDRESSING OTHERS USING NAMES AND TITLES

In Chinese culture, the most common way to address another person is by using his or her complete name, family name + given name,

张艺谋·張藝謀 Zhāng Yìmóu *Yimou Zhang*

or by family name followed by a title,

张先生·張先生 Zhāng xiānsheng *Mr. Zhang*
王医生·王醫生 Wáng yīshēng *Dr. Wang*
朱阿姨 Zhū āyí *Aunt Zhu*

or by title alone,

先生 xiānsheng *Mr.*
医生·醫生 yīshēng *Dr.*
阿姨 āyí *aunt*

The most formal way to address someone is to use his or her complete name followed by a title.

张艺谋先生·張藝謀先生 Zhāng Yìmóu xiānsheng *Mr. Yimou Zhang*
王明德医生·王明德醫生 Wáng Míngdé yīshēng *Dr. Mingde Wang*

Written Practice 3-2

Write the pinyin form of each of the following people's names, using only the family name and title.

1. Wáng Péngfēi (doctor) _____

2. Táng Xīnhuā (teacher) _____

3. Xú Huìkāng (manager) _____

4. Zhāng Píng (Mrs.) _____

5. Lín Dàoyú (Mr.) _____

6. Zhōu Lì (Miss) _____

7. Ráo Xìngróng (principal) _____

8. Mǎ Wēiqīng (driver) _____

ADDRESSING FAMILY MEMBERS USING KINSHIP TERMS

When addressing someone in your immediate family, use the kinship term alone.

爸爸 bàba *dad*
姐姐 jiějie *older sister*

Brothers and sisters usually address each other using the kinship term: 哥哥 gēge (*older brother*), 妹妹 mèimei (*younger sister*), etc. They may also address each other by name, either family name plus given name, or given name alone.

Aunts and uncles may be addressed by the kinship term alone, or by family name followed by the kinship term.

陈阿姨·陳阿姨 Chén āyí *Aunt Chen*
马叔叔·馬叔叔 Mǎ shūshu *Uncle Ma*

Oral Practice

Assume that you are a girl, aged 10. Answer the following questions.

1. You are the oldest of three daughters. How do you address your sisters? → mèimei

2. How do your sisters address you? → jiějie

3. How does your older brother address you? → mèimei

4. How do you address your older brother? → gēge

5. How does your older brother address your father? → bàba OR fùqin

6. How does your father address you? → nǚ'ér

USING KINSHIP TERMS TO ADDRESS PEOPLE OUTSIDE YOUR FAMILY

The terms 爷爷·爺爺 yéye *grandfather,* 奶奶 nǎinai *grandmother,* 叔叔 shūshu *uncle,* and 阿姨 āyí *aunt* are also used as friendly, informal terms of address for people who are not related to you. 爷爷·爺爺 yéye *grandfather* may be used to address any man who is about your grandfather's age, 奶奶 nǎinai *grandmother* may be used to address any woman who is about your grandmother's age, 叔叔 shūshu *uncle* may be used to address any man who is about your father's age, and 阿姨 āyí *aunt* may be used to address anyone who is about your mother's age. The expression 大哥 dà gē *big brother* and, to a lesser extent, the expressions 小弟 xiǎo dì *little brother,* 大姐 dà jiě *big sister,* and 小妹 xiǎo mèi *little sister,* may also be used to address friends who are a bit older or younger than you. When used in this way, these terms can occur with or without a family name.

Written Practice 3-3

Answer the following questions, using pinyin forms.

1. How do you address your two grandfathers? _____

2. You want to ask a woman a question. She is about your mother's age.

   How do you address her? _____

3. Who is older, your nǎinai or your gūgu? _____

4. You want to ask a man a question. He is your grandfather's age.

   How do you address him? _____

ADDRESSING CLOSE FRIENDS

Close friends address each other by using the entire name or, if the given name is a two-syllable name, by using the given name alone. Meiling Chen's friends may call her 陈美玲 · 陳美玲 Chén Měilíng or 美玲 Měilíng. Chun Liu's friends may call her 刘春 · 劉春 Liú Chūn.

   In addition, friends often address each other by 小 xiǎo *little* + Family Name. So, Meiling Chen's friends may call her 小陈 · 小陳 Xiǎo Chén. Chun Liu's friends may call her 小刘 · 小劉 Xiǎo Liú.

   People who are older than 30 may address a friend older than themselves by 老 lǎo *old* + Family Name. Dr. Wang's good friends may call him 老王 Lǎo Wáng. 老 lǎo *old* indicates respect as well as friendship and does not have a negative connotation.

Oral Practice

Your closest friends are (1) Mǎ Jiāměi, (2) Chén Měilì, and (3) Zhāng Xiǎoyīng. Address them using 小 xiǎo *little*.

1. Xiǎo Mǎ

2. Xiǎo Chén

3. Xiǎo Zhāng

What's in a Name?

Western culture and Chinese culture differ in many respects in their use of names. In the West, names are readily shared. One of the first questions you typically ask a new acquaintance is "What is your name?" In Chinese culture, names are more private, and you do not casually ask a person's name. Instead, you may ask an acquaintance how he or she would like to be addressed. Following is a common way to ask this.

我(应该)怎么称呼你? · 我(應該)怎麼稱呼你?
Wǒ (yīnggāi) zěnme chēnghu nǐ?
How do I address you? / How should I address you?

This allows the acquaintance to decide the terms of your relationship, how formal or informal it should be, and how much information to give you about his or her name.

In Western culture, if one of your friends brings friends along when visiting you, he or she introduces them by name. In China, people do not necessarily introduce their friends to each other by name. Instead, they may introduce them by indicating their role or relationship, for example, *This is my roommate,* or *This is my co-worker,* or *This is my cousin.*

In Western culture, people sometimes address their own parents and older relatives by their given names, and may even address the friends of their parents or the parents of their friends by their given names. In Chinese culture, people never address their parents, their older relatives, or people of their parents' generation by their given names; they use a title or kinship term instead. Even spouses and close friends often do not address each other by their given names alone, but use family name and given name together. In Western culture, close friends, especially males, may address each other by their family names alone. In Chinese culture, people never address each other by their family names alone.

Finally, Chinese people traditionally have several different names over the course of their lives. When very young, they are given a baby name—a name with a repeated syllable, such as Línglíng, Dōngdōng, Xiáoxiǎo, or Wéiwéi. When they begin to attend school at the age of five or six, they use a school name. If they establish a career, they may give themselves a professional name—the equivalent of a pen name in Western culture.

QUIZ

1. Answer the following questions.

   a. How does 周利明 Zhōu Lìmíng address his older brother?

   _____

   b. How does his older brother address him? _____

2. Answer the following questions based on the information below.

   周利明 Zhōu Lìmíng is 18 years old. He has two sisters; one is 16, and the other is 19.

   a. How does he address his 16-year-old sister?

   _____

   b. How does she address him? _____

3. Answer the following questions based on the information below.

   周利明 Zhōu Lìmíng is 18 years old. He has two sisters; one is 16, and the other is 19.

   a. How does he address his 19-year-old sister? _____

   b. How does she address him? _____

   c. How does his 16-year-old sister address his 19-year-old sister?

   _____

4. Identify the family name for each of the following people.

   a. 唐新花 Táng Xīnhuā _____

   b. 高蕾 Gāo Lěi _____

5. Following are two Chinese names in English word order. Rewrite the names so that they are in the correct order in Chinese.

   a. Dr. Zhizhen Ma _____

   b. Mr. Yongping Liu _____

6. Rewrite the following names so that they are in the correct order in Chinese.

   a. 医生林美玲·醫生林美玲 yīshēng Lín Měilíng

   _____

   b. 老师爱民孙·老師愛民孫 lǎoshī Àimín Sūn

   _____

7. Select the acceptable way(s) in which you may address your good friend 高蕾 Gāo Lěi, whose family name is 高 Gāo.

   a. 高　Gāo
   b. 高蕾　Gāo Lěi
   c. 蕾　Lěi
   d. 小蕾　Xiǎo Lěi
   e. 小高　Xiǎo Gāo

8. Meiling Chen has two 舅舅 jiùjiu, one 弟弟 dìdi, and one 母亲·母親 mǔqīn. How many children are there in her family, including herself?

   _____

9. Dr. Wang has four children, three boys and one girl.

   a. How many 儿子·兒子 érzi does Dr. Wang have? _____

   b. How many 女儿·女兒 nǚ'ér does Dr. Wang have? _____

10. Professor Ma has three daughters. How many 姐姐 jiějie does her youngest daughter have? _____

CHAPTER 4

Numbers

In this chapter, you will learn about:

The Numbers 1–10 and Zero

Following are the numbers 1–10 and the number *zero* in Mandarin.

1	一	yī	6	六	liù
2	二	èr	7	七	qī
3	三	sān	8	八	bā
4	四	sì	9	九	jiǔ
5	五	wǔ	10	十	shí

zero ○ OR 零 líng

RECITING TELEPHONE NUMBERS AND FAX AND BEEPER NUMBERS

In Mandarin, telephone numbers, fax numbers, and beeper numbers are recited as a series of individual numbers.

The telephone number	*is recited*
3854-1267	sān bā wǔ sì yī èr liù qī
9594-0020	jiǔ wǔ jiǔ sì líng líng èr líng

In Beijing, the number 1 is usually pronounced yāo when it is part of a telephone number.

The telephone number	*is recited*
7827-3566	qī bā èr qī sān wǔ liù liù
9910-3343	jiǔ jiǔ yāo líng sān sān sì sān

Oral Practice

Read aloud the following telephone numbers in Mandarin.

1. 6080-2022 → liù líng bā líng èr líng èr èr

2. 7123-4567 → qī yāo èr sān sì wǔ liù qī OR qī yī èr sān sì wǔ liù qī

3. 9876-5432 → jiǔ bā qī liù wǔ sì sān èr

The Numbers 11–19

The numbers 11–19 are based on the numbers 1–10 and are presented below. Note that each number starts with 十 shí (10): 11 is 十一 shíyī, that is, 10 (+) 1; 12 is 十二 shí'èr, that is, 10 (+) 2; and so on.

11	十一	shíyī	16	十六	shíliù
12	十二	shí'èr	17	十七	shíqī
13	十三	shísān	18	十八	shíbā
14	十四	shísì	19	十九	shíjiǔ
15	十五	shíwǔ			

The Numbers 20–90

Following are the round numbers 20 to 90. Think of these numbers as "2 times 10" (20), "3 times 10" (30), and so on.

20	二十	èrshí	60	六十	liùshí
30	三十	sānshí	70	七十	qīshí
40	四十	sìshí	80	八十	bāshí
50	五十	wǔshí	90	九十	jiǔshí

Following are the numbers 21–25. Note that they are formed the same way as the numbers 11, 12, 13, etc., that is, as 20 (+) 1, 20 (+) 2, and so on.

21	二十一	èrshíyī	24	二十四	èrshísì
22	二十二	èrshí'èr	25	二十五	èrshíwǔ
23	二十三	èrshísān			

All of the numbers from 21 through 99 are formed the same way. Following are several additional numbers.

37	三十七	sānshíqī	62	六十二	liùshí'èr
49	四十九	sìshíjiǔ	99	九十九	jiǔshíjiǔ

Written Practice 4-1

Write the following numbers in Chinese characters and in pinyin.

1. 28 _____
2. 54 _____
3. 77 _____
4. 83 _____
5. 91 _____

Oral Practice

Count from 5 to 95 by fives →

wǔ, shí, shíwǔ, èrshí, èrshíwǔ, sānshí, sānshíwǔ, sìshí, sìshíwǔ, wǔshí, wǔshíwǔ, liùshí, liùshíwǔ, qīshí, qīshíwǔ, bāshí, bāshíwǔ, jiǔshí, jiǔshíwǔ

The Numbers 100–999

The word for 100 is 百 bǎi. Following are the round numbers 100 to 900. Note that there are two ways to say 200: 两百·兩百 liǎng bǎi and 二百 èr bǎi. 两·兩 liǎng is used to indicate *two of something*, and we will see that it can be used to express *thousands* and *ten thousands*, as well as *hundreds*.

100	一百	yī bǎi			
200	两百·兩百	liǎng bǎi	OR	二百	èr bǎi
300	三百	sān bǎi			
400	四百	sì bǎi			
500	五百	wǔ bǎi			
600	六百	liù bǎi			
700	七百	qī bǎi			
800	八百	bā bǎi			
900	九百	jiǔ bǎi			

The numbers from 101 through 999 are expressed as *hundreds + tens + ones.*

	Hundreds + (百 bǎi)	Tens + (十 shí)	Ones
234	二百 èr bǎi OR 两百 · 兩百 liǎng bǎi	三十 sānshí 三十 sānshí	四 sì 四 sì
651	六百 liù bǎi	五十 wǔshí	一 yī
999	九百 jiǔ bǎi	九十 jiǔshí	九 jiǔ

Oral Practice

Count from 100 to 900 by hundreds →

yī bǎi, èr bǎi (OR liǎng bǎi), sān bǎi, sì bǎi, wǔ bǎi, liù bǎi, qī bǎi, bā bǎi, jiǔ bǎi

Written Practice 4-2

Write the following numbers in Chinese characters and in pinyin.

1. 385 _____

2. 218 _____

3. 684 _____

4. 333 _____

5. 792 _____

ZERO AS A PLACEHOLDER

When a number includes a zero that is followed by another number, you can choose either to say the zero (零 líng) or to leave it out. Following are some examples.

303	三百三 sān bǎi sān	OR	三百零三 sān bǎi líng sān		
607	六百七 liù bǎi qī	OR	六百零七 liù bǎi líng qī		

The zero is never pronounced if it occurs at the end of a number, as in 710.

The Numbers 1,000–9,000

The word for 1,000 is 千 qiān. Thousands are counted in the same way as hundreds. Following are the round numbers 1,000 to 9,000.

1,000	一千	yī qiān			
2,000	二千	èr qiān	OR	两千·兩千	liǎng qiān
3,000	三千	sān qiān			
4,000	四千	sì qiān			
5,000	五千	wǔ qiān			
6,000	六千	liù qiān			
7,000	七千	qī qiān			
8,000	八千	bā qiān			
9,000	九千	jiǔ qiān			

Following are several numbers between 1,001 and 9,999. They are expressed as *thousands + hundreds + tens + ones*.

	Thousands + (千 qiān)	Hundreds + (百 bǎi)	Tens + (十 shí)	Ones
1,468	一千 yī qiān	四百 sì bǎi	六十 liùshí	八 bā
2,773	两千·兩千 liǎng qiān OR	七百 qī bǎi	七十 qīshí	三 sān
	二千 èr qiān	七百 qī bǎi	七十 qīshí	三 sān
6,152	六千 liù qiān	一百 yī bǎi	五十 wǔshí	二 èr
8,907	八千 bā qiān	九百 jiǔ bǎi	○ líng	七 qī
9,999	九千 jiǔ qiān	九百 jiǔ bǎi	九十 jiǔshí	九 jiǔ

If a number has two or more zeros in a row followed by a number, you say ○ líng only once.

| 1,001 | 一千
yī qiān | ○
líng | 一
yī | |

Oral Practice

Say the following numbers in Mandarin.

1. 5,828 → 五千八百二十八 wǔ qiān bā bǎi èrshíbā

2. 2,222 → 两千两百二十二·兩千兩百二十二 liǎng qiān liǎng bǎi èrshí'èr

3. 4,320 → 四千三百二十 sì qiān sān bǎi èrshí

4. 9,146 → 九千一百四十六 jiǔ qiān yī bǎi sìshíliù

The Numbers 10,000 and Up

The word for 10,000 is 万·萬 wàn. Beginning with 10,000, numbers are counted differently in Chinese than they are in English. In English, numbers are counted by thousands until you reach the next category, *one million*. That is, you say *nine thousand, ten thousand, eleven thousand*, and so on, all the way up to *nine hundred ninety-nine thousand*. In Mandarin, *ten thousand* is the beginning of a new category, and numbers are counted by ten thousands until you reach the next category, 亿 yì *one hundred million*. We are not going to count that high here, but we will practice saying numbers through the hundred thousands.

Following are the round numbers 10,000 to 90,000.

10,000	一万·一萬	yī wàn			
20,000	两万·兩萬	liǎng wàn	OR	二万·二萬	èr wàn
30,000	三万·三萬	sān wàn			
40,000	四万·四萬	sì wàn			
50,000	五万·五萬	wǔ wàn			
60,000	六万·六萬	liù wàn			
70,000	七万·七萬	qī wàn			
80,000	八万·八萬	bā wàn			
90,000	九万·九萬	jiǔ wàn			

More complex numbers are expressed as the number of each of the following categories: *ten thousands* (万·萬 wàn), *thousands* (千 qiān), *hundreds* (百 bǎi), *tens* (十 shí), and *ones*. Following are the numbers 13,485 and 27,666 in Mandarin.

	Ten thousands + (万·萬 wàn)	Thousands + (千 qiān)	Hundreds + (百 bǎi)	Tens + (十 shí)	Ones
13,485	一万	三千	四百	八十	五
	一萬	三千	四百	八十	五
	yī wàn	sān qiān	sì bǎi	bāshí	wǔ
27,666	两万	七千	六百	六十	六
	兩萬	七千	六百	六十	六
	liǎng wàn	qī qiān	liù bǎi	liùshí	liù

Note that 20,000 can be expressed as either 两万·兩萬 liǎng wàn or 二万·二萬 èr wàn.

If a number has two or more zeros in a row followed by a number, you say 零 líng only once. Following is the number 37,005 in Mandarin.

37,005	三万	七千	零	五
	三萬	七千	零	五
	sān wàn	qī qiān	líng	wǔ

The zero is never pronounced if it occurs at the end of a number. Following is the number 37,000 in Mandarin.

37,000	三万	七千
	三萬	七千
	sān wàn	qī qiān

Oral Practice

Read the following Mandarin numbers aloud, then say what they mean in English.

1. sān wàn bā bǎi bāshí'èr → 30,882
2. liù wàn wǔ qiān jiǔ bǎi líng yī → 65,901
3. yī wàn liǎng qiān sì bǎi bāshíwǔ → 12,485
4. qī wàn bā qiān líng liù → 78,006
5. wǔ wàn liǎng qiān yī bǎi sìshí → 52,140

The category 万 · 萬 wàn (10,000) is used to express numbers up to one hundred million.

100,000	→	一十万 · 一十萬	yī shí wàn
1,000,000	→	一百万 · 一百萬	yī bǎi wàn
10,000,000	→	一千万 · 一千萬	yī qiān wàn
100,000,000	→	万万 · 萬萬	wàn wàn

The number 100,000,000 can also be expressed by the number word 亿 · 億 yì.

Ordinal Numbers

Ordinal numbers indicate sequence: *first, second, third,* etc. In Mandarin, ordinal numbers are formed by adding 第 dì before the number. This method is used for every number. Note that *second* is 第二 dì'èr.

第一	dì yī	*first (1st)*
第二	dì'èr	*second (2nd)*
第三	dì sān	*third (3rd)*
第四	dì sì	*fourth (4th)*
第五	dì wǔ	*fifth (5th)*

Oral Practice

Say the following numbers in Mandarin.

1. 6th → dì liù

2. 10th → dì shí

3. 45th → dì sìshíwǔ

4. 8th → dì bā

5. 12th → dì shí'èr

CULTURE DEMYSTIFIED

Arabic Numerals

In China, Arabic numerals are used as well as Chinese numerals. Large numbers are often written using Arabic numerals; for example, the price of a car or of a house may be written in Arabic numerals. Telephone numbers are almost always written in Arabic numerals, though they are recited in Chinese. For example, the telephone number for emergencies is generally written as 119, but is read (in Beijing) as yāo yāo jiǔ.

QUIZ

Write the following telephone numbers in pinyin.

1. 5316-2323 _____

2. 8406-8888 _____

3. 2262-1789 _____

Write the following numbers in Chinese characters and in pinyin.

4. 679 _____

5. 2,345 _____

6. 28,656 _____

7. 135,890 _____

Write the following numbers in Arabic numerals.

8. 三千一百〇六 sān qiān yī bǎi líng liù _____

9. 四万二百七十 · 四萬二百七十 sì wàn èr bǎi qīshí _____

10. 五千九百〇二 wǔ qiān jiǔ bǎi líng èr _____

CHAPTER 5

Using Pronouns and Nouns

In this chapter, you will learn about:

Pronouns

Mandarin has the following pronouns.

Singular			**Plural**		
我	wǒ	*I, me*	我们 · 我們	wǒmen	*we, us*
你	nǐ	*you*	你们 · 你們	nǐmen	*you*
他	tā	*he, him* (male or gender-neutral)	他们 · 他們	tāmen	*they, them* (male or gender-neutral)
她	tā	*she, her* (female)	她们 · 她們	tāmen	*they, them* (female)
它	tā	*it* (inanimate object)	它们 · 它們	tāmen	*they, them* (inanimate objects)
自己	zìjǐ	*self*			

The Mandarin system of pronouns is very simple. Mandarin uses the same form of pronoun, whether the pronoun serves as the subject of a sentence (*I, he, she, we, they*) or the object of a sentence (*me, him, her, us, them*). Note how the English pronoun changes in the following sentences while the Chinese pronoun remains the same.

我是妹妹。
Wǒ shì mèimei.
I am the younger sister.

妈妈爱**我**。 · 媽媽愛**我**。
Māma ài **wǒ**.
Mom loves me.

In the spoken language, Mandarin pronouns do not distinguish gender (masculine/feminine/neuter). The same pronoun is used, whether it refers to females or males or inanimate objects. However, the third-person pronoun tā (*he, she, it, him, her*) makes a distinction in the written form. Tā is written with three different characters, depending on whether it refers to *he/him* (他), *she/her* (她), or *it* (它). If you hear the following sentence, you cannot tell whether tā is male or female, but when you read the characters, you can tell. Does tā refer to a male or a female in the following sentences?

他是学生。· 他是學生。
Tā shì xuésheng.
Tā *is a student.*

我喜欢他。· 我喜歡他。
Wǒ xǐhuan tā.
I like tā.

The answer is: male. **He** *is a student. I like* **him**.

Mandarin pronouns have singular and plural forms. It is easy to form the plural: Simply add the suffix 们·們 men to the singular form.

我	wǒ	我们·我們	wǒmen
你	nǐ	你们·你們	nǐmen
他	tā	他们·他們	tāmen
她	tā	她们·她們	tāmen
它	tā	它们·它們	tāmen

Written Practice 5-1

Write the plural form of each of the following pronouns in Chinese and in pinyin.

1. 他 tā _____
2. 我 wǒ _____
3. 你 nǐ _____
4. 她 tā _____

REFLEXIVE PRONOUNS

The reflexive pronoun 自己 zìjǐ *self* is somewhat different from English reflexive pronouns such as *myself* or *yourself,* and it is not used as frequently as the English reflexive. Following are the two most common ways 自己 zìjǐ is used.

Immediately After a Pronoun

他不喜欢他自己。· 他不喜歡他自己。
Tā bù xǐhuan **tā zìjǐ**.
He does not like **himself**.

别人会。**我自己不会。** · 别人會。**我自己不會。**
Bié ren huì. **Wǒ zìjǐ** bù huì.
Other people can do (things). ***I myself*** *cannot.*

Immediately Before a Verb

他要自己做。
Tā yào **zìjǐ** zuò.
He wants to do (it) ***himself.***

请你自己写。 · 請你自己寫。
Qǐng **nǐ zìjǐ** xiě.
Please write (it) ***yourself.***

Written Practice 5-2

Complete the following sentences by filling in the blanks to match the English sentences.

1. _____喜欢_____。 · _____喜歡_____。

   _____ xǐhuan _____.

   They like you.

2. _____是学生。 · _____是學生。

   _____ shì xuésheng.

   We are students.

3. 我要_____做。

   Wǒ yào _____ zuò.

   I want to do it myself.

In this overview of pronouns, you might ask yourself, where are the possessive pronouns? Mandarin does not have distinct possessive pronouns. To learn how to indicate possession in Mandarin, see Chapter 12.

Nouns

A Mandarin noun has a single, unchanging form.

- It does not have gender, that is, it does not have different masculine and feminine forms.

- It does not have case, that is, it does not have different forms for the subject and object of a sentence.

- It does not have number, that is, it does not have different forms for singular and plural. Instead, it is *neutral* with respect to number. In the following sentence, for example, the nouns 老师 · 老師 lǎoshī *teacher* and 学生 · 學生 xuésheng *student* can be understood to be either singular or plural—the sentence alone gives no clue.

  老师教学生。· 老師教學生。
  Lǎoshī jiāo xuésheng.
  [*Teachers / the teacher*] *teach*[*es*] [*the student / the students / students*].

When we translate Chinese into English, we have to indicate whether a noun is singular or plural, because English grammar requires that we do so. Chinese grammar does not have such a requirement. When number is not relevant, it is not expressed in Chinese.

Expressing *And*

In English, the word *and* is used to link pronouns, nouns, and verbs. Mandarin, on the other hand, uses different words to link nouns and pronouns than it does to link verbs and verb phrases.

EXPRESSING *AND* WITH 跟 gēn AND 和 hé

The most common words used to link nouns and pronouns are the conjunctions 跟 gēn and 和 hé *and*. 跟 gēn and 和 hé have the same meaning, and the choice of one or the other is determined by speaker preference.

弟弟和妹妹
dìdi hé mèimei
younger brother and younger sister

小白跟他
Xiǎo Bái gēn tā
little Bai and he

我们跟他们 · 我們跟他們
wǒmen gēn tāmen
we and they

我喜欢猫跟狗。· 我喜歡貓跟狗。
Wǒ xǐhuan māo gēn gǒu.
I like cats and dogs.

公共汽车和地铁都很方便。· 公共汽車和地鐵都很方便。
Gōnggòng qìchē hé dìtiě dōu hěn fāngbiàn.
Buses and subways are both very convenient.

跟 gēn and 和 hé are interchangeable in this function. 跟 gēn also functions as a preposition meaning *with*.

我想跟你说话。· 我想跟你說話。
Wǒ xiǎng gēn nǐ shuō huà.
I want to speak with you.

Remember, 跟 gēn and 和 hé only link nouns, pronouns, and noun phrases; they do not link verbs, verb phrases, or sentences. To learn how to express sentences like *My younger brother studies Chinese, and he also studies French,* see Chapter 17.

Although 跟 gēn and 和 hé are easy to use, Mandarin speakers often do not use either word when they want to indicate an *and* relationship between nouns or pronouns. Instead, they simply use nouns or pronouns together without 跟 gēn or 和 hé, especially if the sentence includes 都 dōu *all, both.* (For a detailed discussion of 都 dōu, see below.)

我的爸爸、妈妈都做事。· 我的爸爸、媽媽都做事。
Wǒ de bàba, māma dōu zuò shì.
My mom (and) dad both work.

我星期一、星期二、星期三都很忙。
Wǒ xīngqī yī, xīngqī èr, xīngqī sān dōu hěn máng.
I am very busy Monday, Tuesday, (and) Wednesday.

Written Practice 5-3

Rewrite each of the following sentences, linking the nouns with 跟 gēn or 和 hé, as indicated, to match the English sentence.

1. 男孩子女孩子喜欢吃饺子。· 男孩子女孩子喜歡吃餃子。(和 hé)
   Nán háizi nǚ háizi xǐhuan chī jiǎozi.
   Boys and girls like to eat dumplings.

   _____

2. 历史文学很有意思。· 歷史文學很有意思。(跟 gēn)
   Lìshǐ wénxué hěn yǒu yìsi.
   History and literature are very interesting.

   _____

3. 美国人英国人说英文。· 美國人英國人說英文。(和 hé)
   Měiguórén Yīngguórén shuō Yīngwén.
   Americans and English people speak English.

   _____

4. 我的弟弟我的妹妹很高。(跟 gēn)
   Wǒ de dìdi wǒ de mèimei hěn gāo.
   My younger brother and my younger sister are very tall.

   _____

EXPRESSING *AND* WITH 与·與 yǔ

In literary pieces, the meaning *and* may be expressed by the word 与·與 yǔ. 与·與 yǔ is often used in formal contexts, such as invitations, and it is used in short written texts, such as the titles of books, movies, newspaper or magazine articles, and websites. Following are several examples of the use of 与·與 yǔ in titles.

人与自然·人與自然 rén yǔ zìrán
man and nature

信息与电脑·信息與電腦 xìnxī yǔ diànnǎo
information and computers

环境与发展·環境與發展 huánjìng yǔ fāzhǎn
the environment and development

电影与电视·電影與電視 diànyǐng yǔ diànshì
movies and television

艺术与艺术教育·藝術與藝術教育 yìshù yǔ yìshù jiàoyù
art and art education

民主与法制·民主與法制 mínzhǔ yǔ fǎzhì
democracy and the legal system

Expressing *Both* and *All*

Mandarin uses the word 都 dōu to indicate *both* and *all*. In English, the words *both* and *all* come before the noun they refer to, but in Mandarin, 都 dōu is an adverb and comes before the verb or verb phrase. (See Chapter 16 for more information about 都 dōu.) Following are the sentences that you wrote in Written Practice 5-3 above, but this time with 都 dōu included before the verb phrase. In Mandarin, if the meaning of the sentence involves *both* or *all,* 都 dōu is almost always present.

男孩子和女孩子都喜欢吃饺子。· 男孩子和女孩子都喜歡吃餃子。
Nán háizi hé nǚ háizi dōu xǐhuan chī jiǎozi.
Boys and girls both (all) like to eat dumplings.

历史跟文学都很有意思。· 歷史跟文學都很有意思。
Lìshǐ gēn wénxué dōu hěn yǒu yìsi.
History and literature are both interesting.

美国人和英国人都说英文。· 美國人和英國人都說英文。
Měiguórén hé Yīngguórén dōu shuō Yīngwén.
Americans and English people all speak English.

我的弟弟跟我的妹妹都很高。

Wǒ de dìdi gēn wǒ de mèimei dōu hěn gāo.

My younger brother and my younger sister are both very tall.

Written Practice 5-4

Rewrite each of the following sentences, adding 都 dōu in its proper location to match the English sentence.

1. 我们是学生。· 我們是學生。
   Wǒmen shì xuésheng.
   We are all students.

   _____

2. 他们姓陈。· 他們姓陳。
   Tāmen xìng Chén.
   They are both family-named Chen. (They both have the family name Chen.)

   _____

3. 他们学中文。· 他們學中文。
   Tāmen xué Zhōngwén.
   They all study Chinese.

   _____

4. 我们上大学。· 我們上大學。
   Wǒmen shàng dàxué.
   We all attend college.

   _____

5. 他们是美国人。· 他們是美國人。
   Tāmen shì Měiguórén.
   They are both Americans.

   _____

Indicating the Number of Nouns

Numbers are used by themselves when reciting telephone numbers, doing math, and counting (一 yī *one,* 二 èr *two,* 三 sān *three,* etc.). However, to indicate the number of *nouns*—the number of people, places, concrete objects (such as books, paper, or pencils) or abstract things (such as questions or opinions)—you must place a *classifier* (sometimes called a *measure word*) after the number. The Number + Classifier phrase comes before the noun.

Number + Classifier + Noun

We say that the number + classifier form a *phrase,* because the number and classifier must occur in that order and cannot be separated from each other. If you are talking about the number of people, places, or things, you must place a classifier after the number. You cannot omit the classifier, and you cannot put any other word between the number and classifier. For example, the classifier for 书 · 書 shū *book* is 本 běn. *One book* is expressed in Mandarin as follows.

Number	**Classifier**	**Noun**
一	本	书
一	本	書
yī	běn	shū

You cannot say 一书 · 一書 yī shū.

You cannot omit the classifier, but you *can* omit the noun. In Chinese, nouns are often omitted if they are understood from the context. For example, if I ask you how many books you have, you can answer 一本 yī běn *one.* Note that in English, a number may occur by itself, but in Chinese, when you are talking about the number of people, places, or things, the number must be followed by a classifier.

Before a classifier, the number 2 is always 两 · 兩 liǎng. (For details about the word 两 · 兩 liǎng, see Chapter 4.) To say *two books* in Mandarin, you say 两本书 · 兩本書 liǎng běn shū.

Let us summarize the basic rules of classifiers.

1. To indicate the number of people, places, or things, the number must be followed by a classifier.

2. The order of information is as follows.

Number + Classifier + Noun

3. If the noun is understood from the context, it may be omitted, that is, you can use the following construction.

Number + Classifier

4. Before a classifier, the number 2 is always 两 · 兩 liǎng.

两本书 · 兩本書 liǎng běn shū *two books*

In Mandarin, every noun is associated with at least one classifier. As you learn nouns, it is important to learn the classifiers that go with them. Classifiers sometimes give you information about the noun, and sometimes they contribute to the overall meaning of the phrase. The following sections include more detailed information about classifiers.

THE GENERAL CLASSIFIER 个 · 個 gè

The most common classifier is 个 · 個 gè. 个 · 個 gè is used to indicate the number of people.

一个人 · 一個人 yī gè rén *one person*
三个老师 · 三個老師 sān gè lǎoshī *three teachers*

个 · 個 gè is used in many time expressions.

一个钟头 · 一個鐘頭 yī gè zhōngtóu *one hour*
一个星期 · 一個星期 yī gè xīngqī *one week*
一个月 · 一個月 yī gè yuè *one month*

个 · 個 gè is also used with many abstract nouns.

一个问题 · 一個問題 yī gè wèntí *a question, a problem*
一个思想 · 一個思想 yī gè sīxiǎng *a thought*

个·個 gè has no specific meaning of its own and adds no meaning to a phrase, but if you are counting people or referring to the number of people, you can always use the classifier 个·個 gè. Many other classifiers have meanings of their own, and some nouns require certain classifiers. However, if you cannot remember the classifier that is associated with a noun, use 个·個 gè. It is better to use 个·個 gè than to omit the classifier altogether.

CLASSIFIERS THAT REFER TO THE SHAPE OR CATEGORY OF A NOUN

Some classifiers refer to the shape or category of nouns. These include 本 běn (volume), 支·枝 zhī (a long, thin object), 块·塊 kuài (a lump of something), and 张·張 zhāng (a flat, thin object that is square or rectangular in shape). 本 běn is the classifier for books, 支·枝 zhī is the classifier for pens and pencils, 块·塊 kuài is the classifier for rocks and stones (and dollars), and 张·張 zhāng is the classifier for sheets of paper (and photographs and tables—think of the tabletop).

Number	+ Classifier	+ Noun		
一	本	书		
一	本	書		
yī	běn	shū		
one	volume	book	→	one book
一	支	笔		
一	枝	筆		
yī	zhī	bǐ		
one	long, thin	pen	→	one pen
一	块	石头		
一	塊	石頭		
yī	kuài	shítou		
one	lump	stone	→	one stone
一	张	纸		
一	張	紙		
yī	zhāng	zhǐ		
one	sheet	paper	→	one sheet of paper

Oral Practice

Review numbers in Chapter 4, then read aloud the following phrases in Mandarin.

1. two pens → 两支笔·兩枝筆 liǎng zhī bǐ

2. eight stones → 八块石头·八塊石頭 bā kuài shítou

3. three books → 三本书·三本書 sān běn shū

4. 20 pens → 二十支笔·二十枝筆 èrshí zhī bǐ

5. 50 sheets of paper → 五十张纸·五十張紙 wǔshí zhāng zhǐ

CLASSIFIERS THAT INDICATE THE CONTAINER OR WEIGHT OF A NOUN

Some classifiers measure a noun by indicating the container or the weight of the noun. Examples include 杯 bēi *cup,* 瓶 píng *bottle,* 碗 wǎn *bowl,* 包 bāo *bag,* 克 kè *gram,* and 斤 jīn *½ kilogram*—approximately one pound. Note that these classifiers are often translated in English.

Number + Classifier + Noun

一	杯	水		
yī	bēi	shuǐ		
one	*cup*	*water*	→	*one cup of water*
一	瓶	可乐		
一	瓶	可樂		
yī	píng	kělè		
one	*bottle*	*cola*	→	*one bottle of cola*
一	碗	饭		
一	碗	飯		
yī	wǎn	fàn		
one	*bowl*	*rice*	→	*one bowl of rice*
一	包	糖		
yī	bāo	táng		
one	*bag*	*sugar, candy*	→	*a bag of candy*

Number + Classifier + Noun

一	斤	水果		
yī	jīn	shuǐguǒ		
one	pound	fruit	→	*a pound of fruit*

Oral Practice

Read aloud the following phrases in Mandarin.

1. two bottles of water → 两瓶水·兩瓶水 liǎng píng shuǐ

2. three cups of water → 三杯水 sān bēi shuǐ

3. five pounds of fruit → 五斤水果 wǔ jīn shuǐguǒ

4. 12 bottles of cola → 十二瓶可乐·十二瓶可樂 shí'èr píng kělè

5. 100 grams tea (茶 chá) → 一百克茶 yī bǎi kè chá

CLASSIFIERS THAT INDICATE THE NUMBER OF NOUNS OR SEVERAL NOUNS

Some classifiers indicate the number of nouns or several nouns. These include 双·雙 shuāng *pair*, 套 tào *a set*, and 些 xiē *several, a few*. 些 xiē always occurs with the number one: 一些 yī xiē *several*; it also occurs with the words for *this* and *that* (see below).

Number + Classifier + Noun

一	双	鞋子		
一	雙	鞋子		
yī	shuāng	xiézi		
one	pair	shoes	→	*one pair of shoes*
一	套	衣服		
yī	tào	yīfu		
one	set	clothing	→	*a set of clothes*
一	些	问题		
一	些	問題		
yī	xiē	wèntí		
one	several	question, problem	→	*several questions, several problems*

ONE NOUN, MORE THAN ONE CLASSIFIER

A noun may be associated with more than one classifier, depending on the over-all meaning of the phrase. For example, to say *one **cup** of water,* you say 一杯水 yī bēi shuǐ, and to say *one **bottle** of water,* you say 一瓶水 yī píng shuǐ.

Written Practice 5-5

Write the following noun phrases in Chinese and in pinyin.

1. three questions   _____

2. several questions   _____

3. a cup of water   _____

4. a bowl of rice   _____

5. a piece of candy   _____
   (HINT: A piece is a lump.)

Expressing *This* and *That*

As in English, the Mandarin words for *this* and *that* are used in two different ways. *This* and *that* are used to indicate a specific person, place, or thing, as in the sentences ***This book** is very interesting* and *I want to see **that movie**.* They can also be used as the subject of a sentence without a noun following, as in the sentence ***This** is an easy class.* In the following sections, we discuss these uses of the Mandarin words for *this* and *that*.

EXPRESSING *THIS* NOUN AND *THAT* NOUN WITH 这·這 zhè/zhèi AND 那 nà/nèi

The Mandarin words for *this/these* and *that/those* are 这·這 zhè/zhèi and 那 nà/nèi, respectively. In this usage, the words have alternative pronunciations. Mandarin speakers differ in their preference for the pronunciation zhè or zhèi and the pronunciation nà or nèi, and you should use your Chinese teacher as your model.

To say *this noun*, a classifier is included.

这 · 這 zhè/zhèi + Classifier + Noun

Many Mandarin speakers prefer the pronunciation zhèi when referring to *this (one) noun*, but individual speakers vary in their preference.

    To say *that noun*, a classifier is included.

那 nà/nèi + Classifier + Noun

Many Mandarin speakers prefer the pronunciation nèi when referring to *that (one) noun*, but individual speakers vary in their preference.

Specifier + Classifier + Noun

这	本	书	
這	本	書	
zhèi	běn	shū	
this	Classifier	*book*	→ *this book*
那	个	人	
那	個	人	
nèi	gè	rén	
that	Classifier	*person*	→ *that person*
这	张	纸	
這	張	紙	
zhèi	zhāng	zhǐ	
this	*sheet of*	*paper*	→ *this sheet of paper*
那	支	笔	
那	枝	筆	
nèi	zhī	bǐ	
that	Classifier	*pen*	→ *that pen*
这	些	人	
這	些	人	
zhèi	xiē	rén	
these	Classifier	*people*	→ *these people*
那	些	书	
那	些	書	
nèi	xiē	shū	
those	Classifier	*books*	→ *those books*

When used in this way, 这·這 zhè/zhèi and 那 nà/nèi are called *specifiers,* because they *specify* the identity of the noun that is referred to.

When 这·這 zhè/zhèi or 那 nà/nèi is used with a noun, it must be followed by a classifier.

这本书·這本書 zhè běn shū *this book*
那支笔·那枝筆 nà zhī bǐ *that pen*

You cannot say 这书·這書 zhè shū or 那笔·那筆 nà bǐ. However, as with the construction Number + Classifier + Noun, you can omit the noun if it is understood from the context. For example, if I ask you which pen you would like, you can answer 那支·那枝 nà zhī *that one.* If I ask you which book is yours, you can answer 这本·這本 zhèi běn *this one.* Note that English uses the word *one* in the answer, but that in Mandarin, the word *one* is not part of the expression.

Specifiers can be combined with numbers and classifiers in the same phrase.

Specifier + Number + Classifier + Noun

这	三	本	书
這	三	本	書
zhè	sān	běn	shū
these	*three*	Classifier	*books*
那	两	个	人
那	兩	個	人
nà	liǎng	gè	rén
those	*two*	Classifier	*people*
这	十	张	纸
這	十	張	紙
zhè	shí	zhāng	zhǐ
these	*ten*	*sheets of*	*paper*
那	五	支	笔
那	五	枝	筆
nà	wǔ	zhī	bǐ
those	*five*	Classifier	*pens*

Written Practice 5-6

Rearrange each of the following groups of words in the correct order to match the English phrase.

1. 笔 – 两 – 这 – 支 · 筆 – 兩 – 這 – 枝
   bǐ – liǎng – zhè – zhī
   these two pens

   _____

2. 五 – 那 – 鞋子 – 双 · 五 – 那 – 鞋子 – 雙
   wǔ – nà – xiézi – shuāng
   those five pairs of shoes

   _____

3. 六 – 书 – 本 – 这 · 六 – 書 – 本 – 這
   liù – shū – běn – zhè
   these six books

   _____

4. 这 – 七 – 纸 – 张 · 這 – 七 – 紙 – 張
   zhè – qī – zhǐ – zhāng
   these seven sheets of paper

   _____

5. 那 – 九 – 水 – 杯
   nà – jiǔ – shuǐ – bēi
   those nine glasses of water

   _____

USING *THIS* AND *THAT* AS THE SUBJECT OF A SENTENCE WITH 这 · 這 zhè AND 那 nà

这 · 這 zhè and 那 nà can occur alone, without a classifier and noun following, as the subject of a sentence. In this function, they are sometimes called *demonstratives*, since they *demonstrate*, or point to, a particular object or objects. Note that when they are used as demonstratives, 这 · 這 and 那 can only be pronounced zhè and nà, respectively.

Oral Practice

Read aloud the following sentences in Mandarin. For usage of the verb 是 shì *be*, see Chapter 6.

1. 这是我的书。· 這是我的書。Zhè shì wǒ de shū. → *This is my book.*

2. 那是你的书。· 那是你的書。Nà shì nǐ de shū. → *That is your book.*

3. 这是他的水。· 這是他的水。Zhè shì tā de shuǐ. → *This is his water.*

4. 这是我们的水。· 這是我們的水。Zhè shì wǒmen de shuǐ. → *This is our water.*

5. 那是他们的纸。· 那是他們的紙。Nà shì tāmen de zhǐ. → *That is their paper.*

QUIZ

1. Complete the following sentence by filling in the blanks to match the English sentence.

   _____ 跟_____是朋友。

   _____ gēn _____ shì péngyou.

   She and I are friends.

2. Rewrite Chen Ming's response, adding the missing word.

   Li Li: How many younger brothers do you have?
   Chen Ming: 三。Sān.

   _____

3. Rewrite Chen Ming's response, adding the missing word.

   Li Li: Which book do you want to buy?
   Chen Ming: 我要买那书。· 我要買那書。Wǒ yào mǎi nà shū.

   _____

4. Rewrite the following sentence, adding 都 dōu in its proper location.

   学生和老师喜欢那个电影。· 學生和老師喜歡那個電影。
   Xuésheng hé lǎoshī xǐhuan nàge diànyǐng.
   Students and teachers all like that movie.

   _____

5. Rewrite the following sentence, adding 都 dōu in its proper location.

   我们是朋友。· 我們是朋友。
   Wǒmen shì péngyou.
   We are all friends.

   _____

6. Answer the following question, using the number in parentheses,
   the appropriate classifier, and the noun. Write your answer in Chinese
   and in pinyin.

   How many people are here? (12)

   _____

7. Answer the following question, using the number in parentheses
   and the classifier alone. Write your answer in Chinese and in pinyin.

   How many bowls of rice did you eat? (2)

   _____

8. Select the classifier that cannot be used in the following phrase.

   三 _____ 水   sān _____ shuǐ

   a. 瓶 píng
   b. 碗 wǎn
   c. 些 xiē
   d. 杯 bēi

9. Rewrite the following phrase, adding the number word in parentheses in the correct location.

那个老师 (两) · 那個老師 (兩)
nàge lǎoshī (liǎng)
those two teachers

---

10. Rearrange the following group of words in the correct order to match the English phrase.

个 – 问题 – 五 · 個 – 問題 – 五
gè – wèntí – wǔ
five questions

PART TWO

ACTIONS AND VERBS

CHAPTER 6

Identifying Nouns with Linking Verbs

In this chapter, you will learn about:

Expressing Identity with the Verb 是 shì be

Expressing Family Names with the Verb 姓 xìng family name, be family-named

Expressing Someone's Name with the Verb 叫 jiào call, be called

Expressing Identity with the Verb 是 shì *be*

The verb 是 shì is used to state and negate identities and to ask about identities. The adverb 都 dōu *both, all* is used with 是 shì to indicate the identity of *both* or *all* of the subjects of a sentence.

STATING IDENTITY WITH 是 shì *be*

是 shì links the subject of a sentence with a noun or noun phrase in the predicate, that is, it indicates that the subject is identified by the noun or noun phrase that follows it.

Subject	是 shì *be*	Noun (Phrase)
她	是	老师。
她	是	老師。
Tā	shì	lǎoshī.
She	*is*	*(a) teacher.*
波士顿	是	一个城市。
波士頓	是	一個城市。
Bōshìdùn	shì	yī gè chéngshì.
Boston	*is*	*a city.*

是 shì is commonly used in introducing people. The subject of 是 shì may be the demonstrative 这·這 zhè *this* or 那 nà *that*. (See Chapter 5 for a detailed discussion of expressing *this* and *that* in Chinese.)

Subject	是 shì *be*	Noun (Phrase)
这	是	王老师。
這	是	王老師。
Zhè	shì	Wáng lǎoshī.
This	*is*	*Teacher Wang.*
那	是	陈医生。
那	是	陳醫生。
Nà	shì	Chén yīshēng.
That	*is*	*Dr. Chen.*

Oral Practice

1. Introduce the following people, using the phrase 这是·這是 zhè shì *this is.*

   a. 小王 Xiǎo Wáng *Little Wang* →
   这是小王。· 這是小王。Zhè shì Xiǎo Wáng.

   b. 我的朋友 wǒ de péngyou *my friend* →
   这是我的朋友。· 這是我的朋友。Zhè shì wǒ de péngyou.

2. Link the following subjects and noun phrases, using 是 shì.

   a. 小王 Xiǎo Wáng – 学生·學生 xuésheng *student* →
   小王是学生。· 小王是學生。Xiǎo Wáng shì xuésheng.

   b. 白小春 Bái Xiǎochūn – 老师·老師 lǎoshī *teacher* →
   白小春是老师。· 白小春是老師。Bái Xiǎochūn shì lǎoshī.

NEGATING 是 shì

The negation for 是 shì is always 不 bù, which usually comes right before 是 shì. However, if the sentence includes certain adverbs, such as 都 dōu *both, all* (see below), 不 bù may come before the adverb.

Subject	Negated *be*	Noun
那	不是	陈医生。
那	不是	陳醫生。
Nà	bù shì	Chén yīshēng.
That	*is not*	*Dr. Chen.*
我	不是	英国人。
我	不是	英國人。
Wǒ	bù shì	Yīngguó rén.
I	*am not*	*English.*

Written Practice 6-1

Negate each of the following Mandarin sentences to match the English sentence.

1. 他是我哥哥。
   Tā shì wǒ gēge.
   He is not my older brother.

   _____

2. 我妈妈是老师。 · 我媽媽是老師。
   Wǒ māma shì lǎoshī.
   My mom is not a teacher.

   _____

3. 那是字典。
   Nà shì zìdiǎn.
   That is not a dictionary.

   _____

4. 我的朋友是大学生。 · 我的朋友是大學生。
   Wǒ de péngyou shì dàxuéshēng.
   My friend is not a college student.

   _____

SAYING *ALL, BOTH* AND *NOT ALL, NOT BOTH*

In Chapter 5, you learned that the word 都 dōu is used to express the meanings *both* and *all* in Mandarin. 都 dōu is an adverb and comes before the verb or verb phrase. In affirmative sentences, it comes right before 是 shì.

弟弟和妹妹都是学生。 · 弟弟和妹妹都是學生。
Dìdi hé mèimei dōu shì xuésheng.
Younger sister and younger brother are both students.

他们都是老师。 · 他們都是老師。
Tāmen dōu shì lǎoshī.
They are both (all) teachers.

小白的朋友都是学生。· 小白的朋友都是學生。
Xiǎo Bái de péngyou dōu shì xuésheng.
Little Bai's friends are all students.

Written Practice 6-2

The four statements below are about 王美玲 Wáng Měilíng. Following the example, write a sentence after each statement, declaring that the statement is true for all of Wang Meiling's friends.

EXAMPLE   王美玲是医生。   →   王美玲的朋友都是医生。
王美玲是醫生。   王美玲的朋友都是醫生。
Wáng Měilíng shì yīsheng.   Wáng Měilíng de péngyou dōu shì yīsheng.

Wang Meiling is a doctor.   *All of Wang Meiling's friends are doctors.*

1. 王美玲是中国人。· 王美玲是中國人。
Wáng Měilíng shì Zhōngguó rén.
Wang Meiling is Chinese.

_____

2. 王美玲是老师。· 王美玲是老師。
Wáng Měilíng shì lǎoshī.
Wang Meiling is a teacher.

_____

3. 王美玲是母亲。· 王美玲是母親。
Wáng Měilíng shì mǔqīn.
Wang Meiling is a mother.

_____

4. 王美玲是很好的人。
Wáng Měilíng shì hěn hǎo de rén.
Wang Meiling is a very good person.

_____

In a negative sentence, 都 dōu may come before or after 不 bù, depending on the meaning of the sentence.

都不 dōu bù means *none* (literally, *both/all are not*).

小白的朋友都不是学生。· 小白的朋友都不是學生。
Xiǎo Bái de péngyou dōu bù shì xuésheng.
None of Xiao Bai's friends are students.
　(lit., *All of Xiao Bai's friends are not students.*)

不都 bù dōu means *not all* (literally, *not all are*).

小白的朋友不都是学生。· 小白的朋友不都是學生。
Xiǎo Bái de péngyou bù dōu shì xuésheng.
Not all of Xiao Bai's friends are students.

The meanings and uses of 都 dōu are discussed in more detail in Chapter 5.

Written Practice 6-3

Rewrite each of the following sentences, adding 不都 bù dōu or 都不 dōu bù to match the English sentence.

1. 他们是学生。· 他們是學生。
   Tāmen shì xuésheng.
   They are not all students. (i.e., Some of them are students, some are not.)

   _____

2. 我们是老师。· 我們是老師。
   Wǒmen shì lǎoshī.
   We are all not teachers. (i.e., All of us are something else, not teachers.)

   _____

3. 那是我的钱。· 那是我的錢。
   Nà shì wǒ de qián.
   That money is all not mine. (i.e., None of that money is mine.)

   _____

4. 他们是我的朋友。·他們是我的朋友。

Tāmen shì wǒ de péngyou.

They are not all my friends. (i.e., Some of them are my friends, some aren't.)

ASKING ABOUT IDENTITY: YES-NO QUESTIONS WITH 是 shì

The two most common forms of yes-no questions in Mandarin are 吗·嗎 ma questions and Verb-Not-Verb questions. To form a 吗·嗎 ma yes-no question with 是 shì, 吗·嗎 ma is added to the end of the sentence, adjusting pronouns as necessary.

Statement	ma Question
他是学生。·他是學生。	他是学生吗？·他是學生嗎？
Tā shì xuésheng.	Tā shì xuésheng ma?
He is a student.	*Is he a student?*
我是老师。·我是老師。	你是老师吗？·你是老師嗎？
Wǒ shì lǎoshī.	Nǐ shì lǎoshī ma?
I am a teacher.	*Are you a teacher?*

The most common way to form a Verb-Not-Verb question with 是 shì, is to place 不是 bù shì after 是 shì, that is, to say 是不是 shì bù shì *is or is not.*

Statement	Verb-Not-Verb Question
他是学生。·他是學生。	他是不是学生？·他是不是學生？
Tā shì xuésheng.	Tā shì bù shì xuésheng?
He is a student.	*Is he a student?*
我是老师。·我是老師。	你是不是老师？·你是不是老師？
Wǒ shì lǎoshī.	Nǐ shì bù shì lǎoshī?
I am a teacher.	*Are you a teacher?*

Alternatively, 不是 bù shì can be added to the end of the sentence.

Statement	Verb-Not-Verb Question
他是学生。· 他是學生。	他是学生不是？· 他是學生不是？
Tā shì xuésheng.	Tā shì xuésheng bù shì?
He is a student.	*Is he a student?*
我是老师。· 我是老師。	你是老师不是？· 你是老師不是？
Wǒ shì lǎoshī.	Nǐ shì lǎoshī bù shì?
I am a teacher.	*Are you a teacher?*

Oral Practice

Change the following sentences into yes-no questions with 吗 · 嗎 ma, adjusting pronouns as necessary.

1. 王老师是美国人。· 王老師是美國人。 Wáng lǎoshī shì Měiguó rén. →
   王老师是美国人吗？· 王老師是美國人嗎？ Wáng lǎoshī shì Měiguó rén ma?

2. 他是我的老师。· 他是我的老師。 Tā shì wǒ de lǎoshī. →
   他是你的老师吗？· 他是你的老師嗎？ Tā shì nǐ de lǎoshī ma?

3. 他们是学生。· 他們是學生。 Tāmen shì xuésheng. →
   他们是学生吗？· 他們是學生嗎？ Tāmen shì xuésheng ma?

Written Practice 6-4

Change each of the following 吗 · 嗎 ma yes-no questions into a 是不是 shì bù shì question.

1. 王老师是美国人吗？· 王老師是美國人嗎？
   Wáng lǎoshī shì Měiguó rén ma?
   Is Professor Wang American?

   _____

2. 他是你的老师吗？· 他是你的老師嗎？
   Tā shì nǐ de lǎoshī ma?
   Is he your teacher?

   _____

3. 他们是学生吗？ · 他們是學生嗎？
   Tāmen shì xuésheng ma?
   Are they students?

   _____

4. 那本书是你的吗？ · 那本書是你的嗎？
   Nà běn shū shì nǐ de ma?
   Is that book yours?

   _____

5. 她是你的朋友吗？ · 她是你的朋友嗎？
   Tā shì nǐ de péngyou ma?
   Is she your friend?

   _____

See Chapter 14 for a detailed discussion of yes-no questions and for more practice forming and answering yes-no questions.

是 shì functions differently than the English verb *be*. While the English verb *be* has many functions, 是 shì can only link a subject with a *noun phrase*. You will learn in Chapter 7 that 是 shì cannot be used if the predicate is an adjectival verb, that is, you cannot use 是 shì in Mandarin to express meanings such as *The book is expensive*.

Expressing Family Names with the Verb 姓 xìng *family name, be family-named*

The word 姓 xìng can be used as a noun or as a verb. As a noun, 姓 xìng means *family name*. As a verb, it is used to state one's family name or to ask others for their family names. This section focuses on 姓 xìng as a verb.

USING 姓 xìng TO INTRODUCE A FAMILY NAME

The verb 姓 xìng introduces a person's family name. It can be roughly translated as *be family-named*. The structure of a sentence with 姓 xìng is as follows.

Person	姓 xìng	Family Name
我	姓	高。
Wǒ	xìng	Gāo.
I	*am family-named*	*Gao.* (i.e., *My family name is Gao.*)
他	姓	林。
Tā	xìng	Lín.
He	*is family-named*	*Lin.* (i.e., *His family name is Lin.*)

姓 xìng may only be used to introduce the family name—it may not be used to introduce any other combination of names, and it may never introduce a title. For example, the following sentences are incorrect.

✗ 她姓王美玲。
   Tā xìng Wáng Měilíng.

✗ 她姓老师。· 她姓老師。
   Tā xìng lǎoshī.

✗ 她姓王老师。· 她姓王老師。
   Tā xìng Wáng lǎoshī.

Oral Practice

Indicate the family name of each of the following people, using a complete sentence.

1. 陈美玲 · 陳美玲 Chén Měilíng → 她姓陈。· 她姓陳。 Tā xìng Chén.

2. 王明德 Wáng Míngdé → 他姓王。 Tā xìng Wáng.

3. 张平 · 張平 Zhāng Píng → 他姓张。· 他姓張。 Tā xìng Zhāng.

NEGATING 姓 xìng

姓 xìng is negated with 不 bù *no, not*, which comes right before 姓 xìng.

我不姓高。
Wǒ bù xìng Gāo.
I am not family-named Gao. (i.e., *My family name is not Gao.*)
他不姓林。
Tā bù xìng Lín.
He is not family-named Lin. (i.e., *His family name is not Lin.*)

Written Practice 6-5

For each of the following family names, write a complete Mandarin sentence indicating that it is not your family name.

1. 刘·劉 Liú _____

2. 何 Hé _____

3. 周 Zhōu _____

4. 马·馬 Mǎ _____

ASKING ABOUT FAMILY NAMES

To ask someone his or her family name, the following question is ordinarily used.

你姓什么？· 你姓甚麼？
Nǐ xìng shénme?
What are you family-named? (i.e., *What is your family name?*)

See Chapter 15 for a detailed discussion about asking and answering content questions.

A very polite, formal, and respectful way to ask someone his or her family name is the following.

你贵姓？· 你貴姓？
Nǐ guì xìng?
What is your honorable family name?

This question is often preceded by the introductory 请问·請問 qǐng wèn *may I please ask*. The question 你贵姓？· 你貴姓？ Nǐ guì xìng? is appropriate if the person you are speaking to has higher status than you. Even in formal situations, it is generally not used when speaking to people who have lower status than you.

Oral Practice

Ask the following people their family names.

1. A new student in your class →
   你姓什么？· 你姓甚麼？ Nǐ xìng shénme?

2. A professor whom you meet in the library →
   你贵姓？· 你貴姓？ Nǐ guì xìng?

3. Your new roommate →
   你姓什么？· 你姓甚麼？ Nǐ xìng shénme?

4. A person you are interviewing for a job →
   你姓什么？· 你姓甚麼？ Nǐ xìng shénme?

Expressing Someone's Name with the Verb 叫 jiào *call, be called*

In Chinese, you don't ask someone what his or her name *is*. Instead, you ask what he or she *is called*. In this section, you will learn how to use the verb 叫 jiào *call, be called* to indicate what you are called and to ask others what they are called.

USING 叫 jiào TO INTRODUCE THE WAY A PERSON IS TO BE ADDRESSED

叫 jiào introduces the way in which a person should be addressed (see Chapter 3). 叫 jiào is often translated in Chinese textbooks as (*So and so's*) *name is,* but its use is broader. Following are the most common ways in which 叫 jiào is used.

- 叫 jiào is used to introduce a person's name.

  我叫周利明。
  Wǒ jiào Zhōu Lìmíng.
  I am called Liming Zhou. (i.e., *My name is Liming Zhou.*)

- 叫 jiào is used to introduce a person's nickname.

  他叫小白。
  Tā jiào Xiǎo Bái.
  He is called Little Bai.

叫 jiào *may not* introduce a family name alone: The following sentences are incorrect.

✗ 我叫周。
  Wǒ jiào Zhōu.
✗ 他叫白。
  Tā jiào Bái.

To introduce the family name alone, use 姓 xìng *be family-named.*

NEGATING 叫 jiào

叫 jiào is negated with 不 bù *no, not,* which comes right before 叫 jiào.

我不叫王玲玲。
Wǒ bù jiào Wáng Línglíng.
I am not called Lingling Wang.

ASKING ABOUT A NAME WITH 叫 jiào

To ask someone what he or she is called, the following questions are used.

你叫什么名字？· 你叫甚麼名字？
Nǐ jiào shénme míngzi?
你叫什么？· 你叫甚麼？
Nǐ jiào shénme?
What are you called?

In Chinese culture, it is often appropriate to ask others how they wish to be called. The following formula is used.

我(应该)怎么称呼你？· 我(應該)怎麼稱呼你？
Wǒ (yīnggāi) zěnme chēnghu nǐ?
How do I address you? OR *How should I address you?*

See Chapter 3 for a detailed discussion of Chinese names and titles.
  叫 jiào is also used to tell others to do something.

妈妈叫孩子去睡觉。· 媽媽叫孩子去睡覺。
Māma jiào háizi qù shuì jiào.
Mom told the children to go to sleep.

Oral Practice

Introduce each of the following people, using the information supplied along with 姓 xìng or 叫 jiào, as appropriate.

1. 马·馬 Mǎ → 　　　　　　她姓马。· 她姓馬。
   Tā xìng Mǎ. *Her family name is Ma.*

2. 陈老师·陳老師 Chén lǎoshī → 她叫陈老师。· 她叫陳老師。
   Tā jiào Chén lǎoshī.
   She is called Teacher Chen.

3. 老王 lǎo Wáng → 　　　　他叫老王。
   Tā jiào Lǎo Wáng. *He is called Old Wang.*

Written Practice 6-6

You meet the following people and have a short conversation with them, in which you ask what they are called and they respond. Write each conversation, using 叫 jiào in each question and answer; follow the example.

EXAMPLE   刘春 · 劉春 Liú Chūn
Q: 你叫什么名字？· 你叫甚麼名字？ Nǐ jiào shénme míngzi?
A: 我叫刘春。· 我叫劉春。 Wǒ jiào Liú Chūn.

1. 李丽 · 李麗 Lǐ Lì

   Q: _____

   A: _____

2. 陈爱平 · 陳愛平 Chén Àipíng

   Q: _____

   A: _____

3. 王惠娜 Wáng Huìnà

   Q: _____

   A: _____

4. 周萍 Zhōu Píng

   Q: _____

   A: _____

CULTURE DEMYSTIFIED

Greetings

When Chinese people meet an acquaintance in public (for example, while taking a walk or shopping), they don't say 你好。 Nǐ hǎo. *Hello.* Instead, they typically greet the person by calling (叫 jiào-ing) his or her name.

For example, if you were to see your friend Little Bai while you were walking to the library, you would say 小白。 Xiǎo Bái.

Parents train their children in proper behavior by reminding them to 叫 jiào (call the name or title of) acquaintances when they see them. If a child is with a parent and they meet the child's teacher, the parent prompts the child to greet the teacher as follows.

叫老师。· 叫老師。
Jiào lǎoshī.
Greet your teacher.

The child responds as follows.

老师。· 老師。
Lǎoshī.
Teacher.

If they meet the child's aunt, or a woman about the same age as the child's mother (and therefore the same age as an aunt), the parent prompts the child to greet the aunt as follows.

叫阿姨。
Jiào āyí.
Greet Auntie.

QUIZ

1. Introduce each of the following people, using 这是·這是 Zhè shì *This is . . .*

   a. Teacher Ma

b. Xiaochun Bai (白小春 Bái Xiǎochūn)

   _____

2. Link the following subjects and noun phrases, using 是 shì.

   a. That person – doctor

   _____

   b. This – a book

   _____

3. For each of the following people, write a complete sentence indicating the family name.

   a. 唐新华·唐新華 Táng Xīnhuá

   _____

   b. 周利 Zhōu Lì

   _____

   c. 马嘉美·馬嘉美 Mǎ Jiāměi

   _____

4. Introduce each of the following people, including the information supplied and using either 姓 xìng or 叫 jiào, as appropriate.

   a. 张·張 Zhāng

   _____

   b. 周明德 Zhōu Míngdé

   _____

5. Select the correct Mandarin translation for the following English sentence.

   His name is not Qinglin Bai.

   a. 他不姓白青林。Tā bù xìng Bái Qīnglín.
   b. 他不叫青林白。Tā bù jiào Qīnglín Bái.
   c. 他不叫白青林。Tā bù jiào Bái Qīnglín.

6. Select the correct English translation for the following Mandarin sentence.

他姓张。· 他姓張。Tā xìng Zhāng.

   a. His first name is Zhang.
   b. He is called Little Zhang.
   c. His family name is Zhang.

7. Fill in each blank in the following sentence with 姓 xìng or 叫 jiào, as appropriate, to match the English sentences.

他_____周，_____周明德。

Tā _____ Zhōu, _____ Zhōu Míngdé.

His family name is Zhou. His name is Zhou Mingde.

8. Fill in each blank in the following sentence with 姓 xìng or 叫 jiào, as appropriate, to match the English sentences.

他_____王平。我_____他小王。

Tā _____ Wáng Píng. Wǒ _____ tā Xiǎo Wáng.

His name is Wang Ping. I call him Little Wang.

9. Rewrite the following sentence in the correct word order to match the English sentence. The family name is in bold type.

美玲她白叫。
Měilíng tā **Bái** jiào.
Her name is Meiling Bai.

___

10. Rewrite the following sentence, adding 都 dōu in the appropriate location to match the English sentence.

中文老师不是中国人。· 中文老師不是中國人。
Zhōngwén lǎoshī bù shì Zhōngguó rén.
Not all Chinese teachers are Chinese people.

___

CHAPTER 7

Adjectival and Stative Verbs

In this chapter, you will learn about:

Describing Things with Common Adjectival Verbs
Using Adjectival Verbs with Intensifiers
Adjectival Verbs in the Predicate
The Adjectival Verbs 多 duō many, a lot *and* 少 shǎo few
Expressing Feelings with Stative Verbs
Using Stative Verbs with Intensifiers
Expressing Past States
Comparing Stative Verbs That Have Similar Meanings

Describing Things with Common Adjectival Verbs

Like English, Mandarin has words that describe the qualities of a person, place, or thing—words like *good, bad, big, expensive, cheap, tall,* and *short.* Although the Mandarin words can be translated into English as adjectives, they function as verbs in Mandarin and the word *be* is included in their meaning. These words, as a result, are called adjectival verbs. Following are common Mandarin adjectival verbs, along with their English translations.

好	hǎo	*be good*
坏 · 壞	huài	*be bad*
贵 · 貴	guì	*be expensive*
便宜	piányi	*be cheap*
高	gāo	*be tall*
矮	ǎi	*be short in height*
长 · 長	cháng	*be long*
短	duǎn	*be short in length*
快	kuài	*be fast*
慢	màn	*be slow*
漂亮	piàoliang	*be beautiful*
忙	máng	*be busy*
难 · 難	nán	*be difficult, be hard*
容易	róngyì	*be easy*
聪明 · 聰明	cōngming	*be smart*
笨	bèn	*be stupid*
用功	yònggōng	*be hardworking*
懒 · 懶	lǎn	*be lazy*
高兴 · 高興	gāoxìng	*be happy*
难过 · 難過	nánguò	*be sad*
复杂 · 複雜	fùzá	*be complicated*
简单 · 簡單	jiǎndān	*be simple*

In the following sections, you will learn how to use adjectival verbs to express concepts like *very tall, not tall,* and *That person is tall.*

Using Adjectival Verbs with Intensifiers

To say *very tall* in Chinese, use an adjectival verb with an intensifier such as *very, really,* or *extremely.* Most Mandarin intensifiers come before the adjectival verb, although a few come after the adjectival verb.

INTENSIFIERS THAT COME BEFORE AN ADJECTIVAL VERB

Following is a list of Mandarin intensifiers that come before an adjectival verb, along with their English translations.

很	hěn	*very*
挺	tǐng	*very*
真	zhēn	*really*
太	tài	*too*
非常	fēicháng	*extremely*
特别	tèbié	*especially*
相当·相當	xiāngdāng	*rather*
比较·比較	bǐjiào	*relatively*
有一点·有一點	yǒu yīdiǎn	*a little*
更	gèng	*even more*
越来越·越來越	yuèláiyuè	*more and more*
最	zuì	*most*

Following are examples of phrases composed of Intensifier + Adjectival Verb. As you can see, the word order in Mandarin and English is identical.

真漂亮	zhēn piàoliang	*really pretty*
太贵·太貴	tài guì	*too expensive*
非常快	fēicháng kuài	*extremely fast*
比较容易·比較容易	bǐjiào róngyì	*relatively easy*
越来越好·越來越好	yuèláiyuè hǎo	*better and better*

You can use your knowledge of English to determine whether a particular intensifier from this list can be used with a particular adjectival verb: If you can use the intensifier with the corresponding adjective in English, you can use it with the adjectival verb in Mandarin. For example, if you can say *extremely expensive* in English, you can say 非常贵·非常貴 fēicháng guì in Mandarin.

The Neutral Intensifier 很 hěn

In affirmative sentences, adjectival verbs typically occur with an intensifier. According to Mandarin speakers, using an adjectival verb in an affirmative sentence without an intensifier sounds awkward. The intensifier 很 hěn has come to be used as a "neutral intensifier" in affirmative sentences, filling the intensifier position without adding the full meaning of *very*. If you are not sure which intensifier to use in an affirmative sentence with an adjectival verb, use 很 hěn. When translating from Mandarin to English, you do not always need to translate 很 hěn.

Later in this chapter, you will learn that intensifiers that occur with adjectival verbs can also be used to describe stative verbs.

Oral Practice

Read the following phrases aloud.

1. 特别漂亮 tèbié piàoliang *especially pretty*
2. 相当贵·相當貴 xiāngdāng guì *rather expensive*
3. 最快 zuì kuài *(the) fastest*
4. 比较难·比較難 bǐjiào nán *relatively difficult*

Written Practice 7-1

Rewrite each of the following phrases, adding the Mandarin intensifier for the English word in parentheses. Then translate the phrase into English.

1. 矮 ǎi (*a little*)

   _____

2. 慢 màn (*rather*)

   _____

3. 难·難 nán (*relatively*)

   _____

4. 聪明·聰明 cōngming (*extremely*)

_____

5. 笨 bèn (*really*)

_____

INTENSIFIERS THAT COME AFTER AN ADJECTIVAL VERB

A small number of intensifiers come right after the adjectival verb, becoming part of the adjectival verb in the way that the ending *-er* becomes part of English adjectives like *bigger* and *faster*. No other word can come between the adjectival verb and the intensifier ending. Following are intensifiers that come after an adjectival verb, along with example phrases.

极了·極了 jíle *extremely*

| 好极了·好極了 | hǎojíle | *extremely good* |
| 贵极了·貴極了 | guìjíle | *extremely expensive* |

得很 dehěn *very*

| 好得很 | hǎodehěn | *very good* |
| 贵得很·貴得很 | guìdehěn | *very expensive* |

Intensifiers that come after an adjectival verb are used only when the adjectival verb occurs in the predicate. Later in this chapter, you will learn how they are used in sentences like *That person is tall.*

NEGATING ADJECTIVAL VERBS

Concepts like *not tall, not expensive,* and *not interesting* are expressed by negating the adjectival verb. Most adjectival verbs are negated with the word 不 bù *no, not,* which comes before the adjectival verb.

| 不高 | bù gāo | *not tall* |
| 不贵·不貴 | bù guì | *not expensive* |

Adjectival verb phrases that begin with 有 yǒu, like 有意思 yǒu yìsi *be interesting,* are negated with 没 méi.

没有意思   méi yǒu yìsi   *not interesting*

It is not necessary to use an intensifier with a negated adjectival verb, but intensifiers and negation can both occur before some adjectival verbs; examples of such intensifiers are 很 hěn *very,* 真 zhēn *really,* and 太 tài *too.*

很 hěn usually comes after the negating word and before the adjectival verb.

不 bù	很 hěn	Adjectival Verb
不	很	高
bù	hěn	gāo
not	*very*	*tall*

真 zhēn typically comes before the negating word.

真 zhēn	不 bù	Adjectival Verb
真	不	高
zhēn	bù	gāo
really	*not*	*tall*

太 tài typically comes after the negating word and before the adjectival verb.

不 bù	太 tài	Adjectival Verb
不	太	贵·貴
bù	tài	guì
not	*too*	*expensive*

Oral Practice

Negate the following adjectival verbs and phrases, then say them aloud.

1. 容易 róngyì → 不容易 bù róngyì
2. 高兴·高興 gāoxìng → 不高兴·不高興 bù gāoxìng
3. 矮 ǎi → 不矮 bù ǎi
4. 有意思 yǒu yìsi → 没有意思 méi yǒu yìsi

Adjectival Verbs in the Predicate

In sentences like *That person **is tall***, *My younger brother **is smart***, and *That student **is hardworking***, the predicate (in bold type) identifies some quality of the subject.

In English, the predicate consists of the verb *be* and the adjective that identifies the quality.

That person is tall.
My younger brother is smart.
That student is hardworking.

If the verb *be* is omitted in English, the sentence is ungrammatical.

✗ *That person tall.*
✗ *My younger brother smart.*
✗ *That student hardworking.*

In Mandarin, the predicate consists of the adjectival verb preceded by 很 hěn *very* or another intensifier, or by a negating word. The adjectival verb is the main verb of the predicate, and the predicate does not include the verb 是 shì *be*.

If 是 shì *be* is included, the sentence is ungrammatical. The following Mandarin sentences are grammatical. In the English translations, the verb *be* (*is, are, was, were*) is set in roman type to remind you that it is not included as a separate word in Mandarin.

那个人很高。· 那個人很高。
Nàge rén hěn gāo.
That person is *very tall.*
我的弟弟很聪明。· 我的弟弟很聰明。
Wǒ de dìdi hěn cōngming.
My younger brother is *very smart.*
那个学生很用功。· 那個學生很用功。
Nàge xuésheng hěn yònggōng.
That student is *very hardworking.*

If 是 shì *be* is included in these Mandarin sentences, they are ungrammatical.

✗ 那个人是很高。· 那個人是很高。
  Nàge rén shì hěn gāo.

✗ 我的弟弟是很聪明。· 我的弟弟是很聰明。
  Wǒ de dìdi shì hěn cōngming.

✗ 那个学生是很用功。· 那個學生是很用功。
  Nàge xuésheng shì hěn yònggōng.

Following are additional Mandarin sentences in which the main verb is an adjectival verb. In these examples, the adjectival verb is preceded by the neutral intensifier 很 hěn. Remember that 是 shì *be* is not included in such sentences.

俄国很冷。· 俄國很冷。
Éguó hěn lěng.
Russia is *very cold.*

我的姐姐很漂亮。
Wǒ de jiějie hěn piàoliang.
My older sister is *very pretty.*

那本书很贵。· 那本書很貴。
Nà běn shū hěn guì.
That book is *very expensive.*

今天的考试很难。· 今天的考試很難。
Jīntiān de kǎoshì hěn nán.
Today's test was *very difficult.*

那个人很有名。· 那個人很有名。
Nàge rén hěn yǒu míng.
That person is *very famous.*

Following are examples in which an intensifier other than 很 hěn occurs.

王老师的考试越来越长。· 王老師的考試越來越長。
Wáng lǎoshī de kǎoshì yuèláiyuè cháng.
Professor Wang's tests are *getting longer and longer.*

小陈的妹妹挺漂亮。· 小陳的妹妹挺漂亮。
Xiǎo Chén de mèimei tǐng piàoliang.
Little Chen's younger sister is very pretty.

Written Practice 7-2

Translate the following sentences with intensifiers into English.

1. 他爸爸的车非常大。· 他爸爸的車非常大。
   Tā bàba de chē fēicháng dà.

   _____

2. 那件衣服太贵！· 那件衣服太貴！
   Nà jiàn yīfu tài guì!

   _____

3. 我们的功课越来越难。· 我們的功課越来越難。
   Wǒmen de gōngkè yuèláiyuè nán.

   _____

4. 那个电影真有意思。· 那個電影真有意思。
   Nàge diànyǐng zhēn yǒu yìsi.

   _____

USING INTENSIFIERS THAT FOLLOW THE ADJECTIVAL VERB IN THE PREDICATE

When an adjectival verb is used as the main verb in the predicate, it can occur with the intensifiers that follow the adjectival verb: 极了 · 極了 jíle *extremely* and 得很 dehěn *very*. In the examples that follow, the intensifier is in bold type.

他的女朋友漂亮**极了**。· 他的女朋友漂亮**極了**。
Tā de nǚ péngyou piàoliang **jíle**.
*His girlfriend is **extremely** pretty.*

今天的考试难**得很**。· 今天的考試難**得很**。
Jīntiān de kǎoshì nán **dehěn**.
*Today's test was **very** hard.*

Oral Practice

Read the following sentences aloud, then translate them into English.

1. 那件衣服贵得很。· 那件衣服貴得很。
   Nà jiàn yīfu guì de hěn. →
   That (piece of) clothing is extremely expensive.

2. 王老师的考试难极了。· 王老師的考試難極了。
   Wáng lǎoshī de kǎoshì nánjíle. →
   Professor Wang's tests are extremely difficult.

NEGATING ADJECTIVAL VERBS IN THE PREDICATE

When an adjectival verb serving as the main verb of a sentence is negated, the negation word comes before the adjectival verb or before the preverbal intensifier.

那个人不很高。· 那個人不很高。
Nàge rén bù hěn gāo.
That person is not very tall.

那个饭馆不太贵。· 那個飯館不太貴。
Nàge fànguǎn bù tài guì.
That restaurant is not too expensive.

那个人真不高。· 那個人真不高。
Nàge rén zhēn bù gāo.
That person is really not tall. (i.e., He is fairly short.)

Adjectival verbs that begin with 有 yǒu are always negated with 没 méi.

那本书没有意思。· 那本書沒有意思。
Nà běn shū méi yǒu yìsi.
That book is not interesting.

Written Practice 7-3

Negate the following sentences about your younger brother; do not include an intensifier.

1. 我弟弟很用功。
   Wǒ dìdi hěn yònggōng.
   My younger brother is very hardworking.

   _____

2. 我弟弟很有本事。
   Wǒ dìdi hěn yǒu běnshi.
   My younger brother is very talented.

   _____

3. 我的弟弟很高。
   Wǒ de dìdi hěn gāo.
   My younger brother is very tall.

   _____

4. 我弟弟的衣服很贵。· 我弟弟的衣服很貴。
   Wǒ dìdi de yīfu hěn guì.
   My younger brother's clothing is very expensive.

   _____

The Adjectival Verbs 多 duō *many, a lot* and 少 shǎo *few*

If the main verb of the sentence is an adjectival verb, the order of information is always Subject + Adjectival Verb. The order is the same, no matter what adjectival verb is used. In English, the order of information varies, depending on the adjective. Compare the order of information in the following Mandarin sentences and their English translations, paying particular attention to the order of information in sentences with 多 duō *many, a lot* and 少 shǎo *few*.

Subject	+ Adjectival Verb

贵·貴 guì *expensive*

那本书	很贵。
那本書	很貴。
Nà běn shū	hěn guì.
That book	*is very expensive.*

复杂·複雜 fùzá *complicated*

那个问题	很复杂。
那個問題	很複雜。
Nàge wèntí	hěn fùzá.
That problem	*is very complicated.*

漂亮 piàoliang *pretty*

他的女朋友	很漂亮。
Tā de nǚ péngyou	hěn piàoliang.
His girlfriend	*is very pretty.*

多 duō *many, a lot*

他的书	很多。
他的書	很多。
Tā de shū	hěn duō.
His books	*are numerous.* (i.e., *He has a lot of books.*)

她的问题	不多。
她的問題	不多。
Tā de wèntí	bù duō.
Her problems	*are not many.*
(i.e., *She does not have a lot of problems.*)	

少 shǎo *few*

他的朋友	很少。
Tā de péngyou	hěn shǎo.
His friends	*are few.* (i.e., *He has few friends.*)

王老师的书	不少。
王老師的書	不少。
Wáng lǎoshī de shū	bù shǎo.
Professor Wang's books	*are not few.*
(i.e., *Professor Wang has a lot of books.*)	

Do not get confused by English word order. Remember that 多 duō *many, a lot* and 少 shǎo *few* are adjectival verbs, and when they serve as the main verb of a sentence, the order of information is always Subject + Adjectival Verb.

Written Practice 7-4

Translate the following sentences into English.

1. 姐姐的朋友很多。
   Jiějie de péngyou hěn duō.

   _____

2. 图书馆的书不少。· 圖書館的書不少。
   Túshūguǎn de shū bù shǎo.

   _____

3. 他的问题很多。· 他的問題很多。
   Tā de wèntí hěn duō.

   _____

4. 他的经验太少。· 他的經驗太少。 (经验 · 經驗 jīngyàn *experience*)
   Tā de jīngyàn tài shǎo.

   _____

Expressing Feelings with Stative Verbs

In Mandarin, as in English, verbs are used to express concepts such as *I like that person* and *I don't understand the lesson*. Since these concepts relate to a state, and not to qualities or actions, they are called stative verbs. Following is a list of common stative verbs.

喜欢 · 喜歡	xǐhuan	*like*
想	xiǎng	*want to (do something), would like to (do something)*
要	yào	*want*
希望	xīwàng	*hope*
懂	dǒng	*understand*
信	xìn	*believe*
爱 · 愛	ài	*love*

Using Stative Verbs with Intensifiers

To express ideas such as *I like that book a lot,* you can use stative verbs with intensifiers—much like adjectival verbs covered earlier in this chapter. In Mandarin, the order of intensifier and stative verb is Intensifier + Stative Verb. The intensifier that occurs most commonly with stative verbs is 很 hěn.

Following are examples of intensifiers used with stative verbs. Note that the most natural English translation of the intensifier in these sentences is *very much* or *a lot* and that the intensifier often occurs in a different place in the English sentence than it does in the Mandarin sentence.

我**很想**跟他说话。· 我**很想**跟他說話。
Wǒ **hěn xiǎng** gēn tā shuō huà.
*I **very much want** to speak with him. / I **want** to speak with him **very much.***

她**很像**她妈妈。· 她**很像**她媽媽。
Tā **hěn xiàng** tā māma.
*She **resembles** her mother **a lot.***

我**真爱**你。· 我**真愛**你。
Wǒ **zhēn ài** nǐ.
*I **really love** you.*

我**很喜欢**看电影。· 我**很喜歡**看電影。
Wǒ **hěn xǐhuan** kàn diànyǐng.
*I **like** to watch movies **very much.***

Stative verbs cannot be described with intensifiers that follow the verb—intensifiers like 极了·極了 jíle *extremely* and 得很 dehěn *very.*

Oral Practice

Add the intensifier 很 hěn to the following sentences, then read the sentences aloud.

1. 我想跟他跳舞。 → 我很想跟他跳舞。
   Wǒ xiǎng gēn tā tiào wǔ. Wǒ hěn xiǎng gēn tā tiào wǔ.
   I want to dance with him.

2. 我喜欢唱歌。   →   我很喜欢唱歌。
    我喜歡唱歌。   我很喜歡唱歌。
    Wǒ xǐhuan chàng gē.   Wǒ hěn xǐhuan chàng gē.
    I like to sing.

3. 她爱她的小狗。   →   她很爱她的小狗。
    她愛她的小狗。   她很愛她的小狗。
    Tā ài tā de xiǎo gǒu.   Tā hěn ài tā de xiǎo gǒu.
    She loves her puppy.

Written Practice 7-5

Translate the Mandarin sentences you created in the Oral Practice above into English.

1. _____

2. _____

3. _____

NEGATING STATIVE VERBS

To express an idea such as *I don't like him,* the stative verb is negated with 不 bù; it can never be negated with 没 méi. 不 bù comes right before the stative verb.

我不懂课文。· 我不懂課文。
Wǒ bù dǒng kèwén.
I don't understand the lesson.

我不喜欢他。· 我不喜歡他。
Wǒ bù xǐhuan tā.
I don't like him.

Written Practice 7-6

Write the negated forms of the following Mandarin sentences.

1. 我怕狗。
   Wǒ pà gǒu.
   I am afraid of dogs.

   _____

2. 我要一本字典。
   Wǒ yào yī běn zìdiǎn.
   I want a dictionary.

   _____

3. 我想请他们吃饭。· 我想請他們吃飯。
   Wǒ xiǎng qǐng tāmen chī fàn.
   I want to invite them to eat.

   _____

Expressing Past States

To indicate that a state existed in the past, for example, *I **used to** like him* or ***When I was young**, I was very afraid of dogs,* add an expression that refers to the past. Expressions that indicate the time when a situation takes place always come before the verb phrase. If the verb is a stative verb, time expressions come before a negating word and before an intensifier, if either or both of these are used. In the following examples, the expression that refers to the past is in bold type.

我**以前**很喜欢他。· 我**以前**很喜歡他。
Wǒ **yǐqián** hěn xǐhuan tā.
*I **used to** like him a lot.*

我**小的时候**很怕狗。· 我**小的時候**很怕狗。
Wǒ **xiǎo de shíhou** hěn pà gǒu.
***When I was young**, I was very afraid of dogs.*

Note that there is no grammatical marker that signals the past tense or "completion" of a stative verb in Mandarin. Stative verbs differ from action verbs in this way. (See Chapters 8 and 9 for detailed discussions of action verbs.)

Written Practice 7-7

Rewrite each of the following sentences, adding the past time expression in parentheses. Remember to put the past time expression right before the verb phrase.

1. 我喜欢看电视。(小的时候) · 我喜歡看電視。(小的時候)
   Wǒ xǐhuan kàn diànshì. (xiǎo de shíhou)
   When I was young, I used to like to watch television.

   _____

2. 我不懂中文。(以前)
   Wǒ bù dǒng Zhōngwén. (yǐqián)
   I didn't understand Chinese before.

   _____

3. 他很喜欢吃甜的东西。(以前) · 他很喜歡吃甜的東西。(以前)
   Tā hěn xǐhuan chī tián de dōngxi. (yǐqián)
   Before, he liked to eat sweet things a lot.

   _____

Comparing Stative Verbs That Have Similar Meanings

The following stative verbs have meanings that are similar but different. Pay attention to their meanings and use.

喜欢 · 喜歡 xǐhuan *like* is used to talk about something that you like. It can be followed by a person, place, or thing, or by an action.

我喜欢小狗。· 我喜歡小狗。
Wǒ xǐhuan xiǎo gǒu.
I like puppies.

我喜欢吃中国饭。· 我喜歡吃中國飯。
Wǒ xǐhuan chī Zhōngguó fàn.
I like to eat Chinese food.

要 yào *want* can be followed by a person, place, or thing, or by an action.

我要那本书。· 我要那本書。
Wǒ yào nà běn shū.
I want that book.

我要看电视。· 我要看電視。
Wǒ yào kàn diànshì.
I want to watch television.

想 xiǎng *want to, would like to* is used to talk about something you want to do. It is followed by an action.

我想吃中国饭。· 我想吃中國飯。
Wǒ xiǎng chī Zhōngguó fàn.
I want to eat Chinese food.

我想看电视。· 我想看電視。
Wǒ xiǎng kàn diànshì.
I want to watch television.

想 xiǎng can also mean *think about*. In this case, it is followed by a person, place, or thing.

他想他女朋友。
Tā xiǎng tā nǚ péngyou.
He is thinking about his girlfriend.

Written Practice 7-8

Fill in each blank in the following sentences with the appropriate word to match the English sentences, choosing from (a) 想 xiǎng, (b) 喜欢·喜歡 xǐhuan, and (c) 要 yào.

1. 我＿＿＿在图书馆看书。· 我＿＿＿在圖書館看書。

   Wǒ ＿＿＿ zài túshūguǎn kàn shū.

   I want to study in the library.

2. 我＿＿＿在图书馆看书。· 我＿＿＿在圖書館看書。

   Wǒ ＿＿＿ zài túshūguǎn kàn shū.

   I like to study in the library.

3. 我 ＿＿＿一杯水。

   Wǒ ＿＿＿ yī bēi shuǐ.

   I want a cup of water.

4. 我不＿＿＿考试。· 我不＿＿＿考試。

   Wǒ bù ＿＿＿ kǎoshì.

   I don't like to take tests.

QUIZ

Rewrite each of the following sentences, adding the appropriate intensifier to match the English sentence.

1. 我的哥哥懒。· 我的哥哥懶。
   Wǒ de gēgē lǎn.
   My older brother is rather lazy.

   _____

2. 中文不难。· 中文不難。
   Zhōngwén bù nán.
   Chinese is not too difficult.

   _____

Create a sentence from the following phrases, putting them in the correct order to match the English sentence.

3. 新的 – 快 – 我的 – 电脑 – 非常 · 新的 – 快 – 我的 – 電腦 – 非常
   xīn de – kuài – wǒ de – diànnǎo – fēicháng
   My new computer is extremely fast.

   _____

Rewrite the following sentence, adding negation to match the English sentence.

4. 我的女儿很高。· 我的女兒很高。
   Wǒ de nǚ'ér hěn gāo.
   My daughter is not very tall.

   _____

Highlight the intensifier and adjectival verb in the following sentence, then translate the sentence into English.

5. 那个学生聪明极了。· 那個學生聰明極了。
   Nàge xuésheng cōngmingjíle.

   _____

Rewrite the following sentence, adding 很 hěn in the correct location to match the English sentence.

6. 我想看那个电影。· 我想看那個電影。
   Wǒ xiǎng kàn nàge diànyǐng.
   I want to see that movie very much.

   _____

Create a sentence from the following words, putting them in the correct order to match the English sentence.

7. 信 – 他 – 我 – 不
   xìn – tā – wǒ – bù
   He does not believe me.

_____

Fill in each blank in the following Mandarin sentences with the appropriate word to match the English sentences, choosing from (a) 想 xiǎng, (b) 喜欢·喜歡 xǐhuan, and (c) 要 yào.

8. 我_____睡觉。· 我_____睡覺。

   Wǒ _____ shuì jiào.

   I want to sleep.

9. 我不_____吃鱼。· 我不_____吃魚。

   Wǒ bù _____ chī yú.

   I don't like to eat fish.

10. 我不_____吃鱼。· 我不_____吃魚。

    Wǒ bù _____ chī yú.

    I don't want to eat fish.

CHAPTER 8

Action Verbs: Talking About Habitual, Future, and Ongoing Actions

In this chapter, you will learn about:

Action Verbs and Duration

What is an action? It is something that you did, are doing, or will do—anything that answers the question *What did you do? What are you doing?* or *What will you do?* The verb in the answer is an action verb. Following is a list of action verbs; you can probably add many more verbs to the list.

写·寫	xiě	*write*
唱	chàng	*sing*
买·買	mǎi	*buy, shop*
学·學	xué	*study*
睡	shuì	*sleep*
看	kàn	*watch* (a movie)
听·聽	tīng	*listen to* (music)
站	zhàn	*stand up*
坐	zuò	*sit down*
借	jiè	*borrow, lend*
放	fàng	*put* (a book on the table)

Some actions have *duration,* that is, they take place over time. These actions include 写·寫 xiě *write,* 唱 chàng *sing,* 买·買 mǎi *buy, shop,* 学·學 xué *study,* 睡 shuì *sleep,* 看 kàn *watch* (a movie), and 听·聽 tīng *listen* (to music). If an action has duration, you can say that you are doing the action now, or that you did the action over some period of time.

Some actions do not have duration. They are concluded almost as soon as they are begun. Actions that do not have duration include 站 zhàn *stand up,* 坐 zuò *sit down,* 借 jiè *borrow, lend,* and 放 fàng *put* (a book on the table). An action that does not have duration is sometimes referred to as a *change-of-state* action, since the performance of the action always results in a change.

As we talk about expressing actions in this and the following chapters, we will refer to this distinction between action verbs with duration and action verbs that indicate change of state. These two types of action verbs have much in common, but they sometimes differ in how they function.

Action Verbs and Their Objects

Actions that have duration are always associated with a direct object. Following are examples of action verbs with objects; the objects are in bold type.

看电影 · 看電影	kàn **diànyǐng**	*see **a movie***
吃晚饭 · 吃晚飯	chī **wǎnfàn**	*eat **dinner***
说中国话 · 說中國話	shuō **Zhōngguó huà**	*speak **Chinese***
买东西 · 買東西	mǎi **dōngxi**	*buy **things***

Sometimes, the object of an action verb is not translated into English. Following are some examples of this.

吃饭 · 吃飯	chī **fàn**	*eat*
睡觉 · 睡覺	shuì **jiào**	*sleep*
写字 · 寫字	xiě **zì**	*write*
说话 · 說話	shuō **huà**	*speak, talk*
洗澡	xǐ **zǎo**	*bathe*
走路	zǒu **lù**	*walk*
看书 · 看書	kàn **shū**	*read*
唱歌	chàng **gē**	*sing*
跳舞	tiào **wǔ**	*dance*

The objects in these Mandarin expressions contribute little if any meaning to the verb. They function as placeholders, occurring in the expression unless a more meaningful or specific noun is used. For example, if you want to invite a friend to *eat,* and you do not want to specify what you will be eating, you may say the following.

我想请你吃**饭**。· 我想請你吃**飯**。
Wǒ xiǎng qǐng nǐ chī **fàn**.
*I want to invite you to **eat**.*

But if you want to invite a friend to eat *dinner,* then you use the noun for *dinner,* and you do not use the placeholder object 饭 · 飯 fàn.

我想请你吃**晚饭**。· 我想請你吃**晚飯**。
Wǒ xiǎng qǐng nǐ chī **wǎnfàn**.
*I want to invite you to eat **dinner**.*

If you want to suggest that you eat *dumplings,* you include the word for *dumplings,* 饺子 · 餃子 jiǎozi. Note that the word 饺子 · 餃子 jiǎozi replaces the place-holder object 饭 · 飯 fàn.

我们吃**饺子**吧! · 我們吃**餃子**吧!
Wǒmen chī **jiǎozi** ba!
*Let's eat **dumplings**!*

If you want to *speak* with your friend, you use the noun 话 · 話 huà *talk* as the placeholder object of the verb 说 · 說 shuō *speak, talk.*

我想跟你说**话**。 · 我想跟你說**話**。
Wǒ xiǎng gēn nǐ shuō **huà**.
*I want to **speak** with you.*

But if you want to speak *Chinese* with your friend, you use one of the following sentences.

我想跟你说**中国话**。 · 我想跟你說**中國話**。
Wǒ xiǎng gēn nǐ shuō **Zhōngguó huà**.
我想跟你说**中文**。 · 我想跟你說**中文**。
Wǒ xiǎng gēn nǐ shuō **Zhōngwén**.
*I want to speak **Chinese** with you.*

Many nouns have placeholder meaning in certain contexts, and full meaning in other contexts. For example, you can use the following sentence with the placeholder object 饭 · 飯 fàn to suggest to your friends that you eat, without suggesting a particular type of food.

我们吃**饭**吧! · 我們吃**飯**吧!
Wǒmen chī **fàn** ba!
Let's eat!

In this suggestion, 饭 · 飯 fàn is a placeholder for any kind of food. But when you use the following sentence in a restaurant to request more *rice,* you are using the word 饭 · 飯 fàn in its full meaning of *rice.*

请再来一碗**饭**。 · 請再來一碗**飯**。
Qǐng zài lái yī wǎn **fàn**.
*Please bring another bowl of **rice**.*

Written Practice 8-1

Rewrite each of the following sentences, replacing the placeholder object with the object in parentheses to match the English sentence. The placeholder object is in bold type.

1. 我明天考**试**。(中文) · 我明天考**試**。(中文)
   Wǒ míngtiān kǎo **shì**. (Zhōngwén)
   Tomorrow, I take a Chinese test.

   _____

2. 她喜欢画**画儿**。(山水) · 她喜歡畫**畫兒**。(山水)
   Tā xǐhuan huà **huàr**. (shānshuǐ)
   She likes to paint landscapes.

   _____

3. 他们在图书馆看**书**。(报) · 他們在圖書館看**書**。(報)
   Tāmen zài túshūguǎn kàn **shū**. (bào)
   They read newspapers in the library.

   _____

4. 他跟朋友说**话**。(法文) · 他跟朋友說**話**。(法文)
   Tā gēn péngyou shuō **huà**. (Fǎwén)
   He speaks French with his friends.

   _____

Talking About Habitual Actions

Mandarin does not use any special grammatical structure to indicate habitual actions. The simplest way to indicate that an action happens on a regular basis is to state the action without any time expression at all.

我学中文。· 我學中文。
Wǒ xué Zhōngwén.
I study Chinese.

我上大学。· 我上大學。
Wǒ shàng dàxué.
I attend college.

To indicate that an action happens on a regular basis, you may use the following pattern.

每 měi + Time Noun Phrase + 都 dōu + Verb Phrase

她每天都看报。· 她每天都看報。
Tā měitiān dōu kàn bào.
She reads the news every day.

我每 (一) 个月都回家。· 我每 (一) 個月都回家。
Wǒ měi (yī) gè yuè dōu huí jiā.
I return home once a month.

Note that the number 一 yī *one* may be omitted from the time noun phrase; other numbers must not be omitted. Following is a sentence in which the number is 两·兩 liǎng *two*; it comes before the classifier 个·個 gè and cannot be omitted.

我们每两个星期都考试。· 我們每兩個星期都考試。
Wǒmen měi liǎng gè xīngqī dōu kǎoshì.
We have a test every two weeks.

The most common way to indicate that an action happens regularly is to add an adverb before the verb phrase. The two adverbs that follow are commonly used to indicate that an action happens regularly.

经常·經常 jīngcháng *frequently*

他经常跟朋友吃饭。· 他經常跟朋友吃飯。
Tā jīngcháng gēn péngyou chī fàn.
He frequently eats with his friends.

常 cháng *often*

我常来这儿买东西。· 我常來這兒買東西。
Wǒ cháng lái zhèr mǎi dōngxi.
I often come here to shop.

Written Practice 8-2

Write a Mandarin sentence for each of the following actions, adding the time expression in parentheses to indicate that you perform the action habitually.

1. play ball with friends (经常·經常 jīngcháng)

   _____

2. watch movies (经常·經常 jīngcháng)

   _____

3. eat breakfast (每天 měitiān)

   _____

4. bathe (每天 měitiān)

   _____

INDICATING THAT AN ACTION DOES NOT HAPPEN

To say that an action does not happen, negate the action verb with 不 bù.

她不吃肉。
Tā bù chī ròu.
She doesn't eat meat.

他不学日语。· 他不學日語。
Tā bù xué Rìyǔ.
He doesn't study Japanese.

我们不看电视。· 我們不看電視。
Wǒmen bù kàn diànshì.
We do not watch television.

Written Practice 8-3

Write a Mandarin sentence for each of the following actions, indicating that you do not perform the action.

1. dance   _____

2. sing   _____

3. paint   _____

4. study French   _____

Talking About Future Actions

Mandarin grammar does not require that you explicitly indicate future time. However, sentences that refer to future actions generally include some expression that refers to the future. The most commonly used expressions are those that refer to a specific time, such as *tonight, tomorrow,* and *next week.* Certain verbs and time adverbs may also be used.

TIME EXPRESSIONS THAT REFER TO THE FUTURE

Any expression that refers to time in the future may be used to indicate future time. The time expression comes after the subject and before the verb phrase. This type of time expression can be used with any type of verb. Following are examples of time expressions with action verbs. For more expressions that refer to clock time and calendar time, see Chapter 19.

她明年就毕业。· 她明年就畢業。
Tā míngnián jiù bì yè.
She is graduating next year.

他七月去中国找工作。· 他七月去中國找工作。
Tā qīyuè qù Zhōngguó zhǎo gōngzuò.
He is going to China in July to look for a job.

VERBS THAT SIGNAL FUTURE TIME

The most common verbs that signal future time are the modal verb 会·會 huì and the stative verbs 要 yào *want to, will* and 想 xiǎng *want to, plan to*. As the following examples illustrate, these words can be used with time expressions that refer to future time.

会·會 huì

The modal verb 会·會 huì indicates that an action is possible and, by extension, that it will happen.

明天会下雨。· 明天會下雨。
Míngtiān huì xià yǔ.
It will probably rain tomorrow.

你一定会成功。· 你一定會成功。
Nǐ yīdìng huì chénggōng.
You will certainly succeed.

See Chapter 10 for a detailed discussion of modal verbs and this use of 会·會 huì.

要 yào

要 yào indicates that an action is required and, by extension, that it will happen. 要 yào comes before an action verb. If the action verb has an associated prepositional phrase, 要 yào comes before the prepositional phrase.

我们明天要考试。· 我們明天要考試。
Wǒmen míngtiān yào kǎoshì.
We will have a test tomorrow.

我今天晚上要给我的妈妈打电话。· 我今天晚上要給我的媽媽打電話。
Wǒ jīntiān wǎnshang yào gěi wǒ de māma dǎ diànhuà.
I will give my mother a phone call tonight.

想 xiǎng

When 想 xiǎng comes before an action verb, it indicates that the subject is think-ing about performing the action or wants to perform the action.

我想跟你说话。· 我想跟你說話。
Wǒ xiǎng gēn nǐ shuō huà.
I want to speak with you.

ADVERBS THAT REFER TO THE FUTURE

The adverb 将来·將來 jiānglái *in the future* may be used when talking about actions in the future. The neutral position for 将来·將來 jiānglái is after the sub-ject and before the verb phrase.

我希望**将来**跟她结婚。· 我希望**將來**跟她結婚。
Wǒ xīwàng **jiānglái** gēn tā jiéhūn.
*I hope **in the future** to marry her.*

Written Practice 8-4

Rewrite each of the following sentences, adding the expression(s) in parentheses to match the English sentence.

1. 我去看电影。(明天晚上，想) · 我去看電影。(明天晚上，想)
   Wǒ qù kàn diànyǐng. (míngtiān wǎnshang, xiǎng)
   I want to go to see a movie tomorrow night.

   _____

2. 我们放假。(下个星期) · 我們放假。(下個星期)
   Wǒmen fàng jià. (xià gè xīngqī)
   We will begin vacation next week.

   _____

3. 我登上长城。(将来，会) · 我登上長城。(將來，會)
   Wǒ dēngshàng chángchéng. (jiānglái, huì)
   In the future, I will climb the Great Wall.

   _____

4. 我去中国学习。(九月) · 我去中國學習。(九月)
   Wǒ qù Zhōngguó xuéxí. (jiǔyuè)
   I am going to China in September to study.

INDICATING THAT AN ACTION WILL NOT HAPPEN IN THE FUTURE

The most common way to indicate that an action will not happen in the future is to place 不会 · 不會 bù huì or 不要 bù yào before the action verb. 不会 · 不會 bù huì conveys the sense that it is not possible for an action to happen, and 不要 bù yào conveys the sense that an action won't happen because the subject does not want to perform the action.

我们明天不会考试。 · 我們明天不會考試。
Wǒmen míngtiān bù huì kǎoshì.
We won't have a test tomorrow.

我今天不舒服，不要上课。 · 我今天不舒服，不要上課。
Wǒ jīntiān bù shūfu, bù yào shàng kè.
I am not feeling well today (and) am not going to class.

Note that the expression 不要 bù yào may also mean *do not have to.*

   If 将来 · 將來 jiānglái or 以后 · 以後 yǐhòu occurs in a sentence, it comes before 不会 · 不會 bù huì or 不要 bù yào. A negated sentence with 将来 · 將來 jiānglái or 以后 · 以後 yǐhòu is contrastive, that is, it compares a situation *now* with a situation *in the future.*

我将来不坐飞机了。 · 我將來不坐飛機了。
Wǒ jiānglái bù zuò fēijī le.
In the future, I will not ride on an airplane.

我以后不要穿高跟鞋了。 · 我以後不要穿高跟鞋了。
Wǒ yǐhòu bù yào chuān gāogēnxié le.
I am not going to wear high-heeled shoes again.

Written Practice 8-5

Rewrite the following sentences, indicating that you are not going to perform the actions in the future.

1. 我明天去公园。· 我明天去公園。
   Wǒ míngtiān qù gōngyuán.
   I am going to the park tomorrow.

   _____

2. 我这个周末要回家。· 我這個週末要回家。
   Wǒ zhège zhōumò yào huí jiā.
   I am going home this weekend.

   _____

3. 我今年夏天去中国。· 我今年夏天去中國。
   Wǒ jīnnián xiàtiān qù Zhōngguó.
   I am going to China this summer.

   _____

4. 我今天晚上去图书馆学习。· 我今天晚上去圖書館學習。
   Wǒ jīntiān wǎnshang qù túshūguǎn xuéxí.
   I am going to the library tonight to study.

   _____

Talking About Present-Time Actions and Ongoing Actions

Mandarin has two ways of talking about actions that occur in present time. One way simply locates the action in present time. The other focuses on the ongoing action, indicating that it is *in progress*.

LOCATING ACTIONS IN PRESENT TIME

The adverb 现在 · 現在 xiànzài *now* may be included in any sentence that talks about a situation occurring in present time. The verb can be an action verb, or it can be a stative or adjectival verb. If the verb is an action verb, the sentence usually includes additional information besides the verb. For example, it may include information about the location of the action, about whom the action is happening with, or about who is receiving something as a result of the action.

学生现在在教室考试。· 學生現在在教室考試。
Xuésheng xiànzài zài jiàoshì kǎo shì.
The students are now in the classroom taking a test.

小王现在跟朋友在餐厅吃饭。· 小王現在跟朋友在餐廳吃飯。
Xiǎo Wáng xiànzài gēn péngyou zài cāntīng chī fàn.
Little Wang is eating with her friends in the dining room.

白美玲现在给她的弟弟写信。· 白美玲現在給她的弟弟寫信。
Bái Měilíng xiànzài gěi tā de dìdi xiě xìn.
Bai Meiling is writing a letter to her younger brother right now.

Oral Practice

Add the word 现在 · 現在 xiànzài *now* to each of the following sentences, indicating that the action is happening now. Then read the sentences aloud.

1. 我跟朋友说话。
   我跟朋友說話。
   Wǒ gēn péngyou shuō huà.
   I am speaking with my friends.

   → 我现在跟朋友说话。
     我現在跟朋友說話。
     Wǒ xiànzài gēn péngyou shuō huà.

2. 他们在公园打球。
   他們在公園打球。
   Tāmen zài gōngyuán dǎ qiú.
   They are playing ball in the park.

   → 他们现在在公园打球。
     他們現在在公園打球。
     Tāmen xiànzài zài gōngyuán dǎ qiú.

3. 他在图书馆看书。
   他在圖書館看書。
   Tā zài túshūguǎn kàn shū.
   He is reading in the library.

   → 他现在在图书馆看书。
     他現在在圖書館看書。
     Tā xiànzài zài túshūguǎn kàn shū.

FOCUSING ON ONGOING ACTIONS IN PROGRESS

Mandarin uses a number of expressions to focus on an action in progress. These expressions can only be used with actions that have duration, and they cannot be used with any other kind of verb. When these structures are used, the focus is on the action of the verb itself—not on any detail of the action, such as where or with whom it happens. Following are expressions used to focus on ongoing actions in progress.

The Adverbs 在 zài *now* and 正在 zhèngzài *right now*

在 zài and 正在 zhèngzài are adverbs. They come right before the action verb or before a prepositional phrase that precedes the action verb.

学生正在考试。别进去。· 學生正在考試。別進去。
Xuésheng **zhèngzài** kǎo shì. Bié jìnqu.
学生在考试。别进去。· 學生在考試。別進去。
Xuésheng **zài** kǎo shì. Bié jìnqu.
*The students are taking a test **right now**. Don't enter.*

请等一会儿。他正在跟别人说话。· 請等一會兒。他正在跟別人說話。
Qǐng děng yīhuìr. Tā **zhèngzài** gēn biéren shuō huà.
*Please wait a minute. He is speaking with someone else **right now**.*

The Sentence-Final Particle 呢 ne

呢 ne is a sentence-final particle with several functions. One of these functions is to reinforce the meaning of an ongoing action. It often occurs with 在 zài *now* or 正在 zhèngzài *right now*.

他在说话呢。· 他在說話呢。
Tā zài shuō huà ne.
He is speaking right now.

呢 ne is also used to signal an echo question (see Chapter 14).

The Verb Suffix 着 · 著 zhe

着 · 著 zhe directly follows a verb and indicates that the subject is in the process of performing the action. It may occur in the same sentence with 在 zài *now* or 正在 zhèngzài *right now* and 呢 ne.

他在说着话。· 他在說著話。
Tā zài shuōzhe huà.
He is speaking right now.

我们正在做着作业。· 我們正在做著作業。
Wǒmen zhèngzài zuòzhe zuòyè.
We are doing our homework right now.

着·著 zhe may be used with actions happening in present time, but its use is not restricted to present time. Instead, it is used generally to focus on an action in progress and to indicate that it is ongoing.

The Adverb 还·還 hái *still*

The adverb 还·還 hái may be used to indicate that a situation is continuing. It can be used with 在 zài, 着·著 zhe, and 呢 ne.

他还在这儿呢。· 他還在這兒呢。
Tā hái zài zhèr ne.
He is still here.

我们还在说话呢。· 我們還在說話呢。
Wǒmen hái zài shuō huà ne.
We are still talking.

Written Practice 8-6

Rewrite each of the following sentences, adding 在 zài, 正在 zhèngzài, 着·著 zhe, and/or 呢 ne, as indicated in parentheses, to emphasize the ongoing action in the sentence.

1. 他们唱歌。· 他們唱歌。 Tāmen chàng gē. (正在 zhèngzài, 呢 ne)

   _____

2. 他们吃晚饭。· 他們吃晚飯。 Tāmen chī wǎnfàn. (在 zài, 呢 ne)

   _____

3. 他们做作业。· 他們做作業。 Tāmen zuò zuòyè. (在 zài)

   _____

QUIZ

Rewrite each of the following sentences, replacing the placeholder object in bold type with the object in parentheses. Then write the English translation of each new sentence.

1. 他会写字。(日文) · 他會寫字。(日文)
   Tā huì xiě **zì**. (Rìwén)
   He can write. (*Japanese*)

   _____

2. 我们现在不要说话。(英文) · 我們現在不要說話。(英文)
   Wǒmen xiànzài bù yào shuō **huà**. (Yīngwén)
   We shouldn't speak now. (*English*)

   _____

3. 中国人喜欢打球吗? (篮球) · 中國人喜歡打球嗎? (籃球)
   Zhōngguó rén xǐhuan dǎ **qiú** ma? (lánqiú)
   Do Chinese people like to play ball? (*basketball*)

   _____

Rewrite each of the following sentences, adding the expressions in parentheses to match the English sentence.

4. 我们考试。(每个星期，都) · 我們考試。(每個星期，都)
   Wǒmen kǎoshì. (měi gè xīngqī, dōu)
   We have a test every week.

   _____

5. 他看电视。(每天晚上，都) · 他看電視。(每天晚上，都)
   Tā kàn diànshì. (měitiān wǎnshang, dōu)
   He watches television every night.

   _____

Place each of the following groups of phrases in the correct order to match the English sentence.

6. 我 – 去旅游 – 跟父亲母亲 – 夏天 – 经常 ．
   我 – 去旅遊 – 跟父親母親 – 夏天 – 經常
   wǒ – qù lǚyóu – gēn fùqin mǔqin – xiàtiān – jīngcháng
   I often travel with my father and mother in the summer.

   _____

7. 喝咖啡 – 我 – 不 – 了 – 以后 ．
   喝咖啡 – 我 – 不 – 了 – 以後
   hē kāfēi – wǒ – bù – le – yǐhòu
   I am not going to drink coffee anymore.

   _____

Rewrite each of the following sentences, adding 在 zài, 正在 zhèngzài, 着 · 著 zhe, and/or 呢 ne, as indicated in parentheses, to emphasize the ongoing action in the sentence.

8. 学生考试。· 學生考試。 Xuésheng kǎoshì. (在 zài, 呢 ne)
   The students are taking a test now.

   _____

9. 白老师画画儿。· 白老師畫畫兒。 Bái lǎoshī huà huàr. (正在 zhèngzài)
   Professor Bai is painting now.

   _____

10. 他洗澡。 Tā xǐ zǎo. (正在 zhèngzài)
    He's bathing right now.

    _____

CHAPTER 9

Completed Actions and Actions That Did Not Happen

In this chapter, you will learn about:

Indicating a Completed Action with 了 le
Indicating That an Action Has Not Happened with 没 méi
A Summary of the Use of 了 le *and* 没 méi *in Describing Actions*
Indicating a Past Action with 过·過 guo

Indicating a Completed Action with 了 le

English and many other languages use grammatical tense to indicate that a situation existed or occurred in the past. In Mandarin, there are ways to indicate past time (see Chapter 20), but the distinction between past, present, and future is not as important in Mandarin as it is in English. Instead, Mandarin focuses on whether or not an action happened or is completed.

To indicate that an action happened, add 了 le after the action verb or after the action verb and its object.

THE PLACEMENT OF 了 le

If the object of a verb is specific (for example, *that book*), involves a number (for example, *three books*), or includes a description (for example, 我的车 · 我的車 wǒ de chē *my car*), 了 le generally comes right after the verb.

Verb + 了 le + Object

我昨天看了那个电影。· 我昨天看了那個電影。
Wǒ zuótiān kàn le nàge diànyǐng.
I saw that movie yesterday.

我买了一本书。· 我買了一本書。
Wǒ mǎi le yī běn shū.
I bought a book.

他借了我的车。· 他借了我的車。
Tā jiè le wǒ de chē.
He borrowed my car.

Otherwise, 了 le generally follows the object. This is particularly the case in Verb + Object phrases in which the object does not contribute significant information to the phrase (for example, 吃饭 · 吃飯 chī fàn *eat*, 说话 · 說話 shuō huà *speak*, 看书 · 看書 kàn shū *read*, and 睡觉 · 睡覺 shuì jiào *sleep*).

Verb + Object + 了 le

我在餐厅吃饭了。· 我在餐廳吃飯了。
Wǒ zài cāntīng chī fàn le.
I ate at the cafeteria.

她在图书馆看书了。· 她在圖書館看書了。
Tā zài túshūguǎn kàn shū le.
She read in the library.

As you can see, indicating that an action *happened* often implies that the action happened in the past.

Oral Practice

Add 了 le to each of the following sentences to indicate completed action. Then read the sentence aloud.

1. 我在图书馆做作业。   → 我在图书馆做作业了。
   我在圖書館做作業。   我在圖書館做作業了。
   Wǒ zài túshūguǎn zuò zuòyè.   Wǒ zài túshūguǎn zuò zuòyè le.
                                    I did homework in the library.

2. 我看我的朋友。   → 我看了我的朋友。
   Wǒ kàn wǒ de péngyou.   Wǒ kàn le wǒ de péngyou.
                            I saw my friends.

3. 我们喝两瓶可乐。   → 我们喝了两瓶可乐。
   我們喝兩瓶可樂。   我們喝了兩瓶可樂。
   Wǒmen hē liǎng píng kělè.   Wǒmen hē le liǎng píng kělè.
                            We drank two bottles of cola.

INDICATING THAT AN ACTION HAS ALREADY HAPPENED WITH 已经·已經 yǐjing

To indicate that you have already completed an action, add the adverb 已经·已經 yǐjing *already* before the verb. If the verb is preceded by a preposition phrase, 已经·已經 yǐjing comes before the prepositional phrase. (See Chapter 19 for examples of prepositional phrases.) Note that sentences with 已经·已經 yǐjing often end with sentence-final 了 le.

我们已经吃饭了。· 我們已經吃飯了。
Wǒmen yǐjing chī fàn le.
We have already eaten.

我已经吃早饭了。· 我已經吃早飯了。
Wǒ yǐjing chī zǎofàn le.
I have already eaten breakfast.

我已经跟她说话了。· 我已經跟她說話了。
Wǒ yǐjing gēn tā shuō huà le.
I have already spoken with her.

Written Practice 9-1

For each of the following actions, write a Mandarin sentence indicating that the action has already happened, to match the English sentence.

1. 我看那个电影 · 我看那個電影
   wǒ kàn nàge diànyǐng
   I have already seen that movie.

   _____

2. 我买字典 · 我買字典
   wǒ mǎi zìdiǎn
   I have already bought a dictionary.

   _____

3. 我下课 · 我下課
   wǒ xià kè
   I have already gotten out of class.

   _____

4. 我做作业 · 我做作業
   wǒ zuò zuòyè
   I have already done the homework.

   _____

Indicating That an Action Has Not Happened with 没 méi

Since 了 le signals completion, it is only used with actions that have happened. To indicate that an action did not happen or has not happened, negate the action verb with 没 méi (or 没有 méi yǒu); do not include 了 le in the sentence.

我今天没去图书馆。· 我今天没去圖書館。
Wǒ jīntiān méi qù túshūguǎn.
I didn't go to the library today.

他没吃早饭。· 他没吃早飯。
Tā méi chī zǎofàn.
He didn't eat breakfast.

Written Practice 9-2

Rewrite each of the following sentences, indicating that the action did not happen.

1. 我看了那个电影。· 我看了那個電影。
   Wǒ kàn le nàge diànyǐng.

   _____

2. 我买字典了。· 我買字典了。
   Wǒ mǎi zìdiǎn le.

   _____

3. 我下课了。· 我下課了。
   Wǒ xià kè le.

   _____

4. 我做作业了。· 我做作業了。
   Wǒ zuò zuòyè le.

   _____

INDICATING THAT AN ACTION HAS NOT HAPPENED YET

To say that you haven't done something yet or that something hasn't happened yet, use 还没·還沒 hái méi before the verb. 还·還 hái is an adverb and always comes before the verb or verb phrase. For a detailed discussion of 还·還 hái, see Chapter 17.

他还没吃早饭。· 他還沒吃早飯。
Tā hái méi chī zǎofàn.
He hasn't eaten breakfast yet.

他还没回家。· 他還沒回家。
Tā hái méi huí jiā.
He hasn't gone home yet.

The short negative answer to a question about whether something has happened or not, is 还没有·還沒有 hái méi yǒu. (For a detailed discussion of yes-no questions, see Chapter 14.)

Q: 你吃了早饭吗?
你吃了早飯嗎?
Nǐ chī le zǎofàn ma?
Have you eaten breakfast?

A: 还没有。
還沒有。
Hái méi yǒu.
Not yet.

Q: 你做作业了吗?
你做作業了嗎?
Nǐ zuò zuòyè le ma?
Have you done your homework?

A: 还没有。
還沒有。
Hái méi yǒu.
Not yet.

Written Practice 9-3

For each of the following actions, write a Mandarin sentence indicating that you have not performed the action yet, to match the English sentence.

1. 看电视·看電視 kàn diànshì
   I haven't watched television yet.

   _____

2. 做作业 · 做作業 zuò zuòyè
   I haven't done the homework yet.

   _____

3. 吃晚饭 · 吃晚飯 chī wǎnfàn
   I haven't eaten dinner yet.

   _____

4. 睡觉 · 睡覺 shuì jiào
   I haven't slept yet.

   _____

A Summary of the Use of 了 le and 没 méi in Describing Actions

- To indicate that an action has happened, add 了 le after the action verb or its object.
- To indicate that an action has not happened, add 没 méi before the action verb; do not add 了 le after the action verb or its object.
- To indicate that you have not done something yet, use 还没 · 還沒 hái méi + Action Verb.

Since 了 le indicates that an action happened and 没 méi indicates that an action did not happen or has not happened, 了 le and 没 méi cannot occur together.

Indicating a Past Action with 过 · 過 guo

To indicate that someone has performed an action before, as in *I have read this before,* use 过 · 過 guo after the action verb.

我去过中国。· 我去過中國。
Wǒ qùguo Zhōngguó.
I have been to China before.

我看过那个电影。· 我看過那個電影。
Wǒ kànguo nàge diànyǐng.
I have seen that movie.

过 · 過 guo can be used when the following conditions are met.

- The action is repeatable. Repeatable actions include studying, walking, talking, reading, taking a test, and listening to music. Nonrepeatable actions include being born, dying, graduating from school, and marrying someone.

- The action is not a common occurrence—it does not happen on a regular basis. You can use 过 · 過 guo to say that you have been to China, or that you climbed Mt. Fuji, or that you saw a certain movie, but you do not use 过 · 過 guo to describe actions that you perform on a regular basis, like eating dinner or sleeping.

- Some time has elapsed between the action and the time when you are talking about it. If you just returned from a trip to China, you do not use 过 · 過 guo to say that you have been to China, that is, you would not say 我去过中国。· 我去過中國。 Wǒ qùguo Zhōngguó. If you went to China a year ago, however, this sentence is appropriate.

Written Practice 9-4

For each of the following actions, write a Mandarin sentence indicating that you have performed the action before, using 过 · 過 guo to match the English sentence.

1. 吃法国饭 · 吃法國飯 chī Fǎguó fàn
   I have eaten French food before.

   _____

2. 坐飞机 · 坐飛機 zuò fēijī
   I have flown on an airplane before.

   _____

3. 唱卡拉OK chàng kǎlāOK
   I have sung karaoke before.

   _____

4. 用筷子 yòng kuàizi
I have used chopsticks before.

NEGATING AN ACTION WITH 没 méi + Verb + 过·過 guo

To indicate that you have not performed an action before, negate the action with 没 méi, using 没 méi + Verb + 过·過 guo. If the verb is preceded by a prepositional phrase, 没 méi comes before the prepositional phrase.

我没去过中国。· 我没去過中國。
Wǒ méi qùguo Zhōngguó.
I have never been to China.

我没看过那个电影。· 我没看過那個電影。
Wǒ méi kànguo nàge diànyǐng.
I haven't seen that movie before.

Written Practice 9-5

For each of the following actions, write a Mandarin sentence indicating that you have never performed the action before, to match the English sentence.

1. 吃法国饭·吃法國飯 chī Fǎguó fàn
   I have not eaten French food before.

   _____

2. 坐飞机·坐飛機 zuò fēijī
   I have not flown on an airplane before.

   _____

3. 唱卡拉OK chàng kǎlāOK
   I have not sung karaoke before.

   _____

4. 用筷子 yòng kuàizi
   I have not used chopsticks before.

   _____

USING 过·過 guo WITH 了 le

了 le indicates that an action has happened. Provided all of the conditions for the use of 过·過 guo are met, you can use 过·過 guo and 了 le together to describe the same action in the same sentence. The order in which these elements occur is as follows.

Verb + 过·過 guo + 了 le

When they are used together, 过·過 guo and 了 le are not separated by any other words.

生鱼片我已经吃过了几次。· 生魚片我已經吃過了幾次。
Shēng yú piàn wǒ yǐjing chīguo le jǐ cì.
Sushi I've already eaten a few times.

QUIZ

Rewrite each of the following sentences, adding 了 le to indicate completed action and match the English sentence.

1. 我弟弟吃两碗饭。· 我弟弟吃兩碗飯。
   Wǒ dìdi chī liǎng wǎn fàn.
   My younger brother ate two bowls of rice.

2. 王老师画画儿。· 王老師畫畫兒。
   Wáng lǎoshī huà huàr.
   Professor Wang painted a picture.

3. 他的朋友买飞机票。· 他的朋友買飛機票。
   Tā de péngyou mǎi fēijī piào.
   His friend bought an airplane ticket.

For each of the following actions, write a Mandarin sentence, using 已经·已經 yǐjīng or 还没·還没 hái méi, as appropriate, to match the English sentence.

4. 做作业·做作業 zuò zuòyè
   I haven't done the homework yet.

   _____

5. 洗澡 xǐ zǎo
   I have already bathed.

   _____

6. 考试·考試 kǎo shì
   I have already taken the test.

   _____

For each of the following actions, write a Mandarin sentence indicating that you have performed the action before.

7. 坐飞机·坐飛機 zuò fēijī *ride on an airplane*

   _____

8. 吃中国饭·吃中國飯 chī Zhōngguó fàn *eat Chinese food*

   _____

For each of the following actions, write a Mandarin sentence indicating that you have not performed the action before.

9. 坐飞机·坐飛機 zuò fēijī *ride on an airplane*

   _____

10. 吃中国饭·吃中國飯 chī Zhōngguó fàn *eat Chinese food*

   _____

CHAPTER 10

Indicating Possibility, Ability, and Permission with Modal Verbs

In this chapter, you will learn about:

Rules for Correctly Using 会·會 huì, 能 néng, *and* 可以 kéyǐ
Expressing Probability and Possibility with 会·會 huì
Expressing Ability with 会·會 huì *and* 能 néng
Expressing Permission with 可以 kéyǐ

Rules for Correctly Using 会·會 huì, 能 néng, and 可以 kéyǐ

POSITION OF 会·會 huì, 能 néng, AND 可以 kéyǐ IN THE SENTENCE

The modal verbs 会·會 huì, 能 néng, and 可以 kéyǐ come either before an action verb or before a prepositional phrase that precedes an action verb.

Before an Action Verb

她会说中国话。· 她會說中國話。
Tā huì shuō Zhōngguó huà.
She can speak Chinese.

我的嗓子疼，不能说话。· 我的嗓子疼，不能說話。
Wǒ de sǎngzi téng, bù néng shuō huà.
My throat is sore (and) I cannot speak.

你可以借我的书。· 你可以借我的書。
Nǐ kéyǐ jiè wǒ de shū.
You can borrow my book.

Before a Prepositional Phrase + Action Verb

妈妈说你可以跟我们去看电影。· 媽媽說你可以跟我們去看電影。
Māma shuō nǐ kéyǐ gēn wǒmen qù kàn diànyǐng.
Mom says that you can go to the movies with us.

我的嗓子疼，不能给你们唱歌。· 我的嗓子疼，不能給你們唱歌。
Wǒ de sǎngzi téng, bù néng gěi nǐmen chàng gē.
My throat is sore (and) I can't sing for you.

NEGATION OF 会·會 huì, 能 néng, AND 可以 kéyǐ

不 bù is used to negate 会·會 huì, 能 néng, and 可以 kéyǐ. As you can see in the examples above and in the following examples, 不 bù comes right before 会·會 huì, 能 néng, and 可以 kéyǐ.

她不会说中国话。· 她不會說中國話。
Tā bù huì shuō Zhōngguó huà.
She can't speak Chinese.

我不能跑马拉松。· 我不能跑馬拉松。

Wǒ bù néng pǎo mǎlāsōng.

I can't run a marathon.

你不可以借我的书。· 你不可以借我的書。

Nǐ bù kéyǐ jiè wǒ de shū.

You can't borrow my book.

GIVING SHORT ANSWERS WITH 会·會 huì, 能 néng, AND 可以 kéyǐ

会·會 huì, 能 néng, and 可以 kéyǐ can each be used as a short affirmative answer to a yes-no question. (See Chapter 14 for a detailed discussion of yes-no questions.)

To give the short answer *yes* to a question that includes the modal verb 会·會 huì, 能 néng, or 可以 kéyǐ, simply repeat the modal verb.

Q:	你会说中国话吗？	A:	会。
	你會說中國話嗎？		會。
	Nǐ huì shuō Zhōngguó huà ma?		Huì.
	Can you speak Chinese?		*I can.*
Q:	你能跑马拉松吗？	A:	能。
	你能跑馬拉松嗎？		能。
	Nǐ néng pǎo mǎlāsōng ma?		Néng.
	Can you run a marathon?		*I can.*
Q:	我可以借你的书吗？	A:	可以。
	我可以借你的書嗎？		可以。
	Wǒ kéyǐ jiè nǐ de shū ma?		Kéyǐ.
	Can I borrow your book?		*You can.*

To give the short answer *no* to a question that includes the modal verb 会·會 huì, 能 néng, or 可以 kéyǐ, say 不会·不會 bù huì, 不能 bù néng, or 不可以 bù kéyǐ, respectively.

Q:	你会说中国话吗？	A:	不会。
	你會說中國話嗎？		不會。
	Nǐ huì shuō Zhōngguó huà ma?		Bù huì.
	Can you speak Chinese?		*I cannot.*

Q: 你能跑马拉松吗？　　　　　　A: 不能。
　　你能跑馬拉松嗎？　　　　　　　 不能。
　　Nǐ néng pǎo mǎlāsōng ma?　　　　 Bù néng.
　　Can you run a marathon?　　　　 *I cannot.*

Q: 我可以借你的书吗？　　　　　　A: 不可以。
　　我可以借你的書嗎？　　　　　　　 不可以。
　　Wǒ kéyǐ jiè nǐ de shū ma?　　　　 Bù kéyǐ.
　　Can I borrow your book?　　　　 *You cannot.*

Written Practice 10-1

Reply to each of the following questions with the short answer *no*.

1. 你会用电脑吗？・你會用電腦嗎？
   Nǐ huì yòng diànnǎo ma?
   Can you use a computer?

   _____

2. 你能喝酒吗？・你能喝酒嗎？
   Nǐ néng hē jiǔ ma?
   Can you drink alcohol? (= *Are you physically able to drink?*)

   _____

3. 你可以开车吗？・你可以開車嗎？
   Nǐ kéyǐ kāi chē ma?
   Can you drive? (= *Do you have permission to drive?*)

   _____

Expressing Probability and Possibility with 会・會 huì

会・會 huì is used to indicate that an action will possibly, probably, or definitely occur. In this respect, its use is associated with future time.

明天会下雨。・明天會下雨。
Míngtiān huì xià yǔ.
It will probably rain tomorrow.

我们明天会考试。· 我們明天會考試。
Wǒmen míngtiān huì kǎo shì.
We will have a test tomorrow. OR *We may have a test tomorrow.*

会 · 會 huì can be used with adverbs that indicate that something is possible or probable. These adverbs specify the degree of probability of an action. Following are sentences with the adverbs 也许 · 也許 yéxǔ *perhaps, possibly, maybe,* 可能 kěnéng *perhaps, possibly, maybe,* and 一定 yīdìng *definitely, certainly.* Note that 会 · 會 huì comes after these adverbs.

我这个周末也许会跟朋友去打球。· 我這個週末也許會跟朋友去打球。
Wǒ zhège zhōumò yéxǔ huì gēn péngyou qù dǎ qiú.
This weekend, perhaps I will go and play ball with my friends.

今天晚上的舞会，可能会有很多人来。·
今天晚上的舞會，可能會有很多人來。
Jīntiān wǎnshang de wǔhuì, kěnéng huì yǒu hěn duō rén lái.
A lot of people may come to the dance tonight.
　(lit., *Tonight's dance, perhaps a lot of people will come.*)

我想他一定会请你吃饭。· 我想他一定會請你吃飯。
Wǒ xiǎng tā yīdìng huì qǐng nǐ chī fàn.
I think he will definitely invite you to eat.

Oral Practice

Add 会 · 會 huì to each of the following sentences, indicating that the action will possibly or probably happen, as indicated in the English translations. Then read the sentences aloud.

1. 明天下雪。　　　　　　　→　明天会下雪。
   明天下雪。　　　　　　　　　明天會下雪。
   Míngtiān xià xuě.　　　　　　Míngtiān huì xià xuě.
   　　　　　　　　　　　　　　It may snow tomorrow.

2. 我们今天晚上吃中国饭。　→　我们今天晚上会吃中国饭。
   我們今天晚上吃中國飯。　　　我們今天晚上會吃中國飯。
   Wǒmen jīntiān wǎnshang chī　Wǒmen jīntiān wǎnshang huì chī
   　Zhōngguó fàn.　　　　　　　　Zhōngguó fàn.
   　　　　　　　　　　　　　　We may eat Chinese food tonight.

3. 我明年去中国。   →   我明年会去中国。
　 我明年去中國。   我明年會去中國。
　 Wǒ míngnián qù Zhōngguó.   Wǒ míngnián huì qù Zhōngguó.
　　　　　　　　　　　　　　　　　 I'll probably go to China next year.

Resultative verbs and verbs with potential suffixes are also used to indicate that it is possible or not possible to perform an action. Resultative verbs are outside the scope of this book.

Expressing Ability with 会·會 huì and 能 néng

会·會 huì and 能 néng are used to express ability. 会·會 huì is typically used to indicate mental ability, or ability or knowledge gained from study or practice.

他很会跳舞。· 他很會跳舞。
Tā hěn huì tiào wǔ.
He can really dance.

她会说中国话。· 她會說中國話。
Tā huì shuō Zhōngguó huà.
She can speak Chinese.

能 néng is typically used to indicate the physical ability necessary to perform a particular task.

他今天不舒服，不能吃饭。· 他今天不舒服，不能吃飯。
Tā jīntiān bù shūfu, bù néng chī fàn.
He isn't feeling well today (and) can't eat.

我能跑马拉松。· 我能跑馬拉松。
Wǒ néng pǎo mǎlāsōng.
I can run a marathon.

EXPRESSING GREAT ABILITY WITH 很 hěn ＋ 会·會 huì

When 会·會 huì is used to express ability, it may be modified by the intensifier 很 hěn. (For a detailed discussion of intensifiers with adjectival and stative verbs, see Chapter 7.)

她很会唱歌。· 她很會唱歌。
Tā hěn huì chàng gē.
She can sing very well. OR *She can really sing.*

那个人很会说话。· 那個人很會說話。
Nàge rén hěn huì shuō huà.
That person can really talk. OR *That person is really persuasive.*

Written Practice 10-2

Fill in each blank in the following sentences with the appropriate word to match the English sentences, choosing from (a) 会·會 huì and (b) 能 néng.

1. 他＿＿＿＿用电脑写中文。· 他＿＿＿＿用電腦寫中文。

   Tā ＿＿＿＿ yòng diànnǎo xiě Zhōngwén.

   He can use a computer to type Chinese.

2. 他＿＿＿＿跑马拉松。· 他＿＿＿＿跑馬拉松。

   Tā ＿＿＿＿ pǎo mǎlāsōng.

   He can run a marathon.

3. 王老师＿＿＿＿说英文。· 王老師＿＿＿＿說英文。

   Wáng lǎoshī ＿＿＿＿ shuō Yīngwén.

   Professor Wang can speak English.

Expressing Permission with 可以 kéyǐ

可以 kéyǐ is used to express permission.

你今天可以早一点回家。· 你今天可以早一點回家。
Nǐ jīntiān kéyǐ zǎo yīdiǎn huí jiā.
You can go home a little early today.

Use 可以 kéyǐ to ask for permission to do something.

我可以借你的书吗？· 我可以借你的書嗎？
Wǒ kéyǐ jiè nǐ de shū ma?
Can I borrow your book?

To give a long affirmative reply to a request for permission, use the following.

你可以借我的书。· 你可以借我的書。
Nǐ kéyǐ jiè wǒ de shū.
You can borrow my book.

To give a short affirmative reply to a request for permission, use the following.

可以。
Kéyǐ.
You can.

As an alternative, you may reply affirmatively to a request with the following expression.

行。
Xíng.
OK.

To give a long negative reply to a request for permission, use the following.

你不可以借我的书。· 你不可以借我的書。
Nǐ bù kéyǐ jiè wǒ de shū.
You cannot borrow my book.

To give a short negative reply to a request for permission, use one of the following expressions.

不可以。
Bù kéyǐ.
You cannot.

不行。
Bù xíng.
No. / It's not OK.

行 xíng and 不行 bù xíng are only used in short replies; they cannot be followed by a verb.

INDICATING THAT YOU DO NOT HAVE PERMISSION

To indicate that someone does not have permission to do something, use one of the following constructions.

不可以 bù kéyǐ + Action

你不可以借我的书。· 你不可以借我的書。
Nǐ bù kéyǐ jiè wǒ de shū.
You cannot borrow my book.

不能 bù néng + Action

你不能在图书馆吃饭。· 你不能在圖書館吃飯。
Nǐ bù néng zài túshūguǎn chī fàn.
You cannot eat in the library.

Indicating that you do not have permission to do something is closely related to indicating that the action is prohibited. See Chapter 11 for ways to indicate prohibitions.

Written Practice 10-3

For each of the following phrases, write a Mandarin sentence, adding the modal verb in parentheses to match the English sentence.

1. 在图书馆说话 · 在圖書館說話 zài túshūguǎn shuō huà (可以 kéyǐ)
   You cannot talk in the library.

   _____

2. 在饭馆抽烟 · 在飯館抽煙 zài fànguǎn chōu yān (能 néng)
   You cannot smoke in the restaurant.

   _____

3. 在宿舍做饭 · 在宿舍做飯 zài sùshè zuò fàn (可以 kéyǐ)
   You cannot cook in the dormitory.

   _____

QUIZ

Fill in each blank in the following sentences with the appropriate word to match the English sentences, choosing from (a) 会 · 會 huì, (b) 能 néng, and (c) 可以 kéyǐ.

1. 他的嗓子疼，不_____吃东西。· 他的嗓子疼，不_____吃東西。
   Tā de sǎngzi téng, bù _____ chī dōngxi.
   He has a sore throat (and) cannot eat.

2. 你是十七岁，不_____喝酒。· 你是十七歲，不_____喝酒。
   Nǐ shì shíqī suì, bù _____ hē jiǔ.
   You are 17 years old; you cannot drink.

3. 她_____唱京剧。· 她_____唱京劇。
   Tā _____ chàng Jīng jù.
   She can sing Beijing opera.

4. 你＿＿＿借我的车。·你＿＿＿借我的車。

Nǐ ＿＿＿ jiè wǒ de chē.

You can borrow my car.

5. 那个字太难。我不＿＿＿写。·那個字太難。我不＿＿＿寫。

Nàge zì tài nán. Wǒ bù ＿＿＿ xiě.

That character is too difficult. I can't write it.

For each of the following phrases, write a Mandarin sentence indicating that you cannot perform the action.

6. 抽烟·抽煙 chōu yān *smoke*

_____

7. 在图书馆吃饭·在圖書館吃飯 zài túshūguǎn chī fàn *eat in the library*

_____

Reply negatively to each of the following questions in the shortest acceptable way.

8. 我可以借你的车吗？·我可以借你的車嗎？

Wǒ kéyǐ jiè nǐ de chē ma?

Can I borrow your car?

_____

9. 你会说英文吗？·你會說英文嗎？

Nǐ huì shuō Yīngwén ma?

Can you speak English?

_____

10. 你能跳舞吗？·你能跳舞嗎？

Nǐ néng tiào wǔ ma?

Can you dance?

_____

CHAPTER 11

Expressing Obligations, Suggestions, and Prohibitions

In this chapter, you will learn about:

Expressing Obligations
Expressing Suggestions
Expressing Commands
Expressing Prohibitions

Expressing Obligations

Obligations are actions that people *should* or *must* perform. In Mandarin, as in English, obligations are expressed with a word that comes at the beginning of the verb phrase—before the verb and before a prepositional phrase, if there is one.

EXPRESSING *SHOULD* OR *OUGHT TO*

Following are the Mandarin words that indicate *should* or *ought to*. Just as *should* and *ought to* express the same meaning in English, these Mandarin words are equivalent in meaning. 该·該 gāi is somewhat less formal than 应该·應該 yīnggāi and 应当·應當 yīngdāng. 应·應 yīng is preferred in formal written documents. All of these words may be used to express social and moral obligations.

应该·應該   yīnggāi
该·該   gāi
应当·應當   yīngdāng
应·應   yīng (used in formal written documents)

你应该听父母的话。· 你應該聽父母的話。
Nǐ yīnggāi **tīng fùmǔ de huà**.
*You should **listen to what your parents say***.

你应该帮助你的朋友。· 你應該幫助你的朋友。
Nǐ yīnggāi **bāngzhù nǐ de péngyou**.
*You should **help your friends***.

你该早一点睡觉。· 你該早一點睡覺。
Nǐ gāi **zǎo yīdiǎn shuì jiào**.
*You should **go to sleep a little earlier***.

Written Practice 11-1

Give your younger sister advice about what she should do when studying Chinese. For each of the following phrases, write a Mandarin sentence that expresses the meaning of the English sentence.

1. 每天写字 · 每天寫字
   měitiān xiě zì
   You should write characters every day.

   _____

2. 注意发音 · 注意發音
   zhùyì fāyīn
   You should pay attention to pronunciation.

   _____

3. 练习生词 · 練習生詞
   liànxí shēngcí
   You should study the new words.

   _____

4. 跟你的朋友说中国话 · 跟你的朋友說中國話
   gēn nǐ de péngyou shuō Zhōngguó huà
   You should speak Chinese with your friends.

   _____

EXPRESSING *MUST* OR *HAVE TO*

Following are the Mandarin words that indicate *must* or *have to*.

得	děi (most common in speech)
必得	bìděi (more formal than 得 děi, but often used in speech)
要	yào
必须 · 必須	bìxū (formal)

Note that as a verb, 要 yào means *want*. It can also be used to indicate future time.

These words come before the verb and before a prepositional phrase, if there is one.

你得**明天早上**交作业。· 你得**明天早上**交作業。
Nǐ děi **míngtiān zǎoshang** jiāo zuòyè.
*You must **hand in your homework tomorrow morning**.*

上车以前你得**先**买票。· 上車以前你得**先**買票。
Shàng chē yǐqián nǐ děi **xiān mǎi piào.**
*Before you get on the bus, you must **first buy a ticket**.*

你明天要**早一点**来。· 你明天要**早一點**來。
Nǐ míngtiān yào **zǎo yīdiǎn lái.**
*You must **come a little earlier** tomorrow.*

你必须**回答老师的问题**。· 你必須**回答老師的問題**。
Nǐ bìxū **huídá lǎoshī de wèntí.**
*You must **answer the teacher's questions**.*

Written Practice 11-2

Professor Wang has written a list of things that her students must do before class. Using the following phrases from this list, write complete Mandarin sentences expressing what she told them they must do.

1. 复习生词 · 復習生詞 fùxí shēngcí *review new vocabulary*

   _____

2. 练习汉字 · 練習漢字 liànxí Hànzì *practice Chinese characters*

   _____

3. 做作业 · 做作業 zuò zuòyè *do the homework*

   _____

4. 听录音 · 聽錄音 tīng lùyīn *listen to the recordings*

   _____

EXPRESSING *DO NOT HAVE TO* OR *NEED NOT*

Following are expressions that you can use to say that someone *does not have to* perform some action.

不必	bù bì	*do not have to*
不用	bù yòng	*do not have to*
不要	bù yào	*do not have to*
不须·不須	bù xū	*not be necessary*

Note that 不 is always pronounced with a rising (2nd) tone (bú) before a syllable in 4th tone. Therefore, 不必, 不用, and 不要 are actually pronounced bú bì, bú yòng, and bú yào. In the list above, 不 is presented in its basic, unchanged tone.

These expressions come at the beginning of the verb phrase—before the verb and before a prepositional phrase, if there is one.

在中国，你不必给小费。· 在中國，你不必給小費。
Zài Zhōngguó, nǐ bù bì gěi xiǎofèi.
In China, you do not have to give a tip.

我们是朋友。你不必这么客气。· 我們是朋友。你不必這麼客氣。
Wǒmen shì péngyou. Nǐ bù bì zhème kèqi.
We are friends. You don't have to be so polite.

你不用帮助我。· 你不用幫助我。
Nǐ bù yòng bāngzhù wǒ.
You do not have to help me.

你不须说话。· 你不須說話。
Nǐ bùxū shuō huà.
You do not have to talk.

这是应该的。你不要谢 (我)。· 這是應該的。你不要謝 (我)。
Zhè shì yīnggāi de. Nǐ bù yào xiè (wǒ).
This is an obligation. You do not have to thank me.

Oral Practice

Your friend is visiting you for a few days. Using the following phrases, tell her things that she does not have to do.

1. 做菜 zuò cài (use 不用 bù yòng) →
   你不用做菜。Nǐ bù yòng zuò cài.
   You don't have to cook.

2. 收拾屋子 shōushi wūzi (use 不必 bù bì) →
   你不必收拾屋子。Nǐ bù bì shōushi wūzi.
   You don't have to straighten up your room.

3. 洗盘子·洗盤子 xǐ pánzi (use 不须 bù xū) →
   你不须洗盘子。· 你不須洗盤子。Nǐ bù xū xǐ pánzi.
   You don't have to wash the dishes.

Expressing Suggestions

Two of the most common ways to make suggestions in Mandarin follow.

SUGGESTIONS WITH 吧 ba

You can make a suggestion by ending a statement with the sentence-final particle 吧 ba, which follows the statement without pause.

我们吃饭吧! · 我們吃飯吧!
Wǒmen chī fàn ba!
Let's eat!

你去休息吧。
Nǐ qù xiūxi ba.
Go relax for awhile.

SUGGESTIONS THAT ASK IF AN IDEA IS *ALL RIGHT*

The expressions 怎么样·怎麼樣 zěnmeyàng, 好不好 hǎo bù hǎo, 好吗·好嗎 hǎo ma, 行不行 xíng bù xíng, and 行吗·行嗎 xíng ma are all used to make suggestions. They literally ask if an idea is *all right*. All occur after a pause in speech, and after a comma in written form. They do not occur with 吧 ba.

我们今天晚上去看电影，怎么样？· 我們今天晚上去看電影，怎麼樣？
Wǒmen jīntiān wǎnshang qù kàn diànyǐng, zěnmeyàng?
Let's go see a movie tonight, OK?

我们吃中国菜，好不好？· 我們吃中國菜，好不好？
Wǒmen chī Zhōngguó cài, hǎo bù hǎo?
Let's eat Chinese food, OK?

我们看电视，好不好？· 我們看電視，好不好？
Wǒmen kàn diànshì, hǎo bù hǎo?
Let's watch television, OK?

Oral Practice

Convert the following actions into suggestions, using the expressions in parentheses. Then read your suggestions aloud.

1. 去唱卡拉OK (行吗)
   去唱卡拉OK (行嗎)
   qù chàng kǎlāOK (xíng ma)

   → 我们去唱卡拉OK，行吗？
   我們去唱卡拉OK，行嗎？
   Wǒmen qù chàng kǎlāOK, xíng ma?
   Let's sing karaoke, OK?

2. 请小白吃饭 (好不好)
   請小白吃飯 (好不好)
   qǐng Xiǎo Bái chī fàn (hǎo bù hǎo)

   → 我们请小白吃饭，好不好？
   我們請小白吃飯，好不好？
   Wǒmen qǐng Xiǎo Bái chī fàn,
      hǎo bù hǎo?
   Let's invite Little Bai to eat, OK?

3. 回家 (吧)

   huí jiā (ba)

   → 我们回家吧！
   我們回家吧！
   Wǒmen huí jiā ba!
   Let's go home.

SUGGESTIONS WITH 最好 zuì hǎo

The verb phrase 最好 zuì hǎo *the best thing to do, had better* is used to express the opinion of the speaker about what the listener should do. It comes after the subject, before or after a time expression, and before the verb phrase.

你最好复习功课。· 你最好復習功課。
Nǐ zuì hǎo fùxí gōng kè.
You'd better review the lesson.

你最好多喝水。
Nǐ zuì hǎo duō hē shuǐ.
The best thing for you to do is drink more water.

你最好今天晚上给他打电话。· 你最好今天晚上給他打電話。
Nǐ zuì hǎo jīntiān wǎnshang gěi tā dǎ diànhuà.
You'd better call him tonight.

Written Practice 11-3

Write a Mandarin sentence that converts each of the following actions into a suggestion, using the expression in parentheses to match the English sentence.

1. 听音乐 (怎么样) · 聽音樂 (怎麼樣)
   tīng yīnyuè (zěnmeyàng)
   Let's listen to music tonight.

   _____

2. 坐公共汽车 (最好) · 坐公共汽車 (最好)
   zuò gōnggòngqìchē (zuì hǎo)
   You'd best take the bus.

   _____

3. 去喝咖啡 (好不好)
   qù hē kāfēi (hǎo bù hǎo)
   How about going for coffee?

   _____

4. 看电视 (行不行) · 看電視 (行不行)
   kàn diànshì (xíng bù xíng)
   Let's watch television.

   _____

5. 给我们唱歌 (好吗) · 給我們唱歌 (好嗎)
   gěi wǒmen chàng gē (hǎo ma)
   Why don't you sing us a song?

   _____

Expressing Commands

In a command, the speaker orders the listener to do something. The form of a command in Mandarin is a sentence with no subject.

说! · 說!
Shuō!
Speak!
站住!
Zhànzhù!
Halt!

Commands may end in 吧 ba.

回家吧!
Huí jiā ba!
Go home!

Expressing Prohibitions

In a prohibition, the speaker tells the listener that he or she *should not* or *must not* do something, or that some action is prohibited.

SAYING THAT SOMEONE *SHOULD NOT* PERFORM AN ACTION

To say that someone *should not* perform an action, use 不应该·不應該 bù yīnggāi + Action.

你不应该批评你的父母。· 你不應該批評你的父母。
Nǐ bù yīnggāi pīpíng nǐ de fùmǔ.
You should not criticize (your) parents.

你不应该抽烟。· 你不應該抽煙。
Nǐ bù yīnggāi chōu yān.
You shouldn't smoke.

Written Practice 11-4

Each of the following actions should not be performed while one is studying. Write a Mandarin sentence expressing this prohibition, using 不应该·不應該 bù yīnggāi.

1. 听音乐·聽音樂 tīng yīnyuè *listen to music*

   _____

2. 看电视·看電視 kàn diànshì *watch television*

   _____

3. 跟朋友说话·跟朋友說話 gēn péngyou shuō huà *speak with friends*

   _____

SAYING THAT SOMEONE *MUST NOT* PERFORM AN ACTION

The following expressions are commonly used to say that someone must not perform an action. These expressions come right before the prohibited action and do not occur with a subject.

不要	bù yào	*don't*
别	bié	*don't*

不要喝酒。
Bù yào hē jiǔ.
Don't drink.

别跟他说话。· 别跟他說話。
Bié gēn tā shuō huà.
Don't speak with him.

不要 bù yào and 别 bié occur in informal speech, as well as in writing.

SAYING THAT AN ACTION IS PROHIBITED

To say that an action is prohibited, use one of the following expressions right before the prohibited action; do not include a subject.

不许·不許	bù xǔ	*not permitted*
不准	bù zhǔn	*not permitted, forbidden, prohibited*
禁止	jìnzhǐ	*forbid, prohibit, ban*
严禁·嚴禁	yánjìn	*strictly prohibit*

不许·不許 bù xǔ and 不准 bù zhǔn are relatively formal and do not usually occur in colloquial speech. 禁止 jìnzhǐ and 严禁·嚴禁 yánjìn normally occur in writing, especially in notices and signs that specify prohibited actions.

不许拍照片。· 不許拍照片。
Bù xǔ pāi zhàopiàn.
You are not allowed to take photographs. / Taking photographs is prohibited.

考试的时候，不准偷看别人的考卷。· 考試的時候，不准偷看別人的考卷。
Kǎoshì de shíhou, bù zhǔn tōu kàn biéren de kǎojuàn.
When you are taking a test, it is prohibited to look at another person's test paper.

禁止停车。· 禁止停車。
Jìnzhǐ tíng chē.
It is prohibited to park. / No parking.

严禁酒后开车。· 嚴禁酒後開車。
Yánjìn jiǔ hòu kāi chē.
It is strictly prohibited to drive after drinking. / Don't drink and drive.

Written Practice 11-5

Write Mandarin sentences to indicate that the following actions are prohibited, using the prohibition expressions in parentheses.

1. 在宿舍喝酒 (不准)
   zài sùshè hē jiǔ (bù zhǔn)
   Drinking in the dormitory is prohibited.

   _____

2. 在教室睡觉。(不要) · 在教室睡覺。(不要)
   zài jiàoshì shuì jiào (bù yào)
   Don't sleep in the classroom.

   _____

3. 在图书馆用手机。(别) · 在圖書館用手機。(別)
   zài túshūguǎn yòng shǒujī (bié)
   Don't use a cell phone in the library.

   _____

QUIZ

Rewrite each of the following sentences, adding the appropriate expression of obligation or suggestion from the list below, to match the English sentence.

a. 应该·應該 yīnggāi   d. 不必 bù bì
b. 得 děi   e. 别 bié
c. 不应该·不應該 bù yīnggāi   f. 吧 ba

1. 你在宿舍抽烟。· 你在宿舍抽煙。
   Nǐ zài sùshè chōu yān.
   You should not smoke in the dormitory.

   _____

2. 你请你的老师吃晚饭。· 你請你的老師吃晚飯。
   Nǐ qǐng nǐ de lǎoshī chī wǎnfàn.
   You do not have to invite your teacher to dinner.

   _____

3. 你每天交作业。· 你每天交作業。
   Nǐ měitiān jiāo zuòyè.
   You must hand in your homework every day.

   _____

4. 请你的老师吃晚饭。· 請你的老師吃晚飯。
   Qǐng nǐ de lǎoshī chī wǎnfàn.
   Invite your teacher to dinner!

   _____

5. 在宿舍抽烟。· 在宿舍抽煙。
   Zài sùshè chōu yān.
   Do not smoke in the dormitory.

   _____

6. 你帮助你的弟弟做作业。· 你幫助你的弟弟做作業。
   Nǐ bāngzhù nǐ de dìdi zuò zuòyè.
   You should help your younger brother do his homework.

   _____

Select the correct English translation for each of the following Mandarin sentences.

7. 你不应该跟你的弟弟吵架。· 你不應該跟你的弟弟吵架。
   Nǐ bù yīnggāi gēn nǐ de dìdi chǎo jià.

   a. *Don't fight with your younger brother.*
   b. *You should not fight with your younger brother.*
   c. *You don't have to fight with your younger brother.*

8. 你不要开快车。· 你不要開快車。
   (开快车·開快車 kāi kuài chē *drive a fast car = speed*)
   Nǐ bù yào kāi kuài chē.

   a. *You should not speed.*
   b. *You must not speed.*
   c. *Don't speed.*

9. 我明天得到机场去接我的哥哥。· 我明天得到機場去接我的哥哥。
   Wǒ míngtiān děi dào jīchǎng qù jiē wǒ de gēge.

   a. *I have to go to the airport tomorrow to pick up my older brother.*
   b. *I don't have to go to the airport tomorrow to pick up my older brother.*
   c. *I should go to the airport tomorrow to pick up my older brother.*

10. 你应该每天喝八杯水。· 你應該每天喝八杯水。
    Nǐ yīnggāi měitiān hē bā bēi shuǐ.

    a. *Drink eight glasses of water every day.*
    b. *You should drink eight glasses of water every day.*
    c. *You have to drink eight glasses of water every day.*

PART THREE

NOUNS, QUESTIONS, AND CONNECTIONS

CHAPTER 12

Indicating Possession

In this chapter, you will learn about:

Indicating Possession with 有 yǒu have
Indicating Possession with the Particle 的 de
Possession Phrases That Don't Specify the Thing Possessed
Word Order and Possession

Indicating Possession with 有 yǒu *have*

To say that a subject *has something,* use the word 有 yǒu *have* in the following construction. The subject of 有 yǒu may be a person, place, or thing.

Subject + 有 yǒu + Object

我有一本书。· 我有一本書。
Wǒ yǒu yī běn shū.
I have a/one book.

上海有两个机场。· 上海有兩個機場。
Shànghǎi yǒu liǎng gè jīchǎng.
Shanghai has two airports.

那所房子有两个卧房。· 那所房子有兩個臥房。
Nà suǒ fángzi yǒu liǎng gè wòfáng.
That house has two bedrooms.

Oral Practice

王老师 · 王老師 Wáng Lǎoshī has the following people in her family. Read the list aloud and identify the family members.

1. 她有一个弟弟。· 她有一個弟弟。
   Tā yǒu yī gè dìdi. → *a younger brother*

2. 她有两个孩子。· 她有兩個孩子。
   Tā yǒu liǎng gè háizi. → *two children*

3. 她有两个姐姐。· 她有兩個姐姐。
   Tā yǒu liǎng gè jiějie. → *two older sisters*

4. 她有父亲和母亲。· 她有父親和母親。
   Tā yǒu fùqin hé mǔqin. → *a father and a mother*

Written Practice 12-1

Following is a list of some of 小李 Xiǎo Lǐ's possessions. Write complete sentences that state what 小李 Xiǎo Lǐ has.

1. 电脑·電腦 diànnǎo *computer*

   _____

2. 手机·手機 shǒujī *cell phone*

   _____

3. 电视机·電視機 diànshìjī *television*

   _____

4. 自行车·自行車 zìxíngchē *bicycle*

   _____

NEGATING 有 yǒu

有 yǒu is negated with 没 méi—never with 不 bù.

我没有书。· 我没有書。
Wǒ méi yǒu shū.
I do not have a book.

那所房子没有窗户。· 那所房子没有窗戶。
Nà suǒ fángzi méi yǒu chuānghu.
That house does not have any windows.

Written Practice 12-2

Rewrite each of the following sentences, negating it with 没 méi, to match the English sentences.

1. 小李有哥哥。
   Xiǎo Lǐ yǒu gēge.
   Xiao Li does not have an older brother.

   _____

2. 小李有车。· 小李有車。
   Xiǎo Lǐ yǒu chē.
   Xiao Li does not have a car.

   _____

3. 小李有钱。· 小李有錢。
   Xiǎo Lǐ yǒu qián.
   Xiao Li does not have any money.

   _____

4. 小李有朋友。
   Xiǎo Lǐ yǒu péngyou.
   Xiao Li does not have any friends.

   _____

EXPRESSING *THERE EXISTS* WITH 有 yǒu

If a sentence has no subject, the most natural English translation for 有 yǒu is *there is/are* or *there exists.*

有人在房子里。· 有人在房子裏。
Yǒu rén zài fángzi lǐ.
There are people in the house.

Indicating Possession with the Particle 的 de

I have a book is a complete sentence. Expressions like *my book* and *my sister's friends* are noun phrases that occur within a sentence, as the subject, the object of the verb, or the object of a preposition.

A noun phrase expressing possession contains both the possessor and the thing possessed. In Mandarin, possession phrases typically also include the particle 的 de after the possessor, which can be a noun or a pronoun. The order of information in a possession noun phrase in Mandarin is as follows; in these examples, the possessor is a pronoun.

Possessor	+ 的 de +	Thing Possessed
我	的	书
我	的	書
wǒ	de	shū
my		*book*
他们	的	书
他們	的	書
tāmen	de	shū
their		*book*
我	的	朋友
wǒ	de	péngyou
my		*friend*
你	的	老师
你	的	老師
nǐ	de	lǎoshī
your		*teacher*
他	的	妹妹
tā	de	mèimei
his		*younger sister*

In the following examples, the possessor is a noun.

Possessor + 的 **de** + **Thing Possessed**

老师	的	书
老師	的	書
lǎoshī	de	shū
the teacher's		*book*
妹妹	的	老师
妹妹	的	老師
mèimei	de	lǎoshī
younger sister's		*teacher*
姐姐	的	朋友
jiějie	de	péngyou
older sister's		*friend*

Oral Practice

Read the following Mandarin possession phrases aloud, then translate them into English.

1. 他们的老师·他們的老師 tāmen de lǎoshī → *their teacher*

2. 我的妹妹 wǒ de mèimei → *my younger sister*

3. 你的车·你的車 nǐ de chē → *your car*

4. 他的书·他的書 tā de shū → *his book*

Written Practice 12-3

Translate the following English possession phrases into Mandarin.

1. our friend _____

2. your (*plural*) dad _____

3. their dormitory _____

4. Little Li's bicycle _____

OMITTING 的 de

的 de may be omitted in phrases in which there is a close relationship between the possessor and the thing possessed. For example, 的 de is often omitted in phrases involving a pronoun and a family or family member.

我的妈妈   →   我妈妈
我的媽媽   我媽媽
wǒ de māma   wǒ māma
my mom

我的家   →   我家
wǒ de jiā   wǒ jiā
my family

In most cases, however, 的 de cannot be omitted.

Possession Phrases That Don't Specify the Thing Possessed

In Mandarin, the thing possessed is often omitted if its identity is clear from the context. If the thing possessed is omitted, 的 de must come after the possessor and cannot be omitted. Following are examples in which the thing possessed is omitted. Square brackets indicate where it would go if it were not omitted.

这本书是**我的** [ ]。
這本書是**我的** [ ]。
Zhè běn shū shì **wǒ de** [ ].
*This book is **mine**.*

这是我的椅子。那是**你的** [ ]。
這是我的椅子。那是**你的** [ ]。
Zhè shì wǒ de yǐzi. Nà shì **nǐ de** [ ].
*This is my chair. That (one) is **yours**.*

那个自行车是**小李的** [ ]，不是**我的** [ ]。
那個自行車是**小李的** [ ]，不是**我的** [ ]。
Nàge zìxíngchē shì **Xiǎo Lǐ de** [ ], bù shì **wǒ de** [ ].
*That bicycle is **Xiao Li's**, not **mine**.*

Following are the same sentences with the thing possessed explicitly stated.

这本书是我的书。
這本書是我的書。
Zhè běn shū shì wǒ de shū.
This book is my book.

这是我的椅子。那是你的椅子。
這是我的椅子。那是你的椅子。
Zhè shì wǒ de yǐzi. Nà shì nǐ de yǐzi.
This is my chair. That is your chair.

那个自行车是小李的自行车，不是我的自行车。
那個自行車是小李的自行車，不是我的自行車。
Nàge zìxíngchē shì Xiǎo Lǐ de zìxíngchē, bù shì wǒ de zìxíngchē.
That bicycle is Xiao Li's bicycle, not my bicycle.

Note that when the thing possessed is omitted from the phrase in English, the pronoun takes a special possessive form: *mine, yours, his, hers, its, ours,* or *theirs.* In Mandarin, pronouns do not have a special possessive form. The following chart compares the forms of English and Mandarin pronouns.

Pronoun	**Pronoun + 的 de + Main Noun**	**Pronoun + 的 de**
我	我的 (朋友)	我的
wǒ	wǒ de (péngyou)	wǒ de
I, me	*my (friend)*	*mine*
你	你的 (朋友)	你的
nǐ	nǐ de (péngyou)	nǐ de
you (singular)	*your (friend)*	*yours*
他 / 她 / 它	他的 (朋友)	他的
tā	tā de (péngyou)	tā de
he/she/it, him/her/it	*his/her/its (friend)*	*his/hers/its*
我们 · 我們	我们的 (朋友) · 我們的 (朋友)	我们的 · 我們的
wǒmen	wǒmen de (péngyou)	wǒmen de
we, us	*our (friend)*	*ours*
你们 · 你們	你们的 (朋友) · 你們的 (朋友)	你們的 · 你们的
nǐmen	nǐmen de (péngyou)	nǐmen de
you (plural)	*your (friend)*	*yours*

Pronoun	Pronoun + 的 de + Main Noun	Pronoun + 的 de
他们·他們	他们的 (朋友)·他們的 (朋友)	他们的·他們的
tāmen	tāmen de (péngyou)	tāmen de
they, them	*their* (*friend*)	*theirs*

Oral Practice

Read each of the following sentences aloud, then translate the possession phrase in bold type into English.

1. 那本书是**马老师的**。· 那本書是**馬老師的**。
   Nà běn shū shì **Mǎ lǎoshī de**. → *Professor Ma's*

2. 这些东西都是**他们的**。· 這些東西都是**他們的**。
   Zhè xiē dōngxi dōu shì **tāmen de**. → *theirs*

3. 那本书不是**我的**。· 那本書不是**我的**。
   Nà běn shū bù shì **wǒ de**. → *mine*

4. 这个电脑是**你的**吗？· 這個電腦是**你的**嗎？
   Zhège diànnǎo shì **nǐ de** ma? → *yours*

Written Practice 12-4

Translate the following English phrases into Mandarin.

1. hers   _____

2. yours   _____

3. my younger sister's   _____

4. ours   _____

Word Order and Possession

If you have studied Spanish or French, you have probably noticed that in both of these languages, the particle used in possession phrases is similar in pronunciation to Mandarin 的 de. The order of information in a Spanish or French possession phrase, however, is exactly the opposite of the order in Mandarin. Do not use Spanish or French grammar when speaking Mandarin; in Mandarin, always put the possessor before the thing possessed.

Correct	**Incorrect**
老师的书·老師的書	✗ 书的老师·書的老師
lǎoshī de shū	shū de lǎoshī
the teacher's book	
我哥哥的朋友	✗ 朋友的我哥哥
wǒ gēge de péngyou	péngyou de wǒ gēge
my older brother's friends	

Possession is a type of noun description, and it is one of several ways that you can describe a noun. In Chapter 13, we will discuss descriptions of nouns involving adjectival verbs, such as *a new book,* and descriptions of nouns involving other types of verbs, such as *a book that I like* and *a book that Teacher Chen wrote.*

QUIZ

1. Translate the following Mandarin phrases into English.

    a. 他们的·他們的 tāmen de _____

    b. 你的 nǐ de _____

    c. 我父亲的·我父親的 wǒ fùqin de _____

2. Select the correct Mandarin translation of the phrase *my older brother.*

    a. 哥哥的我 gēge de wǒ

    b. 我哥哥的 wǒ gēge de

    c. 我的哥哥 wǒ de gēge

3. Select the correct Mandarin translation of the phrase *younger sister's teacher.*

   a. 妹妹的老师 · 妹妹的老師   mèimei de lǎoshī
   b. 老师的妹妹 · 老師的妹妹   lǎoshī de mèimei
   c. 妹妹老师的 · 妹妹老師的   mèimei lǎoshī de

4. Place the following words in the correct order to express the English phrase *their dictionaries.*

   的 – 字典 – 他们 · 的 – 字典 – 他們
   de – zìdiǎn – tāmen

   _____

5. Place the following words in the correct order to express the English phrase *older brother's younger sister.*

   妹妹 – 哥哥 – 的
   mèimei – gēge – de

   _____

6. Place the following words in the correct order to express the English phrase *father's daughter.*

   女儿 – 爸爸 – 的 · 女兒 – 爸爸 – 的
   nǚ'ér – bàba – de

   _____

7. Translate the following sentence into Mandarin.

   My teacher has 40 students.

   _____

8. Translate the following sentence into Mandarin.

   Aunt Zhang does not have any younger sisters.

   _____

9. Translate the phrase *older sister's pens* into Mandarin.

   _____

10. Translate the phrase *the teacher's younger brother* into Mandarin.

   _____

CHAPTER 13

Describing Nouns with Adjectival Verbs and Description Clauses

In this chapter, you will learn about:

Describing Nouns with Adjectival Verbs
Describing Nouns with Clauses
Composing Mandarin Noun Phrases with Description Clauses
Translating Mandarin Noun Phrases with Description Clauses into English
Identifying Noun Descriptions When the Main Noun Is Omitted
Translating English Relative Pronouns
Describing a Noun with More Than One Description

Describing Nouns with Adjectival Verbs

As discussed in Chapter 7, qualities are expressed in Mandarin with adjectival verbs. When an adjectival verb describes a noun, it comes before the noun that it describes—called the *main noun*—and is followed by the particle 的 de.

Adjectival Verb + 的 de + Main Noun

高	的	人
gāo	de	rén
a tall person / tall people		

用功	的	学生
用功	的	學生
yònggōng	de	xuésheng
a hardworking student / hardworking students		

Does this construction look familiar? It is the same construction that is used to indicate possession, discussed in Chapter 12. Following are examples of the two patterns, side by side.

Possessor + 的 de + Thing Possessed	**Adjectival Verb + 的 de + Main Noun**
我的朋友	很好的朋友
wǒ de péngyou	hěn hǎo de péngyou
my friend	*a very good friend*
张老师的车	很贵的车
張老師的車	很貴的車
Zhāng lǎoshī de chē	hěn guì de chē
Professor Zhang's car	*a very expensive car*

In Mandarin, all noun descriptions come before the noun. The description and the main noun that follows it form a noun phrase.

USING INTENSIFIERS WITH ADJECTIVAL VERBS

Descriptions involving adjectival verbs typically occur with an intensifier, for example, 很 hěn *very,* 真 zhēn *really,* and 非常 fēicháng *extremely.* In affirmative phrases, when you do not want to add special emphasis, use the neutral intensifier 很 hěn (see Chapter 7).

很聪明的孩子
很聰明的孩子
hěn cōngming de háizi
a very intelligent child / very intelligent children

Following are examples of other intensifiers in noun descriptions.

最高的人
zuì gāo de rén
the tallest person

很有意思的书 · 很有意思的書
hěn yǒu yìsi de shū
a very interesting book / very interesting books

非常漂亮的地方
fēicháng piàoliang de dìfang
an extremely pretty place

挺聪明的孩子 · 挺聰明的孩子
tǐng cōngming de háizi
a very intelligent child

Written Practice 13-1

Match each Mandarin phrase on the left with its English translation on the right.

_____ 1. 比较贵的车 · 比較貴的車
　　　　bǐjiào guì de chē

_____ 2. 挺有意思的电影 · 挺有意思的電影
　　　　tǐng yǒu yìsi de diànyǐng

_____ 3. 非常漂亮的地方
　　　　fēicháng piàoliang de dìfang

_____ 4. 最好的学生 · 最好的學生
　　　　zuì hǎo de xuésheng

a. a very interesting movie
b. the best student
c. a relatively expensive car
d. an extremely beautiful place

Written Practice 13-2

Rewrite each of the following Mandarin phrases, adding the Mandarin equivalent of the intensifier in parentheses.

1. 贵的衣服 · 貴的衣服　guì de yīfu　(extremely)

   _____

2. 用功的学生 · 用功的學生　yònggōng de xuésheng　(very)

   _____

3. 便宜的字典　piányi de zìdiǎn　(rather)

   _____

4. 好的电影 · 好的電影　hǎo de diànyǐng　(relatively)

   _____

NEGATING AN ADJECTIVAL VERB DESCRIPTION

The adjectival verb in a noun description is usually negated with 不 bù.

不太贵的书 · 不太貴的書
bù tài guì de shū
a not-too-expensive book (i.e., *a book that is not too expensive*)

If the adjectival verb phrase begins with 有 yǒu, it is negated with 没 méi.

没有意思的书 · 没有意思的書
méi yǒu yìsi de shū
a not-interesting book (i.e., *a book that is not interesting*)

An intensifier need not be present if the adjectival verb is negated.

不贵的书 · 不貴的書
bù guì de shū
a not-expensive book (i.e., *an inexpensive book*)

Oral Practice

Negate the following phrases, then read the negated phrases aloud.

1. 很漂亮的地方   →   不很漂亮的地方
   hěn piàoliang de dìfang   bù hěn piàoliang de dìfang
   a very beautiful place

2. 有意思的电影   →   没有意思的电影
   有意思的電影   没有意思的電影
   yǒu yìsi de diànyǐng   méi yǒu yìsi de diànyǐng
   an interesting movie

3. 太小的鞋子   →   不太小的鞋子
   tài xiǎo de xiézi   bù tài xiǎo de xiézi
   shoes that are too small

OMITTING 的 de FROM THE NOUN PHRASE

的 de is typically present in a noun phrase with an adjectival verb as descriptor. If 的 de is omitted, the phrase has a special meaning, as in the following examples.

To refer to the White House in Washington D.C., say the following.

白宫   NOT   白的宫
Báigōng   bái de gōng
the White House   *white palace*

To refer to Chinese grain alcohol, say the following.

白酒   NOT   白的酒
báijiǔ   bái de jiǔ
white liquor   *white-colored alcohol*

To refer to red wine, say the following.

红葡萄酒   NOT   红的葡萄酒
紅葡萄酒   紅的葡萄酒
hóng pútaojiǔ   hóng de pútaojiǔ
red wine   *red-colored wine*

To refer to the Red Cross, say the following.

红会 OR 红十字会	NOT	红的会 OR 红十字的会
紅會 OR 紅十字會		紅的會 OR 紅十字的會
Hónghuì OR Hóngshízìhuì		hóng de huì OR hóngshízì de huì
the Red Cross		[no obvious translation]

To refer to an express train or bus, say the following.

快车	NOT	快的车
快車		快的車
kuàichē		kuài de chē
express train; express bus		*a fast car*

OMITTING THE MAIN NOUN

In a noun phrase with an adjectival verb as descriptor, the main noun may be omitted if its identity is clear from the context. In the following pair of sentences, square brackets indicate where the main noun would go if it were not omitted. Can you identify the noun that is omitted in these sentences?

大的鞋子是哥哥的 [ ]。小的 [ ] 是弟弟的 [ ]。
Dà de xiézi shì gēge de [ ]. Xiǎo de [ ] shì dìdi de [ ].
The big shoes are older brother's. The small (ones) are younger brother's.

The answer is: 鞋子 xiézi *shoes.*

Oral Practice

Read the following sentences aloud and identify the omitted nouns. The nouns are given in the Answer Key under Written Practice 13-3.

1. 很有意思的书是他的。没有意思的 [ ] 是我的。
   很有意思的書是他的。没有意思的 [ ] 是我的。
   Hěn yǒu yìsi de shū shì tā de. Méi yǒu yìsi de [ ] shì wǒ de.

2. 最聪明的人是小白。最笨的 [ ] 是我。
   最聰明的人是小白。最笨的 [ ] 是我。
   Zuì cōngming de rén shì Xiǎo Bái. Zuì bèn de [ ] shì wǒ.

3. 最快的车是他的 [ ]。最慢的 [ ] 是我的 [ ]。
   最快的車是他的 [ ]。最慢的 [ ] 是我的 [ ]。
   Zuì kuài de chē shì tā de [ ]. Zuì màn de [ ] shì wǒ de [ ].

Written Practice 13-3

Translate the sentences in the preceding Oral Practice exercise into English.

1. _____

2. _____

3. _____

Describing Nouns with Clauses

Nouns can also be described with clauses, which include an action or stative verb; these are called *description clauses*. They look a lot like sentences and often include the subject or object of the verb, time phrases, and prepositional phrases.

English grammar treats description clauses very differently from descriptions of a noun by another noun (*the students' books*), by a pronoun (*my books*), or by an adjective (*very good books*). In English, description clauses take the form of *relative clauses* and follow the noun that is being described, usually with an intervening relative pronoun (*who, whom, which, where*) or the word *that*. Noun description is much simpler in Mandarin than in English. Mandarin uses the same construction to describe nouns, no matter what kind of description is involved. In the following examples, the verb in the description is in bold type.

Action Verb

[我买] 的书 · [我買] 的書
[wǒ **mǎi**] de shū
the books that [*I **buy***] OR *the books that* [*I **bought***]

Stative Verb

[我们喜欢] 的电影 · [我們喜歡] 的電影
[wǒmen **xǐhuan**] de diànyǐng
the movies that [*we **like***] OR *the movies that* [*we **liked***]

Note that certain English elements do not occur in a Mandarin description clause.

- **Completion and tense.** The verb in the description clause does not include information about completion or tense. Mandarin makes no distinction between the phrases *the books that I am buying* and *the books that I bought.*

- **Articles.** Mandarin description clauses do not include a translation of English *a* or *the.*

- **Introductory words.** In English, description clauses take the form of relative clauses and follow the noun that is being described, usually with an intervening relative pronoun (*who, whom, which, where*) or *that.*

Composing Mandarin Noun Phrases with Description Clauses

In four steps, you can turn noun phrases that include English relative clauses into equivalent Mandarin noun phrases with description clauses. The following English noun phrase, composed of a noun plus a relative clause, will serve as an example: *the student who speaks French.*

STEP 1. IDENTIFY THE MAIN NOUN

The main noun is the noun that the entire noun phrase is about—it is the noun that the relative clause describes. Our example noun phrase is about *the student,* and the relative clause *who speaks French* describes the student. Therefore, *the student* is the main noun. Other examples of noun phrases follow, with the main nouns identified in bold type on the right.

songs that we sang	→	**songs**
the book that I need	→	**the book**
the person whom he respects	→	**the person**
things that I fear	→	**things**
the food that we cooked	→	**the food**

STEP 2: IDENTIFY THE DESCRIPTION

Relative pronouns and *that* are ignored—they are not part of the description and do not get translated into Mandarin. In the phrase *the student who speaks French,* [*speaks French*] is the description. The word *who* is a relative pronoun and, there-fore, is not translated into Mandarin. Following are the five examples of noun phrases listed above, with the main nouns in bold and the description identified in bold italic type on the right.

songs that we sang	→ *we sang*
the book that I need	→ *I need*
the person whom he respects	→ *he respects*
things that I fear	→ *I fear*
the food that we cooked	→ *we cooked*

STEP 3. PLACE THE DESCRIPTION BEFORE THE MAIN NOUN AND ADD 的 de AFTER THE DESCRIPTION

The following example shows completion of Step 3.

[*speaks French*] 的 de **student**

In this step, the noun phrase with English words follows Mandarin word order. The English articles *a* and *the* are ignored, as is tense, since articles and tense do not occur in the Mandarin description clause.

Written Practice 13-4

Rewrite each of the following English noun phrases, placing the description before the main noun and adding 的 de after the description.

1. **songs** that we sang

   _____

2. **the book** that I need

   _____

3. **the person** whom he respects

---

4. **things** that I fear

---

5. **the food** that we cooked

STEP 4. TRANSLATE THE ENGLISH WORDS INTO MANDARIN

[*speaks French*] 的 de **student** → 说法文的学生 · 說法文的學生 ·
shuō Fǎwén de xuésheng

Written Practice 13-5

Translate the phrases that you wrote in Written Practice 13-4 into Mandarin.

1. [*we sang*] 的 de **songs**

---

2. [*I need*] 的 de **book**

---

3. [*he respects*] 的 de **person**

---

4. [*I fear*] 的 de **things**

---

5. [*we cooked*] 的 de **food**

Written Practice 13-6

Each of the following English noun phrases is composed of a noun and a relative clause. Translate them into Mandarin, following the steps outlined above.

1. the airplane ticket that you bought

   _____

2. the candy that my younger sister ate

   _____

3. the tea that we drank

   _____

4. the letter that you wrote

   _____

5. the painting that you are painting

   _____

Translating Mandarin Noun Phrases with Description Clauses into English

In four steps, you can turn Mandarin noun phrases with description clauses into English.

STEP 1. IDENTIFY THE MAIN NOUN IN THE NOUN PHRASE

The main noun is always the noun that comes at the end of the entire phrase, after 的 de. In the following phrase, the main noun is 老师 · 老師 lǎoshī *teacher*.

他们最喜欢的老师 · 他們最喜歡的老師
tāmen zuì xǐhuan de lǎoshī

Oral Practice

Read the following noun phrases aloud and identify the main noun in each phrase.

1. 我借的字典   →   字典
   wǒ jiè de zìdiǎn   zìdiǎn

2. 我买的鞋子 · 我買的鞋子   →   鞋子
   wǒ mǎi de xiézi   xiézi

3. 他唱的歌儿 · 他唱的歌兒   →   歌儿 · 歌兒
   tā chàng de gēr   gēr

4. 她养的猫 · 她養的貓   →   猫 · 貓
   tā yǎng de māo   māo

5. 你们听的音乐 · 你們聽的音樂 →   音乐 · 音樂
   nǐmen tīng de yīnyuè   yīnyuè

STEP 2. IDENTIFY THE DESCRIPTION CLAUSE

The description clause comes right before 的 de. In the following phrase, the description clause is enclosed in brackets.

[他们最喜欢] 的老师 · [他們最喜歡] 的老師
[tāmen zuì xǐhuan] de lǎoshī

Oral Practice

Read the following noun phrases aloud and identify the description clause in each phrase.

1. 我借的字典   →   我借
   wǒ jiè de zìdiǎn   wǒ jiè

2. 我买的鞋子 · 我買的鞋子 →   我买 · 我買
   wǒ mǎi de xiézi   wǒ mǎi

3. 他唱的歌儿 · 他唱的歌兒 →   他唱
   tā chàng de gēr   tā chàng

4. 她养的猫 · 她養的貓   →   她养 · 她養
   tā yǎng de māo   tā yǎng

5. 你们听的音乐 · 你們聽的音樂 → 你们听 · 你們聽
   nǐmen tīng de yīnyuè   nǐmen tīng

STEP 3. TRANSLATE THE WORDS OF THE DESCRIPTION CLAUSE + 的 de + MAIN NOUN INTO ENGLISH

As you perform the translation in this step, be sure to preserve the Mandarin word order.

[他们最喜欢] 的老师 · [他們最喜歡] 的老師
[tāmen zuì xǐhuan] de lǎoshī
→ [they most like] teacher(s)

Written Exercise 13-7

Translate the following Mandarin noun phrases into English, preserving the Mandarin word order.

1. 我借的字典 wǒ jiè de zìdiǎn

   _____

2. 我买的鞋子 · 我買的鞋子 wǒ mǎi de xiézi

   _____

3. 他唱的歌儿 · 他唱的歌兒 tā chàng de gēr

   _____

4. 她养的猫 · 她養的貓 tā yǎng de māo

   _____

5. 你们听的音乐 · 你們聽的音樂 nǐmen tīng de yīnyuè

   _____

STEP 4. REPHRASE THE DESCRIPTION CLAUSE AS A RELATIVE CLAUSE

In this step, place the main noun before the description, then add a relative pronoun or *that* at the beginning of the description clause. In the following example, the main noun is in bold type.

[*I buy*] **shoes** → *(the)* **shoes** *that I buy/bought*

Oral Practice

Following are the answers from Written Exercise 13-7. Place the main noun before the description and rephrase the description clause as a relative clause.

1. [*I borrow*] **dictionary/** → *the* **dictionary/dictionaries** *that I borrow/*
   dictionaries   *borrowed*

2. [*I buy*] **shoes**   → *(the)* **shoes** *that I buy/bought*

3. [*he sings*] **song(s)** → *(the)* **song(s)** *that he sings/sang*

4. [*she raises*] **cat(s)** → *(the)* **cat(s)** *that she raises/raised*

5. [*you listen to*] **music** → *(the)* **music** *that you listen/listened to*

Identifying Noun Descriptions When the Main Noun Is Omitted

When a sentence includes a description clause, 的 de is never omitted. The main noun may be omitted, however, especially in writing. In order to become a good Mandarin reader, you must learn how to interpret a description clause when the main noun is missing.

Often, a main noun is omitted if it refers to something abstract, such as 事情 shìqing (a situation or abstract thing).

昨天发生的 [事情] 我今天才知道。· 昨天發生的 [事情] 我今天才知道。
Zuótiān fāshēng de [shìqing] wǒ jīntiān cái zhīdào.
What happened yesterday (i.e., the thing that happened yesterday) I didn't learn about until today.

A main noun may also be omitted if it is the placeholder object for an action verb (see Chapter 8).

老师说的 [话] 我们都得听。· 老師說的 [話] 我們都得聽。
Lǎoshī shuō de [huà] wǒmen dōu děi tīng.
What the teacher says we all must listen to.
   (i.e., *We must all listen to what the teacher says.*)

A main noun may also be omitted if it is identical to a noun spoken or written earlier, especially if it occurs in the same grammatical position in the sentence as the earlier noun. That is, if the same noun occurs as the subject in several sentences in a row, it can be omitted in all sentences after the first. If the same noun occurs as the object in several sentences in a row, it can be omitted in all sentences after the first. In the second of the two sentences that follow, the main noun is omitted; its location is indicated by square brackets. Can you identify its reference? (The answer is in the English translation.)

小白买的衣服很贵。小王买的 [ ] 很便宜。
小白買的衣服很貴。小王買的 [ ] 很便宜。
Xiǎo Bái mǎi de yīfu hěn guì. Xiǎo Wáng mǎi de [ ] hěn piányi.
The clothing that Little Bai bought is very expensive. (The clothing) that Little Wang bought is very cheap.

Note that the missing noun is the subject of its sentence. It can be omitted in the second sentence precisely because it is identical to the subject of the first sentence.

Oral Practice

Read the following sentences aloud and identify the missing noun in the second sentence of each pair.

1. 喜欢狗的人都养狗。喜欢猫的 [ ] 都养猫。   → 人
   喜歡狗的人都養狗。喜歡貓的 [ ] 都養貓。
   Xǐhuan gǒu de rén dōu yǎng gǒu. Xǐhuan māo de [ ] dōu   rén
      yǎng māo.
   People who like dogs raise dogs. [ ] who like cats raise cats.   *people*

2. 王太太做的菜非常好吃。王先生做的 [ ] 也好吃。 → 菜

   Wáng tàitai zuò de cài fēicháng hǎo chī. Wáng xiānsheng zuò   cài

     de [ ] yě hǎo chī.

   The food that Mrs. Wang cooked is extremely delicious.

    The [ ] that Mr. Wang cooked is also delicious.   *food*

3. 打篮球的学生都很高。打棒球的 [ ] 也很高吗? → 学生

   打籃球的學生都很高。打棒球的 [ ] 也很高嗎?   學生

   Dǎ lánqiú de xuésheng dōu hěn gāo. Dǎ bàngqiú de [ ] yě   xuésheng

     hěn gāo ma?

   The students who play basketball are all very tall. Are the

    [ ] who play baseball also very tall?   *students*

Translating English Relative Pronouns

Do not be tempted to translate English relative pronouns (*who, whom, which, where*) into Mandarin. Mandarin has words for *who, whom, which,* and *where,* but they are content question words (see Chapter 15), not relative pronouns, and they have no place in a Mandarin noun description clause.

Correct	Incorrect	Incorrect
我认识的人	✗ 我认识谁的人	✗ 人谁我认识
我認識的人	✗ 我認識誰的人	✗ 人誰我認識
wǒ rènshi de rén	wǒ rènshi shéi de rén	rén shéi wǒ rènshi
the people whom I met		
我看的电影	✗ 我看什么的电影	✗ 电影什么我看
我看的電影	✗ 我看甚麼的電影	✗ 電影甚麼我看
wǒ kàn de diànyǐng	wǒ kàn shénme de diànyǐng	diànyǐng shénme wǒ kàn
the movies that I saw		

Describing a Noun with More Than One Description

A single noun may be described by more than one description. In this case, the descriptions come one after another *before the main noun*. The main noun occurs only once—after the last description, as follows.

[_____ 的 de] [_____ Classifier] [_____ 的 de] + Noun

Examples of nouns described by multiple descriptions follow. Each description, including the classifier or 的 de, is presented in square brackets. There is no correct or incorrect order for descriptions, as long as they all come before the main noun. Individual speakers have their own preferences about order; use your Chinese teacher's preferred phrase order as your guide.

[那五本] [很贵的] 字典
[那五本] [很貴的] 字典
[nà wǔ běn] [hěn guì de] zìdiǎn
[*those five*] [*very expensive*] *dictionaries*

[两个] [非常便宜的] [新的] 电脑
[兩個] [非常便宜的] [新的] 電腦
[liǎng gè] [fēicháng piányi de] [xīn de] diànnǎo
[*two*] [*extremely cheap*] [*new*] *computers*

[那三个] [很聪明的] 学生
[那三個] [很聰明的] 學生
[nà sān gè] [hěn cōngming de] xuésheng
[*those three*] [*very smart*] *students*

[那个] [很有意思的] 电影
[那個] [很有意思的] 電影
[nàge] [hěn yǒu yìsi de] diànyǐng
[*that*] [*very interesting*] *movie*

Written Practice 13-8

Identify the descriptions in each of the following phrases, then insert square brackets around each of the descriptions, including the classifier or 的 de within the brackets.

1. 我妹妹的三个老师 · 我妹妹的三個老師
   wǒ mèimei de sān gè lǎoshī

   _____

2. 这两本很有意思的书 · 這兩本很有意思的書
   zhè liǎng běn hěn yǒu yìsi de shū

   _____

3. 他的新的电脑 · 他的新的電腦
   tā de xīn de diànnǎo

   _____

4. 张老师的很好的朋友 · 張老師的很好的朋友
   Zhāng lǎoshī de hěn hǎo de péngyou

   _____

QUIZ

1. Rewrite the following phrase, adding the Mandarin equivalent of the English intensifier in parentheses. Then translate the phrase into English.

   聪明的人 · 聰明的人　cōngming de rén　(extremely)

   _____

2. Rearrange the following Mandarin words in the correct order to match the English phrase.

   车 – 的 – 贵 – 非常 · 車 – 的 – 貴 – 非常
   chē – de – guì – fēicháng
   an extremely expensive car

   _____

3. Rearrange the following Mandarin words in the correct order to match the English phrase.

   考试 – 的 – 挺 – 容易 · 考試 – 的 – 挺 – 容易

   kǎoshì – de – tǐng – róngyì

   a very easy test

   _____

4. Identify the missing noun in the following sentence pair, then translate the sentences into English.

   这本书很有意思。那本 [ ] 没有意思。
   這本書很有意思。那本 [ ] 沒有意思。

   Zhè běn shū hěn yǒu yìsi. Nà běn [ ] méi yǒu yìsi.

   _____

5. Rewrite the following Mandarin phrase, negating it to match the English phrase.

   很贵的电影票 · 很貴的電影票

   hěn guì de diànyǐng piào

   a movie ticket that is not very expensive (*an inexpensive movie ticket*)

   _____

6. Rewrite the following English phrases, eliminating *that* as well as *the*, and using Mandarin word order. Then underline the main noun in each phrase.

   a. the teacher that I like   _____

   b. the movie that we saw   _____

   c. the computer that you bought   _____

   d. the Japanese food that you ate _____

7. Translate the English phrases in question 6 into Mandarin, adding 的 de after the description.

   a. _____

   b. _____

   c. _____

   d. _____

8. Identify the main noun in each of the following Mandarin phrases, then translate the phrases into English.

   a. 你用的电脑·你用的電腦 nǐ yòng de diànnǎo

   _____

   b. 我们认识的人·我們認識的人 wǒmen rènshi de rén

   _____

   c. 你不懂的故事 nǐ bù dǒng de gùshi

   _____

   d. 你买的车·你買的車 nǐ mǎi de chē

   _____

9. Rearrange the following Mandarin words in the correct order to match the English phrase.

   借 – 书 – 的 – 我 · 借 – 書 – 的 – 我
   jiè – shū – de – wǒ
   the book that I borrowed

10. Identify the missing noun in the following sentence pair, then translate the sentences into English.

    他买的手机很贵。我买的 [ ] 很便宜。
    他買的手機很貴。我買的 [ ] 很便宜。
    Tā mǎi de shǒujī hěn guì. Wǒ mǎi de [ ] hěn piányi.

    _____

CHAPTER 14

Asking and Answering Yes-No Questions

In this chapter, you will learn about:

Asking Simple Yes-No Questions with 吗·嗎 ma
Asking Yes-No Questions Using the Verb-Not-Verb Construction
Answering Yes-No Questions
Asking and Answering Follow-Up Questions with 呢 ne

Asking Simple Yes-No Questions with 吗·嗎 ma

The simplest way to ask a yes-no question in Mandarin is to end a statement with the question particle 吗·嗎 ma. Think of 吗·嗎 ma as adding the meaning *yes or no?* to the statement. Note that the order of words in Mandarin statements and yes-no questions with 吗·嗎 ma is identical.

Statement	**Yes-No Question with 吗·嗎 ma**
你是学生。	你是学生吗？
你是學生。	你是學生嗎？
Nǐ shì xuésheng.	Nǐ shì xuésheng ma?
You are a student.	*Are you a student?*
他会说中国话。	他会说中国话吗？
他會說中國話。	他會說中國話嗎？
Tā huì shuō Zhōngguó huà.	Tā huì shuō Zhōngguó huà ma?
He can speak Chinese.	*Can he speak Chinese?*
她喜欢看中国电影。	她喜欢看中国电影吗？
她喜歡看中國電影。	她喜歡看中國電影嗎？
Tā xǐhuan kàn Zhōngguó diànyǐng.	Tā xǐhuan kàn Zhōngguó diànyǐng ma?
She likes to watch Chinese movies.	*Does she like to watch Chinese movies?*
他们上大学。	他们上大学吗？
他們上大學。	他們上大學嗎？
Tāmen shàng dàxué.	Tāmen shàng dàxué ma?
They attend college.	*Do they attend college?*

Written Practice 14-1

You have asked your roommate four yes-no questions with 吗·嗎 ma; following are his answers. Write the questions you asked in Mandarin, adjusting pronouns as necessary.

1. 我去过中国。· 我去過中國。
   Wǒ qùguo Zhōngguó.

2. 我喜欢中国电影。· 我喜歡中國電影。
Wǒ xǐhuan Zhōngguó diànyǐng.

_____

3. 我会用筷子吃饭。· 我會用筷子吃飯。
Wǒ huì yòng kuàizi chī fàn.

_____

4. 我有一本中文字典。
Wǒ yǒu yī běn Zhōngwén zìdiǎn.

_____

Asking Yes-No Questions Using the Verb-Not-Verb Construction

The other common way to ask a yes-no question is to use the Verb-Not-Verb question construction, sometimes called the "A-not-A" construction. When asking questions in this way, you say the verb twice, once in affirmative form and once preceded by negation. That is, you say "Verb *not* Verb." In the following examples, the verbs are in bold type.

你是不是学生？· 你是不是學生？
Nǐ **shì** bù **shì** xuésheng?
Are you a student? (lit., *You are or are not a student?*)

他会不会说中国话？· 他會不會說中國話？
Tā **huì** bù **huì** shuō Zhōngguó huà?
Can he speak Chinese?
   (lit., *He can or cannot speak Chinese?*)

你喜欢不喜欢看中国电影？· 你喜歡不喜歡看中國電影？
Nǐ **xǐhuan** bù **xǐhuan** kàn Zhōngguó diànyǐng?
Do you like to watch Chinese movies?
   (lit., *You like or don't like to watch Chinese movies?*)

他们上不上大学？· 他們上不上大學？
Tāmen **shàng** bù **shàng** dàxué?
Do they attend college?
   (lit., *Do they attend or not attend college?*)

As with 吗·嗎 ma yes-no questions, the overall word order in a Verb-Not-Verb question is the same as the word order in its corresponding statement.

Statement	**Verb-Not-Verb Question**
她是学生。	她是不是学生？
她是學生。	她是不是學生？
Tā shì xuésheng.	Tā shì bù shì xuésheng?
She is a student.	*Is she a student?*
他会说中国话。	他会不会说中国话？
他會說中國話。	他會不會說中國話？
Tā huì shuō Zhōngguó huà.	Tā huì bù huì shuō Zhōngguó huà?
He can speak Chinese.	*Can he speak Chinese?*
他们上大学。	他们上不上大学？
他們上大學。	他們上不上大學？
Tāmen shàng dàxué.	Tāmen shàng bù shàng dàxué?
They attend college.	*Do they attend college?*

Do not be misled by English word order! In English, word order in questions is different from word order in statements. When forming questions in Mandarin, use the same word order that you use in the corresponding statement. This is true not only for yes-no questions, but for content questions as well (see Chapter 15).

NEGATING VERB-NOT-VERB QUESTIONS

Mandarin has two words that are used in negation, 不 bù and 没 méi. The negation word that is used in Verb-Not-Verb questions depends on the verb, and for action verbs it also depends on whether or not the action has happened (see Chapter 9). Following are the basic rules for choosing 不 bù or 没 méi.

有 yǒu is always negated with 没 méi.

我有车。· 我有車。
Wǒ yǒu chē.
I have a car.

你有没有车？· 你有没有車？
Nǐ yǒu méi yǒu chē?
Do you have a car?

是 shì *be,* 姓 xìng *be family-named,* and 叫 jiào *call, be called* are negated with 不 bù.

她是不是老师？· 她是不是老師？
Tā shì bù shì lǎoshī?
Is she a teacher?

她姓不姓王？
Tā xìng bù xìng Wáng?
Is his family name Wang?

她叫不叫王美丽？· 她叫不叫王美麗？
Tā jiào bù jiào Wáng Měilì?
Is she called Wang Meili?

Adjectival verbs (Chapter 7), stative verbs (Chapter 7), and modal verbs (Chapter 10) are negated with 不 bù.

他高不高？
Tā gāo bù gāo?
Is he tall?

你喜欢不喜欢那本书？· 你喜歡不喜歡那本書？
Nǐ xǐhuan bù xǐhuan nà běn shū?
Do you like that book?

他会不会说德国话？· 他會不會說德國話？
Tā huì bù huì shuō Déguó huà?
Can he speak German?

Written Practice 14-2

Rewrite the following 吗 · 嗎 ma questions as Verb-Not-Verb questions.

1. 你要吃中国饭吗？· 你要吃中國飯嗎？
   Nǐ yào chī Zhōngguó fàn ma?
   Do you want to eat Chinese food?

   _____

2. 你想看电影吗？· 你想看電影嗎？
   Nǐ xiǎng kàn diànyǐng ma?
   Would you like to see a movie?

   _____

3. 飞机票贵吗？· 飛機票貴嗎？
   Fēijī piào guì ma?
   Are airplane tickets expensive?

   _____

4. 你信他吗？· 你信他嗎？
   Nǐ xìn tā ma?
   Do you believe him?

   _____

An action verb is negated with 不 bù if the sentence refers to a present, future, or habitual action (see Chapter 8).

我们今天考不考试？· 我們今天考不考試？
Wǒmen jīntiān kǎo bù kǎo shì?
Are we taking a test today? (lit., *Do we take a test or not take a test today?*)

你吃不吃辣的？
Nǐ chī bù chī là de?
Do you eat spicy food?

Written Practice 14-3

Ask your roommate whether he regularly performs the following actions, using Verb-Not-Verb questions.

1. 喝咖啡   hē kāfēi   *drink coffee*

   _____

2. 看电视 · 看電視   kàn diànshì   *watch television*

   _____

3. 听音乐 · 聽音樂   tīng yīnyuè   *listen to music*

   _____

4. 打篮球·打籃球 dǎ lánqiú *play basketball*

An action verb is negated with 没 méi if the sentence refers to an action that did not happen (see Chapter 9). A Verb-Not-Verb question that asks whether an event has happened usually takes one of the following forms.

Subject + Verb + 了 le + 没有 méi yǒu
Subject + Verb + 过·過 guo + 没有 méi yǒu

The following examples show the Verb + 了 le + 没有 méi yǒu construction. If the object is neither definite nor specific, 了 le may come after the object (see Chapter 9).

你看了那个电影没有？·你看了那個電影沒有？
Nǐ kàn le nàge diànyǐng méi yǒu?
Did you see that movie or not?

你今天吃早饭了没有？·你今天吃早飯了沒有？
Nǐ jīntiān chī zǎofàn le méi yǒu?
Did you eat breakfast today or not?

The following examples illustrate the Verb + 过·過 guo + 没有 méi yǒu construction.

你去过中国没有？·你去過中國沒有？
Nǐ qùguo Zhōngguó méi yǒu?
Have you been to China before?

你吃过日本饭没有？·你吃過日本飯沒有？
Nǐ chīguo Rìběn fàn méi yǒu?
Have you eaten Japanese food before?

The sentence may also take the following form, although the 没有 méi yǒu ending is more common.

你看过没看过那个电影？·你看過沒看過那個電影？
Nǐ kànguo méi kànguo nàge diànyǐng?
Have you seen that movie?

Written Practice 14-4

Ask your roommate whether he or she performed each of the following actions last night, using Verb-Not-Verb questions. Note that you can only use 了 le in these questions, not 过·過 guo. (Do you know why? See Chapter 9 to review the difference between 了 le and 过·過 guo.)

1. 做作业·做作業 zuò zuòyè *do homework*

   _____

2. 看电影·看電影 kàn diànyǐng *see a movie*

   _____

3. 写信·寫信 xiě xìn *write a letter*

   _____

4. 用电脑·用電腦 yòng diànnǎo *use a computer*

   _____

Answering Yes-No Questions

吗·嗎 ma questions and Verb-Not-Verb questions are answered in the same way.

GIVING THE SHORT ANSWER *NO*

To give the short answer *no,* use the negation word before the verb: Negation + Verb.

Question	Answer
你吃不吃辣的?	不吃。
Nǐ chī bù chī là de?	Bù chī.
Do you eat spicy food?	*No.*

For the verb 有 yǒu, the negation is 没有 méi yǒu.

Question	**Answer**
你有弟弟吗?	没有。
你有弟弟嗎?	
Nǐ yǒu dìdi ma?	Méi yǒu.
Do you have a younger brother?	*No.*
你有机会看那个电影吗?	没有。
你有機會看那個電影嗎?	
Nǐ yǒu jīhuì kàn nàge diànyǐng ma?	Méi yǒu.
Did you have a chance to see that movie?	*No.*

To give the short answer *no* to a question that includes a modal verb (会·會 huì, 能 néng, or 可以 kéyǐ), use the negation word 不 bù before the modal: 不 bù + Modal Verb.

Question	**Answer**
他会说中国话吗?	不会。
他會說中國話嗎?	不會。
Tā huì shuō Zhōngguó huà ma?	Bù huì.
Can he speak Chinese?	*No.*
你能不能跑马拉松?	不能。
你能不能跑馬拉松?	
Nǐ néng bù néng pǎo mǎlāsōng?	Bù néng.
Can you run a marathon?	*No.*
我可以不可以借你的车?	不可以。
我可以不可以借你的車?	
Wǒ kéyǐ bù kéyǐ jiè nǐ de chē?	Bù kéyǐ.
Can I borrow your car?	*No.*

To give the short answer *no* to a question that includes a series of verbs, use the negation word and the first verb in the series.

Question	Answer
你要买书吗?	不要。
你要買書嗎?	
Nǐ yào mǎi shū ma?	Bù yào.
Do you want to buy a book?	*No.* (lit., *don't want*)
你喜欢看电影吗?	不喜欢。
你喜歡看電影嗎?	不喜歡。
Nǐ xǐhuan kàn diànyǐng ma?	Bù xǐhuan.
Do you like to watch movies?	*No.* (lit., *don't like*)
你明天去跳舞吗?	不去。
你明天去跳舞嗎?	
Nǐ míngtiān qù tiào wǔ ma?	Bù qù.
Are you going to go dancing tomorrow?	*No.* (lit., *not going*)

To give the short answer *no* to a question that asks whether an action has happened or is completed, use 没有 méi yǒu (see Chapter 9).

Question	Answer
你看过那个电影没有?	没有。
你看過那個電影沒有?	
Nǐ kànguo nàge diànyǐng méi yǒu?	Méi yǒu.
Have you seen that movie?	*No.*

Written Practice 14-5

Reply to the following questions with the short answer *no*.

1. 你学中文吗? · 你學中文嗎?
   Nǐ xué Zhōngwén ma?
   Do you study Chinese?

   _____

2. 你会做中国饭吗？· 你會做中國飯嗎？
   Nǐ huì zuò Zhōngguó fàn ma?
   Can you cook Chinese food?

   _____

3. 你喜欢不喜欢听音乐？· 你喜歡不喜歡聽音樂？
   Nǐ xǐhuan bù xǐhuan tīng yīnyuè?
   Do you like to listen to music?

   _____

4. 你去过日本吗？· 你去過日本嗎？
   Nǐ qùguo Rìběn ma?
   Have you been to Japan?

   _____

GIVING THE LONG ANSWER *NO*

You can also use a complete sentence to reply *no* to a yes-no question.

Question	**Answer**
我们今天考不考试？	我们今天不考试。
我們今天考不考試？	我們今天不考試。
Wǒmen jīntiān kǎo bù kǎo shì?	Wǒmen jīntiān bù kǎo shì.
Are we taking a test today?	*We are not taking a test today.*
你吃不吃辣的？	我不吃辣的。
Nǐ chī bù chī là de?	Wǒ bù chī là de.
Do you eat spicy food?	*I don't eat spicy food.*
你看过那个电影没有？	我没看过那个电影。
你看過那個電影沒有？	我没看過那個電影。
Nǐ kànguo nàge diànyǐng méi yǒu?	Wǒ méi kànguo nàge diànyǐng.
Have you seen that movie?	*I haven't seen that movie.*

Written Practice 14-6

Reply to the following questions with the long answer *no*.

1. 你学中文吗？· 你學中文嗎？
   Nǐ xué Zhōngwén ma?
   Do you study Chinese?

   _____

2. 你会做中国饭吗？· 你會做中國飯嗎？
   Nǐ huì zuò Zhōngguó fàn ma?
   Can you cook Chinese food?

   _____

3. 你喜欢不喜欢听音乐？· 你喜歡不喜歡聽音樂？
   Nǐ xǐhuan bù xǐhuan tīng yīnyuè?
   Do you like to listen to music?

   _____

4. 你去过日本吗？· 你去過日本嗎？
   Nǐ qùguo Rìběn ma?
   Have you been to Japan?

   _____

GIVING THE SHORT ANSWER *YES*

There is no word for *yes* in Mandarin, but there are ways to reply *yes* to yes-no questions, using a short answer or a long answer. To reply to a question with the short answer *yes*, simply repeat the verb.

Question	Answer
你吃不吃辣的？	吃。
Nǐ chī bù chī là de?	Chī.
Do you eat spicy food?	*Yes.*

If the verb phrase in the question begins with a modal verb (会 · 會 huì, 能 néng, or 可以 kéyǐ), reply *yes* by repeating the modal verb.

Question	Answer
他会说中国话吗？	会。
他會說中國話嗎？	會。
Tā huì shuō Zhōngguó huà ma?	Huì.
Can he speak Chinese?	*Yes.*

If the question includes a series of verbs, reply *yes* by repeating the first verb.

Question	Answer
你要买书吗？	要。
你要買書嗎？	
Nǐ yào mǎi shū ma?	Yào.
Do you want to buy a book?	*Yes.* (lit., *want*)
你喜欢看电影吗？	喜欢。
你喜歡看電影嗎？	喜歡。
Nǐ xǐhuan kàn diànyǐng ma?	Xǐhuan.
Do you like to watch movies?	*Yes.* (lit., *like*)
你明天去跳舞吗？	去。
你明天去跳舞嗎？	
Nǐ míngtiān qù tiàowǔ ma?	Qù.
Are you going to go dancing tomorrow?	*Yes.* (lit., *going*)

If the question asks whether an action has been completed or not and the verb has the suffix 过·過 guo or is followed by 了 le, include 过·過 guo or 了 le in your answer.

Question	Answer
你看过那个电影没有？	看过。
你看過那個電影沒有？	看過。
Nǐ kànguo nàge diànyǐng méi yǒu?	Kànguo.
Have you seen that movie?	*Yes.*
他卖了他的车吗？	卖了。
他賣了他的車嗎？	賣了。
Tā mài le tā de chē ma?	Mài le.
Did he sell his car?	*Yes.*

GIVING THE LONG ANSWER *YES*

You can also use a complete sentence to reply *yes* to a yes-no question.

Question	Answer
我们今天考不考试？	我们今天考试。
我們今天考不考試？	我們今天考試。
Wǒmen jīntiān kǎo bù kǎo shì?	Wǒmen jīntiān kǎo shì.
Are we taking a test today?	*We are taking a test today.*
你吃不吃辣的？	我吃辣的。
Nǐ chī bù chī là de?	Wǒ chī là de.
Do you eat spicy food?	*I eat spicy food.*
你看过那个电影没有？	我看过那个电影。
你看過那個電影沒有？	我看過那個電影。
Nǐ kànguo nàge diànyǐng méi yǒu?	Wǒ kànguo nàge diànyǐng.
Have you seen that movie?	*I have seen that movie.*

Oral Practice

Say aloud the short answer *yes* to each of the following questions.

1. 你是学生吗？ → 是。
   你是學生嗎？
   Nǐ shì xuésheng ma?   Shì.
   Are you a student?

2. 你认识那个老师吗？ → 认识。
   你認識那個老師嗎？   認識。
   Nǐ rènshi nàge lǎoshī ma?   Rènshi.
   Do you know that teacher?

3. 我可以在这儿抽烟吗？ → 可以。
   我可以在這兒抽煙嗎？
   Wǒ kéyǐ zài zhèr chōu yān ma?   Kéyǐ.
   Can I smoke here?

4. 你喜欢跳舞吗？ → 喜欢。
   你喜歡跳舞嗎？   喜歡。
   Nǐ xǐhuan tiào wǔ ma?   Xǐhuan.
   Do you like to dance?

5. 你忙吗?   → 忙。
   你忙嗎?
   Nǐ máng ma?   Máng.
   Are you busy?

Written Practice 14-7

Reply to each of the questions in the preceding Oral Practice with the long answer *yes,* adjusting pronouns as necessary.

1. _____

2. _____

3. _____

4. _____

5. _____

Asking and Answering Follow-Up Questions with 呢 ne

To ask for more information about a person, place, or thing, use a 呢 ne question. 呢 ne questions are follow-up questions that end with the sentence-final word 呢 ne.

In the following examples, the 呢 ne question asks if a situation is true about another subject.

Situation 1: Which people are students?

小王是大学生吗? **小李呢?** · 小王是大學生嗎? **小李呢?**
Xiǎo Wáng shì dàxuéshēng ma? **Xiǎo Lǐ ne?**
*Is Little Wang a college student? (**What about**) Little Li?*

Situation 2: What do your brother and sister study?

你的弟弟学什么? **你的妹妹呢?** · 你的弟弟學甚麼? **你的妹妹呢?**
Nǐ de dìdi xué shénme? **Nǐ de mèimei ne?**
*What does your younger brother study? (**What about**) your younger sister?*

Situation 3: Who are those people?

他是谁？她呢？ · 他是誰？她呢？

Tā shì shéi? **Tā ne?**

*Who is he? (**What about) her?***

In the following examples, the 呢 ne question asks if a situation is true about another object.

Situation 4: What food are you able to cook?

你会做中国饭吗？日本饭呢？ · 你會做中國飯嗎？日本飯呢？

Nǐ huì zuò Zhōngguó fàn ma? **Rìběn fàn ne?**

*Are you able to cook Chinese food? (**What about) Japanese food?***

Situation 5: What sport do you like?

你喜欢打篮球吗？棒球呢？ · 你喜歡打籃球嗎？棒球呢？

Nǐ xǐhuan dǎ lánqiú ma? **Bàngqiú ne?**

*Do you like to play basketball? (**What about) baseball?***

To answer a 呢 ne question, supply the information that is requested by the question. If a 呢 ne question asks whether something is *also* the case, the reply often includes the word 也 yě *also*. (For a detailed discussion of 也 yě *also*, see Chapter 17.)

The following are possible answers to the 呢 ne questions in the five situations above.

Situation 1: Which people are students?

小李也是大学生。 · 小李也是大學生。

Xiǎo Lǐ yě shì dàxuéshēng.

Little Li is also a college student.

Situation 2: What do your brother and sister study?

我的妹妹学历史。 · 我的妹妹學歷史。

Wǒ de mèimei xué lìshǐ.

My younger sister studies history.

Situation 3: Who are those people?

她是白美丽。· 她是白美麗。

Tā shì Bái Měilì.

She is Bai Meili.

Situation 4: What food are you able to cook?

我也会做日本饭。· 我也會做日本飯。

Wǒ yě huì zuò Rìběn fàn.

I am also able to cook Japanese food.

Situation 5: What sport do you like?

我不喜欢打棒球。· 我不喜歡打棒球。

Wǒ bù xǐhuan dǎ bàngqiú.

I don't like to play baseball.

Oral Practice

Each of the following statements is followed by a 呢 ne question. Reply *yes* to each question, using a complete Mandarin sentence.

1. 我是学生。你呢？　　　→　我也是学生。
   我是學生。你呢？　　　　　我也是學生。
   Wǒ shì xuésheng. Nǐ ne?　　Wǒ yě shì xuésheng.
   I am a student. And you?　*I am also a student.*

2. 我学中文。你呢？　　　　→　我也学中文。
   我學中文。你呢？　　　　　　我也學中文。
   Wǒ xué Zhōngwén. Nǐ ne?　　Wǒ yě xué Zhōngwén.
   I study Chinese. What about you?　*I also study Chinese.*

3. 我的老师会说法文。你的老师呢？ → 我的老师也会说法文。
   我的老師會說法文。你的老師呢？　　我的老師也會說法文。
   Wǒ de lǎoshī huì shuō Fǎwén.　　Wǒ de lǎoshī yě huì shuō Fǎwén.
   　Nǐ de lǎoshī ne?
   My teacher can speak French.　*My teacher can also speak French.*
   　What about your teacher?

Written Practice 14-8

Respond to each of the following Mandarin statements by asking a follow-up question to match the English question in bold type.

1. 我已经吃早饭了。· 我已經吃早飯了。
   Wǒ yǐjing chī zǎofàn le.
   I've already eaten breakfast. **What about you?**

   _____

2. 飞机票很贵。· 飛機票很貴。
   Fēijī piào hěn guì.
   Airplane tickets are very expensive. **What about bus tickets?**

   _____

3. 美国电影很有意思。· 美國電影很有意思。
   Měiguó diànyǐng hěn yǒu yìsi.
   American movies are very interesting. **What about Chinese movies?**

   _____

QUIZ

Rewrite the following 吗 · 嗎 ma questions as Verb-Not-Verb questions.

1. 你喝咖啡吗？· 你喝咖啡嗎？
   Nǐ hē kāfēi ma?
   Do you drink coffee?

   _____

2. 你想看电影吗？· 你想看電影嗎？
   Nǐ xiǎng kàn diànyǐng ma?
   Would you like to see a movie?

   _____

3. 你看过那个电影吗？· 你看過那個電影嗎？

Nǐ kànguo nàge diànyǐng ma?

Have you seen that movie?

_____

Rewrite the following Verb-Not-Verb questions as 吗·嗎 ma questions.

4. 你昨天看了电视没有？· 你昨天看了電視沒有？

Nǐ zuótiān kàn le diànshì méi yǒu?

Did you watch television yesterday?

_____

5. 你们已经考试了没有？· 你們已經考試了沒有？

Nǐmen yǐjing kǎoshì le méi yǒu?

Have you taken the test yet?

_____

6. 你喜欢不喜欢坐飞机？· 你喜歡不喜歡坐飛機？

Nǐ xǐhuan bù xǐhuan zuò fēijī?

Do you like to travel by airplane?

_____

Reply to each of the following questions, using the short answer indicated in parentheses.

7. 你周末看了朋友吗？· 你週末看了朋友嗎？

Nǐ zhōumò kàn le péngyou ma?

Did you see your friends on the weekend? (no)

_____

8. 你们喜欢吃中国菜吗？· 你們喜歡吃中國菜嗎？

Nǐmen xǐhuan chī Zhōngguó cài ma?

Do you like to eat Chinese food? (yes)

_____

Respond to the following Mandarin statements by asking a follow-up question to match the English question in bold type.

9. 数学很难。· 數學很難。

   Shùxué hěn nán.

   Math is very difficult. ***What about history?***

   _____

10. 小王想去。

   Xiǎo Wáng xiǎng qù.

   Little Wang wants to go. ***What about Little Zhang?***

   _____

CHAPTER 15

Asking and Answering
Content Questions

In this chapter, you will learn about:

Mandarin Content Question Words
Asking Questions with Content Question Words

Mandarin Content Question Words

Content questions ask *who, what, when, where, why,* and *how.* In English, these are sometimes called *wh-*questions, because most of the question words begin with *wh.*

Following is a list of Mandarin content question words, along with their English equivalents.

谁 · 誰	shéi	*who?*
什么 · 甚麼	shénme	*what?*
什么时候 · 甚麼時候	shénme shíhou	*when?*
几点钟 · 幾點鐘	jǐ diǎn zhōng	*when? (at what hour?)*
哪儿 · 哪兒	nǎr	*where?*
哪里 · 哪裏	nǎli	*where?*
什么地方 · 甚麼地方	shénme dìfang	*where?*
哪	nǎ	*which?*
几 · 幾	jǐ	*how much? how many?*
多少	duōshao	*how much? how many?*
怎么 · 怎麼	zěnme	*how?*

Asking Questions with Content Question Words

In Mandarin, the order of information in statements and questions is the same. The content question word is placed where the answer would be placed in a statement. This is different from English, where content question words always come at the beginning of the question.

The following sections illustrate the use of each of the content question words listed above. Each question is paired with a possible answer. Compare the position of the question word and its answer in each pair of sentences.

ASKING *WHO* WITH 谁·誰 shéi

To inquire about a person, you can use 谁·誰 shéi in a variety of ways.

谁·誰 shéi as the Subject of a Sentence

Question	Answer
谁喜欢看电影?	小王喜欢看电影。
誰喜歡看電影?	小王喜歡看電影。
Shéi xǐhuan kàn diànyǐng?	**Xiǎo Wáng** xǐhuan kàn diànyǐng.
Who *likes to watch movies?*	***Little Wang*** *likes to watch movies.*

谁·誰 shéi as the Object of a Verb

Question	Answer
他是谁?	他是毛老师。
他是誰?	他是毛老師。
Tā shì **shéi**?	Tā shì **Máo lǎoshī**.
Who *is he?*	*He is* ***Professor Mao***.

谁·誰 shéi as the Object of a Preposition

Question	Answer
你想跟谁说话?	我想跟小王说话。
你想跟誰說話?	我想跟小王說話。
Nǐ xiǎng gēn **shéi** shuō huà?	Wǒ xiǎng gēn **Xiǎo Wáng** shuō huà.
Whom *do you want to speak with?*	*I want to speak with* ***Little Wang***.

ASKING *WHAT* WITH 什么·甚麼 shénme

To inquire about a place or thing, you can use 什么·甚麼 shénme.

什么·甚麼 shénme as the Subject of a Sentence

Question	Answer
什么菜好吃?	四川菜好吃。
甚麼菜好吃?	
Shénme cài hǎo chī?	**Sìchuān** cài hǎo chī.
What *food is good to eat?*	***Sichuan*** *food is good to eat.*

什么 · 甚麼 shénme as the Object of a Verb

Question	Answer
那是什么？	那是字典。
那是甚麼？	
Nà shì **shénme**?	Nà shì **zìdiǎn**.
***What** is that?*	*That is **a dictionary**.*

什么 · 甚麼 shénme as the Object of a Preposition

Question	Answer
你对什么有兴趣？	我对文学有兴趣。
你對甚麼有興趣？	我對文學有興趣。
Nǐ duì **shénme** yǒu xìngqù?	Wǒ duì **wénxué** yǒu xìngqù.
***What** are you interested in?*	*I am interested in **literature**.*

Written Practice 15-1

Answer each of the following questions, using the word or phrase in parentheses and writing a complete Mandarin sentence. Be sure to use the appropriate pronoun in your answer.

1. 谁会说德国话？(我) · 誰會說德國話？(我)
   Shéi huì shuō Déguó huà? (wǒ)

   _____

2. 那个人是谁？(我的老师) · 那個人是誰？(我的老師)
   Nàge rén shì shéi? (wǒ de lǎoshī)

   _____

3. 你喜欢吃什么？(日本菜) · 你喜歡吃甚麼？(日本菜)
   Nǐ xǐhuan chī shénme? (Rìběn cài)

   _____

4. 他跟谁说话？(他的女朋友) · 他跟誰說話？(他的女朋友)
   Tā gēn shéi shuō huà? (tā de nǚ péngyou)

   _____

5. 他给你什么？(一张地图) · 他給你甚麼？(一張地圖)
   Tā gěi nǐ shénme? (yī zhāng dìtú)

   _____

ASKING *WHEN* WITH 什麼時候 · 甚麼時候 shénme shíhou AND 几点钟 · 幾點鐘 jǐ diǎn zhōng

什么時候 · 甚麼時候 shénme shíhou and 几点钟 · 幾點鐘 jǐ diǎn zhōng are both used to ask about time. Since 几点钟 · 幾點鐘 jǐ diǎn zhōng asks specifically about clock time (see Chapter 19), the answer has to be phrased in terms of clock time. 什么时候 · 甚麼時候 shénme shíhou is a more general expression and can be used whenever the English question word *when* is used. The answer to a 什么时候 · 甚麼時候 shénme shíhou question can be any type of time expression.

Since these two expressions refer to time, they are placed after the subject and before the verb phrase.

Question	Answer
你早上几点钟起床?	我早上六点半起床。
你早上幾點鐘起床?	我早上六點半起床。
Nǐ zǎoshang **jǐ diǎn zhōng** qǐ chuáng?	Wǒ zǎoshang **liù diǎn bàn** qǐ chuáng.
What time do you get up in the morning?	*I get up **at 6:30** in the morning.*
你什么时候有空?	我明天下午有空。
你甚麼時候有空?	
Nǐ **shénme shíhou** yǒu kòng?	Wǒ **míngtiān xiàwǔ** yǒu kòng.
When do you have free time?	*I have free time **tomorrow**.*

Oral Practice

Ask your roommate questions based on the following activities, using 什么时候 · 甚麼時候 shénme shíhou or 几点钟 · 幾點鐘 jǐ diǎn zhōng.

1. 下课 · 下課 xià kè → 你几点钟下课?
   你幾點鐘下課?
   Nǐ jǐ diǎn zhōng xià kè?
   OR 你什么时候下课?
   你甚麼時候下課?
   Nǐ shénme shíhou xià kè?
   When do you get out of class?

2. 毕业 · 畢業 bì yè → 你什么时候毕业?
   你甚麼時候畢業?
   Nǐ shénme shíhou bì yè?
   When do you graduate?

3. 放假 fàng jià → 你什么时候放假？
你甚麼時候放假？

Nǐ shénme shíhou fàng jià?

When do you start vacation?

4. 起床 qǐ chuáng → 你几点钟起床？
你幾點鐘起床？

Nǐ jǐ diǎn zhōng qǐ chuáng?

OR

你什么时候起床？
你甚麼時候起床？

Nǐ shénme shíhou qǐ chuáng?

When do you get out of bed?

ASKING *WHERE* WITH 哪儿·哪兒 nǎr, 哪里·哪裏 nǎli, AND 什么地方·甚麼地方 shénme dìfang

哪儿·哪兒 nǎr, 哪里·哪裏 nǎli, and 什么地方·甚麼地方 shénme dìfang ask the question *where?* They all mean exactly the same thing. 哪儿·哪兒 nǎr is more common than 哪里·哪裏 nǎli in northern China, especially around Beijing, and 哪里·哪裏 nǎli is more common than 哪儿·哪兒 nǎr in southern China and in Taiwan. Since these expressions refer to location, they are placed after the subject and before the verb phrase. In questions with prepositional phrases, they typically occur with the preposition 在 zài *at, on*. (For a detailed discussion of how to express location, see Chapter 18.)

Question	Answer
你想在哪儿吃饭？	我想在学生中心吃饭。
你想在哪兒吃飯？	我想在學生中心吃飯。
Nǐ xiǎng **zài nǎr** chī fàn?	Wǒ xiǎng **zài xuésheng zhōngxīn** chī fàn.
Where do you want to eat?	*I want to eat **in the student center**.*
你在哪里吃饭？	我在餐厅吃饭。
你在哪裏吃飯？	我在餐廳吃飯。
Nǐ **zài nǎli** chī fàn?	Wǒ **zài cāntīng** chī fàn.
Where do you eat?	*I eat **in the cafeteria**.*
你在什么地方买课本？	我在书店买课本。
你在甚麼地方買課本？	我在書店買課本。
Nǐ **zài shénme dìfang** mǎi kèběn?	Wǒ **zài shūdiàn** mǎi kèběn.
Where do you buy textbooks?	*I buy textbooks **at the bookstore**.*

Written Practice 15-2

For each of the following statements involving location, write the question that would elicit the statement as the answer, using the question word or phrase in parentheses.

1. 我在宿舍用电脑。(什么地方·甚麼地方 shénme dìfang)
   我在宿舍用電腦。
   Wǒ zài sùshè yòng diànnǎo.
   I use a computer in the dormitory.

   _____

2. 我在家看电视。(哪儿·哪兒 nǎr)
   我在家看電視。
   Wǒ zài jiā kàn diànshì.
   I watch television at home.

   _____

3. 我在公园打球。(哪里·哪裏 nǎli)
   我在公園打球。
   Wǒ zài gōngyuán dǎ qiú.
   I play ball in the park.

   _____

4. 我在图书馆读书。(哪儿·哪兒 nǎr)
   我在圖書館讀書。
   Wǒ zài túshūguǎn dú shū.
   I study in the library.

   _____

5. 我在学校吃午饭。(什么地方·甚麼地方 shénme dìfang)
   我在學校吃午飯。
   Wǒ zài xuéxiào chī wǔfàn.
   I eat lunch at school.

   _____

ASKING *WHICH* WITH 哪 **nǎ**

哪 nǎ *which* is used to ask about the identity of a person, place, or thing. It is always followed by a classifier, the choice of which depends on the noun that follows.

你要哪本书？· 你要哪本書？
Nǐ yào nǎ běn shū?
Which book do you want?

她买了哪双鞋？· 她買了哪雙鞋？
Tā mǎi le nǎ shuāng xié?
Which pair of shoes did she buy?

The answer to a 哪 nǎ question identifies the noun that is being asked about. It often includes the specifier 这 · 這 zhè *this* or 那 nà *that*.

我要这本书。· 我要這本書。
Wǒ yào zhè běn shū.
I want this book.

她买了那双红颜色的鞋。· 她買了那雙紅顏色的鞋。
Tā mǎi le nà shuāng hóng yánsè de xié.
She bought that pair of red shoes.

Oral Practice

Read the following questions with 哪 nǎ aloud, then answer them in Mandarin.

1. 哪个人？   → 那个人
   哪個人？   那個人
   nǎge rén?   nàge rén
   which person?   *that person*

2. 哪张照片？   → 那张照片
   哪張照片？   那張照片
   nǎ zhāng zhàopiàn?   nà zhāng zhàopiàn
   which photograph?   *that photograph*

3. 哪五个电影？   →   那五个电影
     哪五個電影？   那五個電影
     nǎ wǔ gè diànyǐng?   nà wǔ gè diànyǐng
     which five movies?   *those five movies*

ASKING *HOW MUCH* WITH 几·幾 jǐ AND 多少 duōshao

几·幾 jǐ and 多少 duōshao can both be translated as *how much* or *how many*, but they have somewhat different meanings and usages.

几·幾 jǐ

几·幾 jǐ is used to ask about relatively small numbers, when the speaker expects the answer to be less than 10 or 20.

几·幾 jǐ questions *the number only* and must be followed by a classifier.

你要买几瓶可乐？· 你要買**幾**瓶可樂？
Nǐ yào mǎi **jǐ** píng kělè?
How many *bottles of cola do you want to buy?*

多少 duōshao

多少 duōshao has a more general meaning than 几·幾 jǐ. It is used to ask about a number when there is no expectation about whether the answer will be a large or small number. 多少 duōshao is not followed by a classifier.

你认识**多少**人？· 你認識**多少**人？
Nǐ rènshi **duōshao** rén?
How many *people do you know?*

你这个月看了**多少**电影？· 你這個月看了**多少**電影？
Nǐ zhège yuè kàn le **duōshao** diànyǐng?
How many *movies have you seen this month?*

你有**多少**钱？· 你有**多少**錢？
Nǐ yǒu **duōshao** qián?
How much *money do you have?*

Answers to 几・幾 jǐ and 多少 duōshao questions have the same form and must include a number and a classifier.

Question	Answer
你要买几瓶可乐?	我要买五瓶可乐。
你要買**幾**瓶可樂?	我要買五瓶可樂。
Nǐ yào mǎi **jǐ** píng kělè?	Wǒ yào mǎi **wǔ** píng kělè.
How many *bottles of cola do you want to buy?*	*I want to buy **five** bottles of cola.*
你认识多少人?	我认识六个人。
你認識**多少**人?	我認識六個人。
Nǐ rènshi **duōshao** rén?	Wǒ rènshi **liù gè** rén.
How many *people do you know?*	*I know **six** people.*
你上个月看了多少电影?	我上个月看了八个电影。
你上個月看了**多少**電影?	我上個月看了八個電影。
Nǐ shàng gè yuè kàn le **duōshao** diànyǐng?	Wǒ shàng gè yuè kàn le **bā gè** diànyǐng.
How many *movies did you see last month?*	*Last month, I saw **eight** movies.*

Written Practice 15-3

For each of the following statements involving quantity, write the question that would elicit the statement as the answer, using the question word in parentheses.

1. 我有三十块钱。・我有三十塊錢。(多少 duōshao)
   Wǒ yǒu sānshí kuài qián.
   I have 30 dollars.

   _____

2. 我昨天看了两个电影。・我昨天看了兩個電影。(几・幾 jǐ)
   Wǒ zuótiān kàn le liǎng gè diànyǐng.
   I watched two movies yesterday.

   _____

3. 我买了五本书。· 我買了五本書。(几· 幾 jǐ)
    Wǒ mǎi le wǔ běn shū.
    I bought five books.

---

4. 我想请六个朋友吃饭。· 我想請六個朋友吃飯。(几· 幾 jǐ)
    Wǒ xiǎng qǐng liù gè péngyou chī fàn.
    I am planning to invite six friends to eat.

---

5. 我吃了二十五个饺子。· 我吃了二十五個餃子。(多少 duōshao)
    Wǒ chī le èrshíwǔ gè jiǎozi.
    I ate 25 dumplings.

ASKING *HOW* WITH 怎么·怎麼 zěnme

怎么·怎麼 zěnme *how* questions are usually answered with long explanations, not merely with a single word or phrase. In these questions, 怎么·怎麼 zěnme always comes right before the verb phrase. The object of the verb is often included before the subject, as the topic of the sentence.

从这儿到公园**怎么**走？· 從這兒到公園**怎麼**走？
Cóng zhèr dào gōngyuán **zěnme** zǒu?
How *do you go from here to the park?*

中国话**怎么**说？· 中國話**怎麼**說？
Zhōngguó huà **zěnme** shuō?
How *do you say (it) in Chinese?*

这个字**怎么**写？· 這個字**怎麼**寫？
Zhège zì **zěnme** xiě?
How *do you write this character?*

Oral Practice

Ask how to perform each of the following actions, using 怎麼·怎么 zěnme *how*. Note that the English word *it* is not translated in Mandarin.

1. 用 yòng → 怎么用？· 怎麼用？
   Zěnme yòng?
   How do you use it?

2. 卖·賣 mài → 怎么卖？· 怎麼賣？
   Zěnme mài?
   How is it sold?

3. 说·說 shuō → 怎么说？· 怎麼說？
   Zěnme shuō?
   How do you say it?

4. 走 zǒu → 怎么走？· 怎麼走？
   Zěnme zǒu?
   How do you go?

QUIZ

Your friend has invited you to eat dinner with her. Ask her the following questions in Mandarin.

1. When are we eating dinner?

_____

2. Where are we eating dinner?

_____

3. Whom are we eating dinner with?

_____

4. Who invited us to eat dinner?

_____

You and your older brother are going to a movie. Ask him the following questions in Mandarin.

5. What time does the movie start?

   _____

6. Where is the movie theater?
   (电影院 · 電影院 diànyǐngyuàn *movie theater*)

   _____

7. How much money is a movie ticket?

   _____

Ask the following 怎么 · 怎麼 zěnme questions in Mandarin. Note that the English word *it* is not translated.

8. How do you write it?

   _____

9. How do you cook it?

   _____

10. How do you read it?

   _____

CHAPTER 16

Expressing *All* or *Both* in Relation to Nouns

In this chapter, you will learn about:

The Location of 都 dōu *in the Sentence*

Using 都 dōu *to Say* Both *or* All *of the Object of a Verb*

Emphasizing Every *with* 所有的 suóyǒu de

Using 都 dōu *to Say* None (of)

Expressing Not All *with* 不都 bù dōu

The Location of 都 dōu in the Sentence

都 dōu is an adverb and must come before the verb phrase.

If the verb is the first word in the verb phrase, 都 dōu comes before the verb, which is in bold type in the following example.

我们都喜欢唱歌。· 我們都**喜歡**唱歌。
Wǒmen dōu **xǐhuan** chàng gē.
*We both/all **like** to sing.*

If the verb is preceded by an intensifier, 都 dōu comes before the intensifier, which is in bold type in the following example.

我们都**很**喜欢吃中国饭。· 我們都**很**喜歡吃中國飯。
Wǒmen dōu **hěn** xǐhuan chī Zhōngguó fàn.
*We all like to eat Chinese food **very much**.*

If the verb phrase begins with a prepositional phrase, 都 dōu comes before the prepositional phrase, which is in bold type in the following example.

我们昨天都**跟朋友**吃饭了。· 我們昨天都**跟朋友**吃飯了。
Wǒmen zuótiān dōu **gēn péngyou** chī fàn le.
*Yesterday we both/all ate **with our friends**.*

If the verb phrase begins with an adverbial phrase, 都 dōu comes before the adverbial phrase, which is in bold type in the following example.

学生都**好好地**学习。· 學生都**好好地**學習。
Xuésheng dōu **hǎohāo de** xuéxí.
*The students both/all studied **hard**.*

都 dōu can be translated in several ways in English. In the sentences above, it is translated as either *both* or *all*, depending on whether the subject refers to two or more than two people. No matter how 都 dōu is translated in English, it must come before the verb phrase in Mandarin.

Oral Practice

Read each of the following sentences aloud, adding 都 dōu in the appropriate location.

1. 我的朋友很用功。 → 我的朋友都很用功。
   Wǒ de péngyou hěn yònggōng.   Wǒ de péngyou dōu hěn yònggōng.

2. 我们看过那本书。 → 我们都看过那本书。
   我們看過那本書。   我們都看過那本書。
   Wǒmen kànguo nà běn shū.   Wǒmen dōu kànguo nà běn shū.

3. 美国的汽车很贵吗? → 美国的汽车都很贵吗?
   美國的汽車很貴嗎?   美國的汽車都很貴嗎?
   Měiguó de qìchē hěn guì ma?   Měiguó de qìchē dōu hěn guì ma?

4. 我和我妹妹喜欢看电影。 → 我和我妹妹都喜欢看电影。
   我和我妹妹喜歡看電影。   我和我妹妹都喜歡看電影。
   Wǒ hé wǒ mèimei xǐhuan kàn   Wǒ hé wǒ mèimei dōu xǐhuan kàn
   diànyǐng.   diànyǐng.

Using 都 dōu to Say *Both* or *All* of the Object of a Verb

In the examples above, 都 dōu indicates *both/all* of the subject of the sentence.

都 dōu can also be used to indicate *both/all* of the object of the verb. When 都 dōu refers to the object, the object is typically topicalized, that is, it comes before the subject of the sentence. In the following examples, the object is in bold type.

中国饭我都喜欢。· **中國飯**我都喜歡。
Zhōngguó fàn wǒ dōu xǐhuan.
Chinese food, I like (it) all.

那两个电影我都看过。· **那兩個電影**我都看過。
Nà liǎng gè diànyǐng wǒ dōu kànguo.
Those two movies, I have seen them both.

那些电影我都看过。· **那些電影**我都看過。
Nà xiē diànyǐng wǒ dōu kànguo.
Those (several) movies, I have seen them all.

Written Practice 16-1

Rewrite each of the following sentences, placing the object of the verb at the beginning of the sentence and adding 都 dōu before the verb, to match the English sentence.

1. 我认识那些人。· 我認識那些人。
   Wǒ rènshi nà xiē rén.
   Those people, I know them all.

   _____

2. 我已经看过那两本书。· 我已經看過那兩本書。
   Wǒ yǐjing kànguo nà liǎng běn shū.
   Those two books, I've read them both.

   _____

3. 我去过法国，也去过西班牙。· 我去過法國，也去過西班牙。
   Wǒ qùguo Fǎguó, yě qùguo Xībānyá.
   France and Spain, I've been to both.

   _____

4. 我坐过飞机，也坐 过船。· 我坐過飛機，也坐過船。
   Wǒ zuòguo fēijī, yě zuòguo chuán.
   Airplane and ship, I've traveled on both.

   _____

Emphasizing *Every* with 所有的 suóyǒu de

The expression 所有的 suóyǒu de comes right before a noun and adds the meaning *every*; it typically occurs in the same sentence with 都 dōu. This kind of *redundancy*, in which two words in the sentence mean the same thing, is very common in Mandarin.

所有的菜都很好吃。
Suóyǒu de cài dōu hěn hǎo chī.
All of the dishes are very delicious.

所有的女孩子都喜欢他。· 所有的女孩子都喜歡他。
Suóyǒu de nǚháizi dōu xǐhuan tā.
All of the girls like him.

Written Practice 16-2

Rewrite each of the following sentences, adding 所有的 suóyǒu de and 都 dōu.

1. 学生考试了。· 學生考試了。
   Xuésheng kǎo shì le.
   All of the students took a test.

   _____

2. 学生病了。· 學生病了。
   Xuésheng bìng le.
   All of the students got sick.

   _____

3. 学生学中文吗？· 學生學中文嗎？
   Xuésheng xué Zhōngwén ma?
   Do all of the students study Chinese?

   _____

4. 孩子喜欢看电视。· 孩子喜歡看電視。
   Háizi xǐhuan kàn diànshì.
   All of the children like to watch television.

   _____

Using 都 dōu to Say *None (of)*

Mandarin does not have a separate word for *none*. The most common way to indicate *none (of)* is to use 都 dōu + Negation Word (lit., *all not*). The negation word that is used depends on the verb, and for action verbs, on whether or not the action has happened. For detailed discussions of verbs and negation, see Chapters 6–11.

都不 dōu bù *not all, none*

我们都不喜欢他。· 我們都不喜歡他。
Wǒmen dōu bù xǐhuan tā.
None of us likes him. (lit., *We all do not like him.*)

我们都不会跳舞。· 我們都不會跳舞。
Wǒmen dōu bù huì tiào wǔ.
None of us can dance. (lit., *We all cannot dance.*)

我们都不喜欢考试。· 我們都不喜歡考試。
Wǒmen dōu bù xǐhuan kǎoshì.
None of us likes to take tests. (lit., *We all don't like to take tests.*)

他们都不吃肉。· 他們都不吃肉。
Tāmen dōu bù chī ròu.
None of them eats meat. (lit., *They all do not eat meat.*)

都没 dōu méi *none, not any*

我们都没有钱。· 我們都沒有錢。
Wǒmen dōu méi yǒu qián.
None of us has money. (lit., *We all do not have money.*)

他们都没有空。· 他們都沒有空。
Tāmen dōu méi yǒu kòng.
None of them has free time. (lit., *They all do not have free time.*)

我们都没睡觉。· 我們都沒睡覺。
Wǒmen dōu méi shuì jiào.
None of us has slept. (lit., *We all have not slept.*)

When you want to say *none of* the object, the object must come before the verb. It often comes before the subject as well, at the beginning of the sentence. The object is in bold type in the following examples.

那个饭馆的饭，我都不喜欢。· **那個飯館的飯**，我都不喜歡。
Nàge fànguǎn de fàn, wǒ dōu bù xǐhuan.
*I don't like any of **that restaurant's food**.*
　　(lit., **The food in that restaurant**, I like none of it.)

那些电影，我都没看过。· **那些電影**，我都沒看過。
Nà xiē diànyǐng, wǒ dōu méi kànguo.
*I haven't seen any of **those movies**.*
　　(lit., **Those movies**, I have seen none of them.)

Written Practice 16-3

Rewrite each of the following sentences, adding 都不 dōu bù or 都没 dōu méi to express the meaning of the English sentence.

1. 学生喜欢考试。· 學生喜歡考試。
   Xuésheng xǐhuan kǎoshì.
   No student likes tests.

   _____

2. 孩子喜欢睡觉。· 孩子喜歡睡覺。
   Háizi xǐhuan shuì jiào.
   No child likes to sleep.

   _____

3. 我们坐过飞机。· 我們坐過飛機。
   Wǒmen zuòguo fēijī.
   None of us has been on a plane.

   _____

4. 他们怕狗。· 他們怕狗。
   Tāmen pà gǒu.
   None of them is afraid of dogs.

   _____

SAYING *NOT EVEN A LITTLE* WITH 一点·一點 yīdiǎn

To say *not even a little of* an object, add the phrase 一点·一點 yīdiǎn before the object noun phrase. As in the examples above, the object noun phrase must come before the verb. When 一点·一點 yīdiǎn is used, however, the object noun phrase typically comes after the subject—not at the beginning of the sentence. The object noun phrase is in bold type in the following examples.

他一点饭都没吃。· 他一點飯都沒吃。
Tā **yīdiǎn fàn** dōu méi chī.
*He didn't eat **even a little of the food**.*

我一点钱都没有。· 我一點錢都沒有。
Wǒ **yīdiǎn qián** dōu méi yǒu.
*I don't **even** have **a little money**.*

Written Practice 16-4

Write a Mandarin sentence from each of the following groups of phrases, adding 一点·一點 yīdiǎn and 都 dōu to match the English sentence.

1. 他 – 咖啡 – 喝
   tā – kāfēi – hē
   He does not drink any coffee at all.

   _____

2. 他 – 鱼 – 吃 · 他 – 魚 – 吃
   tā – yú – chī
   He doesn't eat any fish at all.

   _____

3. 我 – 电视 – 看 · 我 – 電視 – 看
   wǒ – diànshì – kàn
   I don't watch any television at all.

   _____

4. 她 – 作业 – 做 · 她 – 作業 – 做
   tā – zuòyè – zuò
   She didn't do any homework at all.

   _____

Expressing *Not All* with 不都 bù dōu

To indicate that a situation is true for some, but not all, of the subjects or objects, use 不都 bù dōu *not all* before the verb phrase.

他们不都喜欢他。· 他們不都喜歡他。
Tāmen bù dōu xǐhuan tā.
They don't all like him.
   (i.e., *Some people like him, and some people don't.*)

我不都懂。
Wǒ bù dōu dǒng.
I don't understand everything.
　(i.e., *I understand some of it, but not the whole thing.*)

If 不都 bù dōu refers to the object of the verb, the object often comes before the verb.

他的电影，我不都喜欢。· 他的電影，我不都喜歡。
Tā de diànyǐng, wǒ bù dōu xǐhuan.
His movies, I don't like all of them.
　(i.e., *I like some of them, but not all of them.*)

Written Practice 16-5

Rewrite each of the following sentences, adding 不都 bù dōu to match the English sentence.

1. 学生喜欢考试。· 學生喜歡考試。
    Xuésheng xǐhuan kǎoshì.
    Not all of the students like tests.

    _____

2. 孩子喜欢睡觉。· 孩子喜歡睡覺。
    Háizi xǐhuan shuì jiào.
    Not all children like to sleep.

    _____

3. 我们学中文。· 我們學中文。
    Wǒmen xué Zhōngwén.
    We don't all study Chinese.

    _____

4. 他们怕狗。· 他們怕狗。
    Tāmen pà gǒu.
    Not all of them are afraid of dogs.

    _____

QUIZ

Rewrite each of the following sentences, adding 都 dōu, 都不 dōu bù, 都没 dōu méi, or 不都 bù dōu to match the English sentence.

1. 车太贵。· 車太貴。
   Chē tài guì.
   All of the cars are too expensive.

   _____

2. 王老师的考试很难。· 王老師的考試很難。
   Wáng lǎoshī de kǎoshì hěn nán.
   None of Professor Wang's tests is very difficult.

   _____

3. 中国饭我喜欢。· 中國飯我喜歡。
   Zhōngguó fàn wǒ xǐhuan.
   I don't like all Chinese food. (i.e., I like some, but not all, Chinese food.)

   _____

4. 他写的书我看过。· 他寫的書我看過。
   Tā xiě de shū wǒ kànguo.
   I have read all of the books that he has written.

   _____

5. 他写的书我看过。· 他寫的書我看過。
   Tā xiě de shū wǒ kànguo.
   I have not read any of the books that he has written.

   _____

6. 车太贵。· 車太貴。
   Chē tài guì.
   Not all of the cars are too expensive.

   _____

7. 我的朋友会开车。· 我的朋友會開車。
   Wǒ de péngyou huì kāi chē.
   All of my friends can drive.

   _____

Rewrite each of the following sentences, adding 所有的 suóyǒu de and 都 dōu to match the English sentence.

8. 菜太辣。
   Cài tài là.
   All of the dishes are too spicy.

   _____

9. 电影我看过。 · 電影我看過。
   Diànyǐng wǒ kànguo.
   I've seen all of the movies before.

   _____

10. 学生去过长城。 · 學生去過長城。
    Xuésheng qùguo Chángchéng.
    All of the students have been to the Great Wall before.

    _____

CHAPTER 17

Linking Verbs and Verb Phrases with *And* and *Only*

In this chapter, you will learn about:

Expressing And *in Mandarin*
Expressing In Addition *with* 还·還 hái
Indicating Two Qualities with 又 yòu + AV₁ + 又 yòu + AV₂
Saying Only *with* 只 zhǐ, 就 jiù, *and* 才 cái

Expressing *And* in Mandarin

English uses the single word *and* to connect nouns or noun phrases (*cats and dogs, my older sister and my younger brother*), verbs or verb phrases (*read and write, go to China and study Chinese*), prepositions (*in and out*), adjectives (*small and fast*), and adverbs (*quickly and quietly*). Mandarin does not have a word as versatile as English *and*. Instead, it uses different words in different constructions to connect different types of phrases.

The words and patterns that we introduce in this chapter are 也 yě *also,* 还·還 hái *in addition,* and 又 … 又 yòu . . . yòu. 也 yě, 还·還 hái, and 又 yòu are adverbs, and each of them comes at the very beginning of the verb phrase, before the verb or before any adverbial modifier or prepositional phrase that comes before the verb. These adverbs never come before the subject or before any other noun or noun phrase.

EXPRESSING *AND* WITH 也 yě

也 yě may occur with any kind of verb or verb phrase.

也 yě Before a Stative Verb

我喜欢唱歌，也喜欢跳舞。· 我喜歡唱歌，也喜歡跳舞。
Wǒ xǐhuan chàng gē, yě xǐhuan tiào wǔ.
I like to sing and also like to dance.

也 yě Before a Modal Verb

她会说中国话，也会说俄国话。· 她會說中國話，也會說俄國話。
Tā huì shuō Zhōngguó huà, yě huì shuō Éguó huà.
She can speak Chinese and can also speak Russian.

也 yě Before an Action Verb

那个书店卖书，也卖电脑。· 那個書店賣書，也賣電腦。
Nàge shūdiàn mài shū, yě mài diànnǎo.
That bookstore sells books and also sells computers.

也 yě Before an Adjectival Verb

你的妹妹很聪明，也很用功。· 你的妹妹很聰明，也很用功。
Nǐ de mèimei hěn cōngming, yě hěn yònggōng.
Your younger sister is very smart and also very hardworking.

In these examples, 也 yě is used to say two things about the same subject. You can also use 也 yě to say the same thing about two different subjects. In the following examples, note that 也 yě comes before the second verb phrase—not before the second subject.

我喜欢唱歌。她也喜欢唱歌。· 我喜歡唱歌。她也喜歡唱歌。
Wǒ xǐhuan chàng gē. Tā yě xǐhuan chàng gē.
I like to sing. She also likes to sing.

我会开车。他也会开车。· 我會開車。他也會開車。
Wǒ huì kāi chē. Tā yě huì kāi chē.
I can drive. He can also drive.

SAYING TWO THINGS ABOUT THE SAME SUBJECT WITH 也 yě VP₁ 也 yě VP₂

When saying two things about the same subject, 也 yě may be used before each of the verb phrases. This construction can be translated as *both VP₁ and also VP₂*, although the first 也 yě is often not translated at all.

我也喜欢唱歌，也喜欢跳舞。· 我也喜歡唱歌，也喜歡跳舞。
Wǒ yě xǐhuan chàng gē, yě xǐhuan tiào wǔ.
I like to sing and also like to dance.

她也会说中国话，也会说俄国话。· 她也會說中國話，也會說俄國話。
Tā yě huì shuō Zhōngguó huà, yě huì shuō Éguó huà.
She can speak Chinese and can also speak Russian.

When this construction is used with an adjectival verb, the verb is typically preceded by an intensifier.

你的妹妹也很聪明，也很用功。· 你的妹妹也很聰明，也很用功。
Nǐ de mèimei yě hěn cōngming, yě hěn yònggōng.
Your younger sister is both very smart and also very hardworking.

Oral Practice

Read each of the following sentences aloud, then translate it into English.

1. 这个菜也好看也好吃 。　　　　　　→　*This dish looks good and tastes*
   這個菜也好看也好吃。　　　　　　　　*good.*
   Zhège cài yě hǎo kàn yě hǎo chī.

2. 这个房间也有暖气也有空调。　　　→　*This room has heating and*
   這個房間也有暖氣也有空調。　　　　　*air-conditioning.*
   Zhège fángjiān yě yǒu nuǎnqì
   　　yě yǒu kōngtiáo.

3. 他也会唱歌，也会跳舞。　　　　　→　*He can sing and dance.*
   他也會唱歌，也會跳舞。
   Tā yě huì chàng gē, yě huì tiào wǔ.

4. 那个地方也有山也有水，很漂亮。　→　*That place has both mountains*
   那個地方也有山也有水，很漂亮。　　　*and water. (It's) very pretty.*
   Nàge dìfang yě yǒu shān yě yǒu shuǐ,
   　　hěn piàoliang.

Written Practice 17-1

Rewrite each of the following sentences, adding 也 yě to match the English sentence.

1. 我的朋友都喜欢看电影。我喜欢看电影。
   我的朋友都喜歡看電影。我喜歡看電影。
   Wǒ de péngyou dōu xǐhuan kàn diànyǐng. Wǒ xǐhuan kàn diànyǐng.
   My friends all like to watch movies. I also like to watch movies.

   _____

2. 我的朋友都有手机。我有手机。
   我的朋友都有手機。我有手機。
   Wǒ de péngyou dōu yǒu shǒujī. Wǒ yǒu shǒujī.
   My friends all have cell phones. I also have a cell phone.

   _____

3. 我喜欢唱歌。我喜欢跳舞。
   我喜歡唱歌。我喜歡跳舞。
   Wǒ xǐhuan chàng gē. Wǒ xǐhuan tiào wǔ.
   I like to sing. I also like to dance.

---

4. 我去过中国。我去过日本。
   我去過中國。我去過日本。
   Wǒ qùguo Zhōngguó. Wǒ qùguo Rìběn.
   I've been to China. I've also been to Japan.

Expressing *In Addition* with 还·還 hái

As a connecting word, 还·還 hái introduces a situation that follows another situation.

　　还·還 hái may introduce an additional action.

弟弟吃了二十个饺子，还吃了一碗饭。
弟弟吃了二十個餃子，還吃了一碗飯。
Dìdi chī le èrshí gè jiǎozi, hái chī le yī wǎn fàn.
Younger brother ate 20 dumplings and, in addition, ate one bowl of rice.

　　还·還 hái may indicate that an action continues into the future.

她在中国住了一年，还想多住几年。
她在中國住了一年，還想多住幾年。
Tā zài Zhōngguó zhù le yīnián, hái xiǎng duō zhù jǐ nián.
She lived in China for a year and still wants to live there a few more years.

我弟弟吃了二十个饺子，还要多吃。
我弟弟吃了二十個餃子，還要多吃。
Wǒ dìdi chī le èrshí gè jiǎozi, hái yào duō chī.
My brother ate 20 dumplings and still wants to eat some more.

还·還 hái may introduce additional information.

我有一个哥哥，还有一个弟弟。
我有一個哥哥，還有一個弟弟。
Wǒ yǒu yī gè gēge, hái yǒu yī gè dìdi.
I have an older brother and, in addition, (I) have a younger brother.

还·還 hái also means *still,* in the sense that a situation is ongoing.

他还在这儿。·他還在這兒。
Tā hái zài zhèr.
He is still here.

For more details on the use of 还·還 hái in ongoing situations, see Chapter 8.

Written Practice 17-2

Rewrite each of the following sentences, adding 还·還 hái to match the English sentence.

1. 我们吃了豆腐，吃了青菜。·我們吃了豆腐，吃了青菜。
   Wǒmen chī le dòufu, chī le qīngcài.
   We ate doufu, and we also ate green vegetables.

   _____

2. 我想买鞋，想买大衣。·我想買鞋，想買大衣。
   Wǒ xiǎng mǎi xié, xiǎng mǎi dàyī.
   I want to buy shoes, and I also want to buy an overcoat.

   _____

3. 我昨天晚上看了书，做了作业。·我昨天晚上看了書，做了作業。
   Wǒ zuótiān wǎnshang kàn le shū, zuò le zuòyè.
   Last night I read a book, and in addition I did homework.

   _____

4. 他学中文。他学日文。·他學中文。他學日文。
Tā xué Zhōngwén. Tā xué Rìwén.
He studies Chinese and also studies Japanese.

USING 还有·還有 hái yǒu TO EXPRESS *IN ADDITION* BETWEEN SENTENCES

还有·還有 hái yǒu comes at the beginning of the second of two sentences to introduce additional information.

小高学习很好。还有，他很会打球。·小高學習很好。還有，他很會打球。
Xiǎo Gāo xuéxí hěn hǎo. Hái yǒu, tā hěn huì dǎ qiú.
Little Gao is a good student. In addition, he can really play ball.

Indicating Two Qualities with 又 yòu + AV₁ + 又 yòu + AV₂

To indicate that a person, place, or thing has two qualities, use the following construction.

Subject + 又 yòu + Adjectival Verb₁ + 又 yòu + Adjectival Verb₂

又 yòu typically comes right before the adjectival verb without any intensifiers. 又 yòu must be used before each of the adjectival verbs in the sequence.

他的哥哥又高又大。
Tā de gēge yòu gāo yòu dà.
His older brother is both tall and big.

那个饭馆的饭又便宜又好吃。·那個飯館的飯又便宜又好吃。
Nàge fànguǎn de fàn yòu piányi yòu hǎo chī.
The food in that restaurant is both cheap and delicious.

Written Practice 17-3

Rewrite each of the following sentences, adding 又 yòu before each of the adjectival verbs. Then translate the sentence into English.

1. 这件衣服便宜好。· 這件衣服便宜好。
   Zhè jiàn yīfu piányi hǎo.

   _____

2. 今天的天气冷湿。· 今天的天氣冷濕。
   Jīntiān de tiānqì lěng shī. (冷 lěng *cold*; 湿 · 濕 shī *damp, humid*)

   _____

3. 你的鞋脏臭。· 你的鞋髒臭。
   Nǐ de xié zāng chòu. (脏 · 髒 zāng *dirty*; 臭 chòu *smelly*)

   _____

4. 那个人聪明用功。· 那個人聰明用功。
   Nàge rén cōngming yònggōng.

   _____

Saying *Only* with 只 zhǐ, 就 jiù, and 才 cái

The adverbs 只 zhǐ, 就 jiù, and 才 cái come right before the verb phrase, either before the verb (or modal verb) or, if the verb phrase begins with a prepositional phrase, before the prepositional phrase.

我只看了一个电影。· 我只看了一個電影。
Wǒ zhǐ kàn le yī gè diànyǐng.
I only saw one movie.

我才睡五个小时。· 我才睡五個小時。
Wǒ cái shuì wǔ gè xiǎoshí.
I only slept for five hours.

我就会说中国话。· 我就會說中國話。
Wǒ jiù huì shuō Zhōngguó huà.
I can only speak Chinese.

我就喜欢吃意大利面。· 我就喜歡吃意大利麵。
Wǒ jiù xǐhuan chī Yìdàlì miàn.
I only like to eat spaghetti.

我只在餐厅吃午饭。· 我只在餐廳吃午飯。
Wǒ zhǐ zài cāntīng chī wǔfàn.
I only eat lunch in the cafeteria.

If 只 zhǐ, 就 jiù, or 才 cái occurs with a time phrase, the time phrase must begin with the preposition 在 zài *at, on.*

我只在周末看电影。· 我只在週末看電影。
Wǒ zhǐ zài zhōumò kàn diànyǐng.
I only watch movies on the weekend.

只 zhǐ, 就 jiù, and 才 cái never come before a noun.

SAYING *ONLY* WITH 只 zhǐ AND 就 jiù

只 zhǐ and 就 jiù are identical in meaning when expressing the meaning *only*. The choice of one or the other adverb is determined by speaker preference.

Oral Practice

Read each of the following sentences aloud, replacing 只 zhǐ with 就 jiù or 就 jiù with 只 zhǐ.

1. 我只有一个弟弟。　→　我就有一个弟弟。
   我只有一個弟弟。　　　我就有一個弟弟。
   Wǒ zhǐ yǒu yī gè dìdi.　Wǒ jiù yǒu yī gè dìdi.
   I only have one younger brother.

2. 他就会写十个汉字。　→　他只会写十个汉字。
   他就會寫十個漢字。　　　他只會寫十個漢字。
   Tā jiù huì xiě shí gè Hànzì.　Tā zhǐ huì xiě shí gè Hànzì.
   He can only write 10 characters.

3. 我只喜欢跳舞。 → 我就喜欢跳舞。
   我只喜歡跳舞。 　　 我就喜歡跳舞。
   Wǒ zhǐ xǐhuan tiào wǔ. 　 Wǒ jiù xǐhuan tiào wǔ.
   I only like to dance.

4. 他只买了一双鞋。 → 他就买了一双鞋。
   他只買了一雙鞋。 　　 他就買了一雙鞋。
   Tā zhǐ mǎi le yī shuāng xié. 　 Tā jiù mǎi le yī shuāng xié.
   He only bought one pair of shoes.

Written Practice 17-4

Rewrite each of the following sentences, adding 只 zhǐ or 就 jiù, as indicated in parentheses, to match the English sentence.

1. 他喜欢打球。· 他喜歡打球。
   Tā xǐhuan dǎ qiú.
   He only likes to play ball. (只 zhǐ)

   _____

2. 他们是小学生。·· 他們是小學生。
   Tāmen shì xiǎoxuéshēng.
   They are only elementary school students. (就 jiù)

   _____

3. 我会做美国饭。·· 我會做美國飯。
   Wǒ huì zuò Měiguó fàn.
   I can only cook American food. (只 zhǐ)

   _____

4. 我们可以在家看电视。· 我們可以在家看電視。
   Wǒmen kéyǐ zài jiā kàn diànshì.
   We can only watch television at home. (就 jiù)

   _____

SAYING *ONLY* WITH 才 cái

才 cái means *only*, but its meaning varies somewhat from that of 只 zhǐ and 就 jiù. 才 cái also indicates that the information is in some way less than the speaker or the listener expects. It is typically used in sentences that express quantity, and the verb phrase typically includes a number. Note that even when a sentence refers to a completed action, the sentence does not include 了 le.

我才学一年。· 我才學一年。
Wǒ cái xué yī nián.
I've only studied for one year.

现在才十点。· 現在才十點。
Xiànzài cái shídiǎn.
It's only 10 o'clock.

我妹妹才六岁。· 我妹妹才六歲。
Wǒ mèimei cái liù suì.
My younger sister is only six years old.

Written Practice 17-5

Rewrite each of the following sentences, adding 才 cái to match the English sentence.

1. 我吃了一口。
   Wǒ chī le yī kǒu.
   I have only eaten one bite.

   _____

2. 我做了一个菜。· 我做了一個菜。
   Wǒ zuò le yī gè cài.
   I have only cooked one dish.

   _____

3. 我看了半个电影。· 我看了半個電影。
   Wǒ kàn le bàn gè diànyǐng.
   I only watched half a movie.

   _____

4. 我写了一个字。· 我寫了一個字。
   Wǒ xiě le yī gè zì.
   I have only written one character.

SAYING *ONLY* WITH 只有 zhǐ yǒu

To say that a situation is true *only for the subject,* add the phrase 只有 zhǐ yǒu before the subject.

只有小李打了电话。· 只有小李打了電話。
Zhǐ yǒu Xiǎo Lǐ dǎ le diànhuà.
Only Little Li made a phone call.

只有王老师会说日本话。· 只有王老師會說日本話。
Zhǐ yǒu Wáng lǎoshī huì shuō Rìběn huà.
Only Professor Wang can speak Japanese.

只有小白喜欢那个电影。· 只有小白喜歡那個電影。
Zhǐ yǒu Xiǎo Bái xǐhuan nàge diànyǐng.
Only Little Bai liked that movie.

Oral Practice

Read each of the following sentences aloud, adding 只有 zhǐ yǒu before the subject to match the English sentence.

1. 小王做了作业。 → 只有小王做了作业。
   小王做了作業。 　　 只有小王做了作業。
   Xiǎo Wáng zuò le zuòyè. 　Zhǐ yǒu Xiǎo Wáng zuò le zuòyè.
   　　　　　　　　　　　 Only Little Wang did the homework.

2. 小王吃了早饭。 → 只有小王吃了早饭。
   小王吃了早飯。 　　 只有小王吃了早飯。
   Xiǎo Wáng chī le zǎofàn. 　Zhǐ yǒu Xiǎo Wáng chī le zǎofàn.
   　　　　　　　　　　　 Only Little Wang ate breakfast.

3. 小李睡了八个小时。 → 只有小李睡了八个小时。
   小李睡了八個小時。   只有小李睡了八個小時。
   Xiǎo Lǐ shuì le bā gè xiǎoshí.   **Zhǐ yǒu Xiǎo Lǐ shuì le bā gè xiǎoshí.**
   Only Little Li slept for eight hours.

4. 小白有手机。 → 只有小白有手机。
   小白有手機。   只有小白有手機。
   Xiǎo Bái yǒu shǒujī.   **Zhǐ yǒu Xiǎo Bái yǒu shǒujī.**
   Only Little Bai has a cell phone.

QUIZ

Rewrite each of the following sentences, adding the word(s) in parentheses to match the English sentence.

1. 她的男朋友高大。
   Tā de nán péngyou gāo dà. (又 … 又 yòu … yòu)
   Her boyfriend is tall and big.

   _____

2. 台北的地铁很方便很干净。· 臺北的地鐵很方便很乾淨。
   Táiběi de dìtiě hěn fāngbiàn hěn gānjìng. (也 … 也 yě … yě)
   Taipei's subways are convenient and clean.

   _____

3. 他们喜欢吃中餐, 喜欢吃西餐。· 他們喜歡吃中餐, 喜歡吃西餐。
   Tāmen xǐhuan chī Zhōngcān, xǐhuan chī xīcān. (还·還 hái)
   They like to eat Chinese food, and they also like to eat Western food.

   _____

4. 我的汽车旧破。· 我的汽車舊破。
   Wǒ de qìchē jiù pò. (又 … 又 yòu … yòu)
   My car is both old and broken.

   _____

5. 我喜欢喝红茶，喜欢喝绿茶。· 我喜歡喝紅茶，喜歡喝綠茶。
   Wǒ xǐhuan hē hóngchá, xǐhuan hē lǜchá. (也　yě)
   I like to drink black tea, and I also like to drink green tea.
      (Note that in Chinese, *black tea* is called 红茶 · 紅茶 hóng chá *red tea*.)

_____

Following are descriptions of Little Wang's activities last week. Rewrite each of the sentences, using 只 zhǐ, 就 jiù, or 才 cái, as indicated in parentheses.

6. 小王看了四个电影。(就) · 小王看了四個電影。(就)
   Xiǎo Wáng kàn le sì gè diànyǐng. (jiù)

_____

7. 小王买了六本书。(只) · 小王買了六本書。(只)
   Xiǎo Wáng mǎi le liù běn shū. (zhǐ)

_____

8. 小王吃了九个饺子。(才) · 小王吃了九個餃子。(才)
   Xiǎo Wáng chī le jiǔ gè jiǎozi. (cái)

_____

Write a sentence to say that each of the following situations is only true for Little Bai. Then translate the sentence into English.

9. 能吃辣的　néng chī là de　*is able to eat hot and spicy food*

_____

10. 没睡觉 · 没睡覺　méi shuì jiào　*did not sleep*

_____

PART FOUR

TIME AND SPACE, ACTIONS AND COMPARISONS

CHAPTER 18

Location and Distance

In this chapter, you will learn about:

Location Words

The following list contains the most common location words in Mandarin. Each word is composed of a base word (the first syllable) and a suffix (the second syllable). Most base words can occur with more than one suffix. The list illustrates the most common suffixes: 头·頭 tou, 边·邊 bian, and 面 mian. The choice of suffix depends on the region of China and the preference of the speaker. Since all the variations with the same base word have the same meaning, you should follow the guidance of your teacher and your Chinese textbook in your choice of suffix.

	头·頭 tou	边·邊 bian	面 mian
in front	前头·前頭 qiántou	前边·前邊 qiánbian	前面 qiánmian
behind	后头·後頭 hòutou	后边·後邊 hòubian	后面·後面 hòumian
inside	里头·裏頭 lǐtou	里边·裏邊 lǐbian	里面·裏面 lǐmian
outside	外头·外頭 wàitou	外边·外邊 wàibian	外面 wàimian
above, on top	上头·上頭 shàngtou	上边·上邊 shàngbian	上面 shàngmian
below, under	下头·下頭 xiàtou	下边·下邊 xiàbian	下面 xiàmian
left side		左边·左邊 zuǒbian	
right side		右边·右邊 yòubian	
beside		旁边·旁邊 pángbiān	
across			对面·對面 duìmiàn
between		中间·中間 zhōngjiān	

Note that the last five location words in the list occur only with a single suffix.

COMPASS DIRECTION WORDS

The base words for compass directions are one syllable long and occur with a suffix. There are regional variations in the preferred suffix.

Compass directions are normally recited in the order 东南西北·東南西北 dōng nán xī běi *east, south, west, north* or 东西南北·東西南北 dōng xī nán běi *east, west, south, north.* The combination compass direction words, such as *northeast* and *southwest,* are formed by combining two different base words. The combination words may occur with an additional suffix but often occur without one.

	Short Form	**边·邊 bian**	**面 mian**
east	东·東 dōng	东边·東邊 dōngbian	东面·東面 dōngmian
south	南 nán	南边·南邊 nánbian	南面 nánmian
west	西 xī	西边·西邊 xībian	西面 xīmian
north	北 běi	北边·北邊 běibian	北面 běimian
northeast	东北·東北 dōngběi	东北边·東北邊 dōngběibian	
southeast	东南·東南 dōngnán	东南边·東南邊 dōngnánbian	
northwest	西北 xīběi	西北边·西北邊 xīběibian	
southwest	西南·西南 xīnán	西南边·西南邊 xīnánbian	

Indicating Location with a Location Phrase: 在 zài + Location Word

Mandarin location words are nouns, and in location expressions they typically occur in the phrase 在 zài + Location Word. Note that this phrase may be translated into English with different prepositions, depending on the location word. In Mandarin, 在 zài indicates a general location, and the location word that follows provides more precise information about whether the location is *at, on, in, over, under,* and so on.

The following construction is used to say that a person, place, or thing is at a particular location.

Subject + 在 zài + Location Word (including suffix)

我的狗在外头。· 我的狗在外頭。
Wǒ de gǒu zài wàitou.
My dog is (located) outside.

孩子都在里头。· 孩子都在裏頭。
Háizi dōu zài lǐtou.
The children are all (located) inside.

我的房间在左边。· 我的房間在左邊。
Wǒ de fángjiān zài zuǒbian.
My room is (located) on the left.

小李的房间在右边。· 小李的房間在右邊。
Xiǎo Lǐ de fángjiān zài yòubian.
Little Li's room is (located) on the right.

小王的房间在中间。· 小王的房間在中間。
Xiǎo Wáng de fángjiān zài zhōngjiān.
Little Wang's room is (located) in between.

小陈的房间在对面。· 小陳的房間在對面。
Xiǎo Chén de fángjiān zài duìmiàn.
Little Chen's room is (located) across (from us).

火车站在北边。· 火車站在北邊。
Huǒchēzhàn zài běibian.
The train station is (located) in the north.

飞机场在南边。· 飛機場在南邊。
Fēijīchǎng zài nánbian.
The airport is (located) in the south.

我家在西南。
Wǒ jiā zài xīnán.
My home is (located) in the southwest.

Written Practice 18-1

Write a complete Mandarin sentence indicating where each of the following people, places, or things is located, using the information in parentheses.

1. 图书馆·圖書館 túshūguǎn (in the south)

   _____

2. 我的宿舍 wǒ de sùshè (in front)

   _____

3. 加拿大 Jiānádà (in the north)

   _____

4. 我的狗 wǒ de gǒu (outside)

   _____

5. 我的妹妹 wǒ de mèimei (inside)

   _____

6. 公园·公園 gōngyuán (on the west side)

   _____

Indicating Location with Respect to a Reference Point

The location of a person, place, or thing is often indicated with respect to some reference point, for example, *behind **the house*** or *under **the book***. Mandarin uses the following construction to indicate the reference point, which is in bold type in the examples that follow. When the location phrase comes first in the sentence, 在 zài may be omitted.

(在 zài +) Reference Point + 的 de + Location Word

(在)**房子**的后头 · (在)**房子**的後頭
(zài) **fángzi** de hòutou
*behind **the house***

(在)**书**的下头 · (在)**書**的下頭
(zài) **shū** de xiàtou
*under **the book***

(在)**我**的右边 · (在)**我**的右邊
(zài) **wǒ** de yòubian
*on/to **my** right*

(在)**宿舍**的东边 · (在)宿舍的東邊
(zài) **sùshè** de dōngbian
*to the east of **the dormitory***

Written Practice 18-2

Write a Mandarin phrase indicating the location of each of the following people, places, or things, matching the English phrase in parentheses. The reference point is in bold italic type.

1. 图书馆 · 圖書館 túshūguǎn (*inside **the library***)

   _____

2. 餐厅 · 餐廳 cāntīng (*next to **the cafeteria***)

   _____

3. 公园 · 公園 gōngyuán (*to the north of **the park***)

   _____

4. 书店·書店 shūdiàn (*in front of **the bookstore***)

_____

5. 学校·學校 xuéxiào (*across from **the school***)

_____

6. 你 nǐ (*on **your** right*)

_____

To say that a person, place, or thing is located *in the park* or *across from the library*, simply add the person, place, or thing as the subject of the location expression.

Subject + 在 zài + Reference Point + 的 de + Location Word

我的宿舍在图书馆的北边。· 我的宿舍在圖書館的北邊。
Wǒ de sùshè zài túshūguǎn de běibian.
My dorm is (located) to the north of the library.

餐厅在大学的西北边。· 餐廳在大學的西北邊。
Cāntīng zài dàxué de xīběibian.
The cafeteria is (located) on the northwest side of the college.

公共汽车站在书店的对面。· 公共汽車站在書店的對面。
Gōnggòng qìchēzhàn zài shūdiàn de duìmiàn.
The bus stop is (located) across from the bookstore.

学生中心在餐厅的右边。· 學生中心在餐廳的右邊。
Xuésheng zhōngxīn zài cāntīng de yòubian.
The student center is (located) to the right of the cafeteria.

邮局在学生中心的后面。· 郵局在學生中心的後面。
Yóujú zài xuésheng zhōngxīn de hòumian.
The post office is (located) behind the student center.

Written Practice 18-3

Rearrange each of the following groups of phrases into a complete Mandarin sentence to match the English sentence.

1. 房子的上头 – 在 – 我的猫
   房子的上頭 – 在 – 我的貓
   fángzi de shàngtou – zài – wǒ de māo
   My cat is on the house.

   _____

2. 图书馆 – 的 – 你的车 – 在 – 后面
   圖書館 – 的 – 你的車 – 在 – 後面
   túshūguǎn – de – nǐ de chē – zài – hòumian
   Your car is behind the library.

   _____

3. 的 – 在 – 书店 – 南边 – 图书馆
   的 – 在 – 書店 – 南邊 – 圖書館
   de – zài – shūdiàn – nánbian – túshūguǎn
   The library is (to the) south of the bookstore.

   _____

4. 在 – 的 – 宿舍 – 书店 – 对面
   在 – 的 – 宿舍 – 書店 – 對面
   zài – de – sùshè – shūdiàn – duìmiàn
   The bookstore is across from the dormitory.

   _____

5. 电脑 – 的 – 我 – 宿舍 – 里头 – 的 – 在
   電腦 – 的 – 我 – 宿舍 – 裏頭 – 的 – 在
   diànnǎo – de – wǒ – sùshè – lǐtou – de – zài
   My computer is in the dormitory.

   _____

THE SHORT FORM OF LOCATION WORDS

Each of the following location words has a short form, without a suffix.

in front	前头·前頭	qiántou	→	前	qián
behind	后头·後頭	hòutou	→	后·後	hòu
inside	里头·裏頭	lǐtou	→	里·裏	lǐ
outside	外头·外頭	wàitou	→	外	wài
above, on top	上头·上頭	shàngtou	→	上	shàng
below, under	下头·下頭	xiàtou	→	下	xià

The short form is used when the location phrase includes a reference point. The short form comes right after the reference point, without 的 de. 前 qián *in front* and 后·後 hòu *behind* are less commonly used than the short forms of the other location words.

房子的里头 → 房子里
房子的裏頭 房子裏
fángzi de lǐtou fángzi lǐ
inside the house

门的外头 → 门外
門的外頭 門外
mén de wàitou mén wài
outside the door

书的上头 → 书上
書的上頭 書上
shū de shàngtou shū shàng
on the book

桌子的下头 → 桌子下
桌子的下頭 桌子下
zhuōzi de xiàtou zhuōzi xià
under the table

图书馆的前头 → 图书馆前
圖書館的前頭 圖書館前
túshūguǎn de qiántou túshūguǎn qián
in front of the library

宿舍的后头   →   宿舍后
宿舍的後頭   宿舍後
sùshè de hòutou   sùshè hòu
behind the dormitory

Written Practice 18-4

Rewrite each of the following sentences, using the short form of the location word.

1. 他们在门的外头。· 他們在門的外頭。
   Tāmen zài mén de wàitou.
   They are outside the door.

   _____

2. 学生在图书馆的里头。· 學生在圖書館的裏頭。
   Xuésheng zài túshūguǎn de lǐtou.
   The students are in the library.

   _____

3. 你的猫在房子的上头。· 你的貓在房子的上頭。
   Nǐ de māo zài fángzi de shàngtou.
   Your cat is on the house.

   _____

4. 他的书包在桌子的下头。· 他的書包在桌子的下頭。
   Tā de shūbāo zài zhuōzi de xiàtou.
   His book bag is under the table.

   _____

Talking About Things That Exist at a Location

Mandarin uses the following construction to indicate the existence of a person, place, or thing at a location, such as *there are people in the house.*

在 zài + Location Word + 有 yǒu + Noun Phrase

在图书馆的后头有一个小公园。· 在圖書館的後頭有一個小公園。

Zài túshūguǎn de hòutou yǒu yī gè xiǎo gōngyuán.

Behind the library there is a small park.

When 在 zài is the first word of the sentence, it can be omitted.

房子里有很多人。· 房子裏有很多人。

Fángzi lǐ yǒu hěn duō rén.

Inside the house there are a lot of people.

This information can also be expressed with the 有 yǒu phrase first and the 在 zài phrase second. In this order, 在 zài must not be omitted.

有 yǒu + Noun Phrase + 在 zài + Location Word

有一个小公园在图书馆的后头。· 有一個小公園在圖書館的後頭。

Yǒu yī gè xiǎo gōngyuán zài túshūguǎn de hòutou.

There is a small park behind the library.

有很多人在房子里。· 有很多人在房子裏。

Yǒu hěn duō rén zài fángzi lǐ.

There are a lot of people inside the house.

Written Practice 18-5

Help 小王 Xiǎo Wáng describe his dorm room. Using the construction 在 zài + Location Word + 有 yǒu + Noun Phrase, write a Mandarin sentence indicating the existence of each of the following objects at the location indicated in the English sentence.

1. 床 chuáng *bed* (窗户 chuānghu *window*)
   There is a bed under the window.

2. 桌子 zhuōzi *table*
There is a small table in front of the bed.

_____

3. 椅子 yǐzi *chair* (一把椅子 yī bǎ yǐzi)
There are two chairs to the right of the table.

_____

4. 电话机·電話機 diànhuàjī *telephone*
There is a telephone on the table.

_____

5. 电视机·電視機 diànshìjī *television*
There is a television between the chairs.

_____

Indicating the Place Where an Action Happens

To indicate the place where an action happens, as in *I eat in the cafeteria*, place 在 zài + Location Word before the action verb. When the location phrase is used in this way, 在 zài is a preposition and can generally be translated into English as *at*, *in*, or *on*.

我在图书馆学习。· 我在圖書館學習。
Wǒ zài túshūguǎn xuéxí.
I study at the library.

我的朋友在餐厅吃饭。· 我的朋友在餐廳吃飯。
Wǒ de péngyou zài cāntīng chī fàn.
My friends eat at the cafeteria.

小陈在宿舍做作业。· 小陳在宿舍做作業。
Xiǎo Chén zài sùshè zuò zuòyè.
Little Chen does homework in the dormitory.

Location words and compass directions can also indicate the place where an action happens.

我在外头等你。· 我在外頭等你。
Wǒ zài wàitou děng nǐ.
I am waiting for you outside.

他们在里头吃饭。· 他們在裏頭吃飯。
Tāmen zài lǐtou chī fàn.
They are eating inside.

他们在北边旅行。· 他們在北邊旅行。
Tāmen zài běibian lǚxíng.
They are vacationing in the north.

他在南边工作。· 他在南邊工作。
Tā zài nánbian gōngzuò.
He works in the south.

Written Practice 18-6

Rewrite each of the following Mandarin sentences, including the location in parentheses. Then translate the new sentence into English.

1. 我的朋友打球。(公园·公園 gōngyuán)
   Wǒ de péngyou dǎ qiú.
   (*in **the park***)

   _____

2. 他们唱歌。· 他們唱歌。(宿舍 sùshè)
   Tāmen chàng gē.
   (*in front of **the dormitory***)

   _____

3. 我们上课了。· 我們上課了。(书店·書店 shūdiàn)
   Wǒmen shàng kè le.
   (*behind **the bookstore***)

   _____

4. 他们跳舞了。· 他們跳舞了。(桌子 zhuōzi)
   Tāmen tiào wǔ le.
   (*on **the table***)

_____

5. 他们卖衣服。· 他們賣衣服。(火车站·火車站 huǒchēzhàn)
   Tāmen mài yīfu.
   (*north of **the train station***)

_____

Using Location Phrases to Describe People, Places, and Things

A location phrase can serve as the description of a person, place, or thing. As with all noun descriptions in Mandarin, the description, followed by 的 de, comes before the *main noun*—the person, place, or thing that is being described. (To review the constructions used to describe nouns, see Chapters 7, 12, and 13.) When the description is a location phrase, the construction is as follows.

Location Phrase + 的 de + Main Noun

In the following examples, a location phrase describes a noun, which is in bold type. 在 zài may be omitted from the description phrase.

在北边的**宿舍** · 在北邊的**宿舍**
zài běibian de **sùshè**
the dormitory *to the north*

在图书馆的北边的**宿舍** · 在圖書館的北邊的**宿舍**
zài túshūguǎn de běibian de **sùshè**
the dormitory *to the north of the library*

在里头的**人** · 在裏頭的**人**
zài lǐtou de **rén**
the people *inside*

在房子里头的人 · 在房子裏頭的人
zài fángzi lǐtou de **rén**
*the **people** inside the house*

在房子里的人 · 在房子裏的人
zài fángzilǐ de **rén**
*the **people** inside the house*

Note that when a location phrase comes *before* a noun, it describes the noun.

在北边的公园 · 在北邊的公園
zài běibian de gōngyuán
the park in the north

When a location phrase comes *after* a noun, it indicates a location with respect to that noun.

在公园的北边 · 在公園的北邊
zài gōngyuán de běibian
to the north of the park

Written Practice 18-7

Translate the following phrases into English.

1. 桌子上的水果
   zhuōzi shàng de shuíguǒ

   _____

2. 图书馆外头的自行车 · 圖書館外頭的自行車
   túshūguǎn wàitou de zìxíngchē

   _____

3. 书店后头的餐厅 · 書店後頭的餐廳
   shūdiàn hòutou de cāntīng

   _____

4. 北京的北边的大学·北京的北邊的大學
   Běijīng de běibian de dàxué

   _____

5. 饭馆里的人·飯館裏的人
   fànguǎn lǐ de rén

   _____

Words That Indicate Distance

The following list contains the most commonly used units of distance in Mandarin. China uses the metric system, but also has its own traditional unit of distance, the 里 lǐ, translated as _mile_ or _Chinese mile._ All of these units are directly preceded by a number and may optionally be followed by the noun 路 lù _road._

里 lǐ	general term for mile; usually refers to a Chinese mile
华里·華里 huálǐ	Chinese mile; ½ kilometer; approximately ⅓ American mile
英里 yīnglǐ	British mile, American mile
公里 gōnglǐ	kilometer
米 mǐ	meter

Expressing the Distance Between Two Locations

Mandarin uses the following construction to express the distance between location A and location B.

Location A + 离·離 lí + Location B (+ 有 yǒu) + Distance
我家离图书馆有三公里。· 我家離圖書館有三公里。
Wǒ jiā lí túshūguǎn yǒu sān gōnglǐ.
My house is three kilometers from the library.

大学离机场有五十里路。· 大學離機場有五十里路。

Dàxué lí jīchǎng yǒu wǔshí lǐ lù.

The college is 50 miles from the airport.

纽约离波士顿有一百八十英里。· 紐約離波士頓有一百八十英里。

Niǔyuē lí Bōshìdùn yǒu yī bǎi bāshí yīnglǐ.

New York is 180 miles from Boston.

Written Practice 18-8

Write a complete Mandarin sentence expressing the distance between the two locations in each of the following items, as indicated.

1. 公园 · 公園 gōngyuán *park*
   大学 · 大學 dàxué *college*
   10 kilometers

   _____

2. 飞机场 · 飛機場 fēijīchǎng *airport*
   火车站 · 火車站 huǒchēzhàn *train station*
   5 American miles

   _____

3. 宿舍 sùshè *dormitory*
   图书馆 · 圖書館 túshūguǎn *library*
   100 meters

   _____

4. 书店 · 書店 shūdiàn *bookstore*
   公共汽车站 · 公共汽車站 gōnggòng qìchēzhàn *bus station*
   3 Chinese miles

   _____

5. 大学 · 大學 dàxué *college*
   书店 · 書店 shūdiàn *bookstore*
   2 kilometers

   _____

Expressing *Near* and *Far*

Mandarin uses the following construction to indicate that location A is *near* location B.

Location A + 离 · 離 lí + **Location B** + 很近 hěn jìn
(*Location A is very near Location B.*)

图书馆离我的宿舍很近。· 圖書館離我的宿舍很近。
Túshūguǎn lí wǒ de sùshè hěn jìn.
The library is near my dormitory.

学生中心离书店很近。· 學生中心離書店很近。
Xuésheng zhōngxīn lí shūdiàn hěn jìn.
The student center is very near the bookstore.

Since 近 jìn *close* is an adjectival verb, it is often preceded by 很 hěn (see Chapter 7).

The following construction is used to indicate that location A is *far from* location B.

Location A + 离 · 離 lí + **Location B** + 很远 · 很遠 hěn yuǎn
(*Location A is very far from Location B.*)

我家离大学很远。· 我家離大學很遠。
Wǒ jiā lí dàxué hěn yuǎn.
My house is very far from the college.

飞机场离大学很远。· 飛機場離大學很遠。
Fēijīchǎng lí dàxué hěn yuǎn.
The airport is far from the college.

To indicate that a location is near *here* or far from *here*, use one of the following constructions.

Near Here

Location A 离这儿很近。	OR	Location A 离这里很近。
Location A 離這兒很近。		Location A 離這裏很近。
Location A lí zhèr hěn jìn.		Location A lí zhèli hěn jìn.
Location A is close to here.		

Far from Here

Location A 离这儿很远。	OR	Location A 离这里很远。
Location A 離這兒很遠。		Location A 離這裏很遠。
Location A lí zhèr hěn yuǎn.		Location A lí zhèli hěn yuǎn.
Location A is far from here.		

Note that 这儿 · 這兒 zhèr *here* and 这里 · 這裏 zhèli *here* are equivalent in meaning and usage.

图书馆离这儿很近。· 圖書館離這兒很近。
Túshūguǎn lí zhèr hěn jìn.
The library is close to here.

飞机场离这里很远。· 飛機場離這裏很遠。
Fēijīchǎng lí zhèli hěn yuǎn.
The airport is far from here.

Written Practice 18-9

Write a complete Mandarin sentence indicating that the two locations in each of the following items are near each other or far from each other, as indicated by the phrase in parentheses. Then translate the sentence into English.

1. 中国饭馆，这儿 (很近)
   中國飯館，這兒 (很近)
   Zhōngguó fànguǎn, zhèr (hěn jìn)

   _____

2. 大学，我家 (很远)
   大學，我家 (很遠)
   dàxué, wǒ jiā (hěn yuǎn)

   _____

3. 公园，大学 (很近)
   公園，大學 (很近)
   gōngyuán, dàxué (hěn jìn)

   _____

4. 公园，这里 (很远)
   公園，這裏 (很遠)
   gōngyuán, zhèli (hěn yuǎn)

   _____

5. 宿舍，餐厅 (很近)
   宿舍，餐廳 (很近)
   sùshè, cāntīng (hěn jìn)

   _____

ASKING ABOUT *NEAR* AND *FAR*

Mandarin uses the following constructions to ask if location A is far from location B.

Location A 离 Location B 远吗?	OR Location A 离 Location B 远不远?
Location A 離 Location B 遠嗎?	Location A 離 Location B 遠不遠?
Location A lí Location B yuǎn ma?	Location A lí Location B yuǎn bù yuǎn?

Is it far from location A to location B?

你家离大学远吗?	OR 你家离大学远不远?
你家離大學遠嗎?	你家離大學遠不遠?
Nǐ jiā lí dàxué yuǎn ma?	Nǐ jiā lí dàxué yuǎn bù yuǎn?

Is your home far from the college?

Oral Practice

Read each of the following questions aloud, then answer *no,* using a complete sentence.

1. 你家离书店远不远?　　　→　我家离书店不远。
   你家離書店遠不遠?　　　　　我家離書店不遠。
   Nǐ jiā lí shūdiàn yuǎn bù yuǎn?　　Wǒ jiā lí shūdiàn bù yuǎn.

2. 公园离这儿远吗?　　　　→　公园离这儿不远。
   公園離這兒遠嗎?　　　　　　公園離這兒不遠。
   Gōngyuán lí zhèr yuǎn ma?　　Gōngyuán lí zhèr bù yuǎn.

3. 书店离你家近吗？   →   书店离我家不近。
書店離你家近嗎？   書店離我家不近。
Shūdiàn lí nǐ jiā jìn ma?   Shūdiàn lí wǒ jiā bù jìn.

4. 大学离飞机场远不远？   →   大学离飞机场不远。
大學離飛機場遠不遠？   大學離飛機場不遠。
Dàxué lí fēijīchǎng yuǎn bù yuǎn?   Dàxué lí fēijīchǎng bù yuǎn.

5. 你家离大学近吗？   →   我家离大学不近。
你家離大學近嗎？   我家離大學不近。
Nǐ jiā lí dàxué jìn ma?   Wǒ jiā lí dàxué bù jìn.

ASKING ABOUT DISTANCE

Mandarin uses the following construction to ask how far location A is from location B.

Location A 离 · 離 Location B (有)多远 · 多遠？
Location A lí Location B (yǒu) duō yuǎn?
How far is it from location A to location B?

中国离美国有多远？ · 中國離美國有多遠？
Zhōngguó lí Měiguó yǒu duō yuǎn?
How far is China from America?

你的宿舍离公共汽车站有多远？ · 你的宿舍離公共汽車站有多遠？
Nǐ de sùshè lí gōnggòng qìchēzhàn yǒu duō yuǎn?
How far is your dorm from the bus stop?

If the distance between locations is relatively close, the following construction may also be used.

Location A 离 · 離 Location B (有)几里路 · 幾里路？
Location A lí Location B (yǒu) jǐ lǐ lù?
How many miles is it from location A to location B?

Written Practice 18-10

Each of the following statements indicates the distance between two locations. For each statement, write a Mandarin question that asks for the distance. If the distance is more than 20 miles/kilometers/meters, use the question expression 多远·多遠 duō yuǎn. If the distance is less than 20 miles/kilometers/meters, use the question word 几·幾 jǐ. (See Chapter 15 to review the content question word 几·幾 jǐ *how much, how many.*)

1. 学生中心离图书馆有两百米。· 學生中心離圖書館有兩百米。
   Xuésheng zhōngxīn lí túshūguǎn yǒu liǎng bǎi mǐ.

   _____

2. 我家离大学有七英里。· 我家離大學有七英里。
   Wǒ jiā lí dàxué yǒu qī yīnglǐ.

   _____

3. 飞机场离这儿有一百公里。· 飛機場離這兒有一百公里。
   Fēijīchǎng lí zhèr yǒu yībǎi gōnglǐ.

   _____

4. 公园离学校有三里路。· 公園離學校有三里路。
   Gōngyuán lí xuéxiào yǒu sān lǐ lù.

   _____

5. 餐厅离宿舍有二十五米。· 餐廳離宿舍有二十五米。
   Cāntīng lí sùshè yǒu èrshíwǔ mǐ.

   _____

QUIZ

Combine each of the following groups of phrases into a complete Mandarin sentence, indicating where the action is performed.

1. my older brother – eats lunch – in front of the library

   _____

2. they – play ball – to the north of the dormitory

   _____

Combine each of the following groups of phrases into a complete Mandarin sentence, indicating where the place is located.

3. my dorm – next to the library

   _____

4. the park – southwest of the university

   _____

Rearrange each of the following groups of phrases into a complete Mandarin sentence to match the English sentence.

5. 在 – 大学 – 一个好饭馆 – 的 – 有 – 西边
   在 – 大學 – 一個好飯館 – 的 – 有 – 西邊
   zài – dàxué – yī gè hǎo fànguǎn – de – yǒu – xībian
   There is a good restaurant to the west of the university.

   _____

6. 餐厅 – 在 – 里 – 有 – 书店
   餐廳 – 在 – 裏 – 有 – 書店
   cāntīng – zài – lǐ – yǒu – shūdiàn
   There is a cafeteria inside the bookstore.

   _____

Following is the distance between certain campus locations.

Cafeteria to student center   45 meters
Bookstore to dormitories   1 Chinese mile
Dormitories to library   2 kilometers

7. Write three questions, asking if it is far between the two locations in each pair above.

    a. _____

    b. _____

    c. _____

8. Write three questions, asking how far it is between the two locations in each pair above.

    a. _____

    b. _____

    c. _____

9. Answer *yes* to each question in question 7, using a complete Mandarin sentence.

    a. _____

    b. _____

    c. _____

10. Answer each question in question 8, using a complete Mandarin sentence that indicates the distance between the two locations.

    a. _____

    b. _____

    c. _____

CHAPTER 19

Talking About Time

In this chapter, you will learn about:

Talking About Hours and Minutes
Reciting Time
Talking About the Parts of the Day
Combining Time Expressions
Talking About Weeks and the Days of the Week
Counting Days and Referring to Surrounding Days
Talking About Months and the Dates of the Month
Talking About Years
Reciting Complete Dates: Year, Month, and Date

Talking About Hours and Minutes

Mandarin has two words for *hour*: 钟头·鐘頭 zhōngtóu and 小时·小時 xiǎoshí. To count the number of hours, use one of the following constructions.

Number + 个·個 **gè** + 钟头·鐘頭 **zhōngtóu**
Number + 个·個 **gè** + 小时·小時 **xiǎoshí**

一个钟头·一個鐘頭	yī gè zhōngtóu	*one hour*
一个小时·一個小時	yī gè xiǎoshí	*one hour*
两个钟头·兩個鐘頭	liǎng gè zhōngtóu	*two hours*
两个小时·兩個小時	liǎng gè xiǎoshí	*two hours*
三个钟头·三個鐘頭	sān gè zhōngtóu	*three hours*
三个小时·三個小時	sān gè xiǎoshí	*three hours*

To indicate *half an hour*, say 半个钟头·半個鐘頭 bàn gè zhōngtóu or 半个小时·半個小時 bàn gè xiǎoshí. To indicate a certain number of hours *and a half*, use one of the following constructions.

Number + 个·個 **gè** + 半 **bàn** + 钟头·鐘頭 **zhōngtóu**
Number + 个·個 **gè** + 半 **bàn** + 小时·小時 **xiǎoshí**

两个半钟头·兩個半鐘頭	liǎng gè bàn zhōngtóu	*2½ hours*
四个半钟头·四個半鐘頭	sì gè bàn zhōngtóu	*4½ hours*
五个半小时·五個半小時	wǔ gè bàn xiǎoshí	*5½ hours*

The word for minute is 分 fēn. In counting the number of minutes, 分 fēn follows the number.

一分	yī fēn	*one minute*
两分·兩分	liǎng fēn	*two minutes*
三分	sān fēn	*three minutes*
二十分	èrshí fēn	*20 minutes*

分 fēn follows the number because it is a classifier. 分 fēn may be followed by the noun 钟·鐘 zhōng *clock,* although 钟·鐘 zhōng is often omitted. Examples of the full phrase, including the word 钟·鐘 zhōng, follow. If 钟·鐘 zhōng is used and the phrase includes minutes, the word 分 fēn must also be used.

Number + 分 fēn + 钟·鐘 zhōng

一分钟·一分鐘	yī fēn zhōng	*one minute*
两分钟·兩分鐘	liǎng fēn zhōng	*two minutes*
三分钟·三分鐘	sān fēn zhōng	*three minutes*

Oral Practice

Read the following phrases aloud, then translate them into English.

1. 七个钟头·七個鐘頭   → *7 hours*
   qī gè zhōngtóu

2. 三个半小时·三個半小時   → *3½ hours*
   sān gè bàn xiǎoshí

3. 十五分钟·十五分鐘   → *15 minutes*
   shíwǔ fēn zhōng

Written Practice 19-1

Translate the following Mandarin phrases into English.

1. 两个小时·兩個小時 liǎng gè xiǎoshí

   _____

2. 十个钟头·十個鐘頭 shí gè zhōngtóu

   _____

3. 一分 yī fēn

   _____

4. 五十九分 wǔshíjiǔ fēn

   _____

Reciting Time

RECITING TIME ON THE HOUR

To recite time on the hour, use the following construction. (Note that the word 钟·鐘 zhōng *clock* is optional.)

Number + 点钟·點鐘 diǎn zhōng

一点钟·一點鐘	yī diǎn zhōng	*1 o'clock*
两点钟·兩點鐘	liǎng diǎn zhōng	*2 o'clock*
三点钟·三點鐘	sān diǎn zhōng	*3 o'clock*
四点钟·四點鐘	sì diǎn zhōng	*4 o'clock*
五点钟·五點鐘	wǔ diǎn zhōng	*5 o'clock*
六点钟·六點鐘	liù diǎn zhōng	*6 o'clock*
七点钟·七點鐘	qī diǎn zhōng	*7 o'clock*
八点钟·八點鐘	bā diǎn zhōng	*8 o'clock*
九点钟·九點鐘	jiǔ diǎn zhōng	*9 o'clock*
十点钟·十點鐘	shí diǎn zhōng	*10 o'clock*
十一点钟·十一點鐘	shíyī diǎn zhōng	*11 o'clock*
十二点钟·十二點鐘	shí'èr diǎn zhōng	*12 o'clock*

To ask *what time it is,* use one of the following questions.

几点钟？· 幾點鐘？ Jǐ diǎn zhōng?
几点？· 幾點？ Jǐ diǎn?

To ask *what time it is now,* add the word 现在·現在 xiànzài *now* to one of the questions above.

现在(是)几点钟？· 現在(是) 幾點鐘？
Xiànzài (shì) jǐ diǎn zhōng?

Oral Practice

For each of the following times, (1) ask what time it is now and (2) answer the question in Mandarin.

1. 3 o'clock → Q: 现在几点钟？· 现在幾點鐘？
   Xiànzài jǐ diǎn zhōng?
   A: 三点钟。· 三點鐘。
   Sān diǎn zhōng.

2. 1 o'clock → Q: 现在几点？· 現在幾點？
   Xiànzài jǐ diǎn?
   A: 一点。· 一點。
   Yī diǎn.

3. 7 o'clock → Q: 现在是几点钟？· 現在是幾點鐘？
   Xiànzài shì jǐ diǎn zhōng?
   A: 七点钟。· 七點鐘。
   Qī diǎn zhōng.

4. 6 o'clock → Q: 现在几点钟？· 現在幾點鐘？
   Xiànzài jǐ diǎn zhōng?
   A: 六点钟。· 六點鐘。
   Liù diǎn zhōng.

RECITING TIME IN HOURS AND MINUTES

There are three ways to recite time in hours and minutes in Mandarin.

Hour Plus Minutes

The most common way to recite time in Mandarin is to state the hour followed by the minutes. Any number of minutes from 1 to 59 can be recited in this format. If the number of minutes is 11 or greater, the word for *minute*, 分 fēn, is optional.

八点十分 · 八點十分	bā diǎn shí fēn	8:10
四点十五(分) · 四點十五(分)	sìdiǎn shíwǔ (fēn)	4:15
三点二十五(分) · 三點二十五(分)	sān diǎn èrshí wǔ (fēn)	3:25
六点四十(分) · 六點四十(分)	liù diǎn sìshí (fēn)	6:40
九点五十五(分) · 九點五十五(分)	jiǔ diǎn wǔshí wǔ (fēn)	9:55

Written Practice 19-2

Write the following times in Arabic numerals. For example, write 八点十分 · 八點十分 bā diǎn shífēn as 8:10.

1. 十一点七分 · 十一點七分 shíyī diǎn qī fēn _____

2. 四点四十 · 四點四十 sìdiǎn sìshí _____

3. 一点五十九分 · 一點五十九分 yī diǎn wǔshí jiǔ fēn _____

4. 五点三十四 · 五點三十四 wǔ diǎn sānshí sì _____

Half Past, Quarter Past, and *Three Quarters Past*

To indicate *half past the hour,* use the word 半 bàn *half, half past.*

九点半 · 九點半   jiǔ diǎn bàn   9:30
十二点半 · 十二點半   shí èr diǎn bàn   12:30

To indicate *a quarter past the hour,* use the expression 一刻 yī kè *one quarter.*

八点一刻 · 八點一刻   bā diǎn yī kè   8:15
十点一刻 · 十點一刻   shí diǎn yī kè   10:15

To indicate *three quarters past the hour,* use the expression 三刻 sān kè *three quarters.*

两点三刻 · 兩點三刻   liǎng diǎn sān kè   2:45
五点三刻 · 五點三刻   wǔ diǎn sān kè   5:45

Oral Practice

Read each of the following Mandarin phrases aloud, then recite the time in English.

1. 十点半·十點半 shí diǎn bàn   → 10:30

2. 六点三刻·六點三刻 liù diǎn sān kè   → 6:45

3. 十二点一刻·十二點一刻 shí'èr diǎn yī kè → 12:15

Minutes Past the Hour, Using 过·過 guò

To indicate minutes past the hour up to but not including half past the hour, add the word 过·過 guò *past* before the minutes. If 过·過 guò is used, the word 分 fēn *minute* is usually included.

八点过十分·八點過十分	bā diǎn guò shí fēn	8:10
三点过二十五分·三點過二十五分	sān diǎn guò èrshí wǔ fēn	3:25

过·過 guò is never used with 半 bàn *half past,* and it is rarely used with 刻 kè *quarter.* That is, you can recite the time 3:20 as either 三点二十·三點二十 sān diǎn èrshí or 三点过二十分·三點過二十分 sān diǎn guò èrshí fēn, but you should recite the time 3:30 only as 三点半·三點半 sān diǎn bàn.

Written Practice 19-3

Write each of the following times in Mandarin, adding 过·過 guò, 半 bàn, or 一刻 yī kè to the time expression.

1. 1:25 _____

2. 8:17 _____

3. 9:15 _____

4. 2:30 _____

Reciting Minutes to the Hour

To express minutes to the hour, use the word 差 chà followed by the number of minutes to the hour.

差一分九点·差一分九點   chà yī fēn jiǔ diǎn   *one minute to nine* (= 8:59)

差 chà + Minutes can be used for any number of minutes to the hour from 1 to 29. If 差 chà is used, the word 分 fēn *minute* is usually included after the number of minutes. 差 chà does not occur with 半 bàn *half past*. The expression 差 chà + Minutes may come before or after the hour.

To indicate a quarter to the hour, use the expression 差一刻 chà yī kè.

差 chà + Minutes + Hour

差五分六点·差五分六點   chà wǔ fēn liù diǎn   *5 minutes to 6* (= 5:55)
差十分四点·差十分四點   chà shí fēn sì diǎn   *10 minutes to 4* (= 3:50)
差一刻五点·差一刻五點   chà yī kè wǔ diǎn   *a quarter to 5* (= 4:45)

Hour + 差 chà + Minutes

六点差五分·六點差五分   liù diǎn chà wǔ fēn   *5 minutes to 6* (= 5:55)
四点差十分·四點差十分   sì diǎn chà shí fēn   *10 minutes to 4* (= 3:50)
五点差一刻·五點差一刻   wǔ diǎn chà yī kè   *a quarter to 5* (= 4:45)

Written Practice 19-4

Write each of the following times in Mandarin, using 差 chà.

1. 7:50   ————————————————————————

2. 2:45   ————————————————————————

3. 8:35   ————————————————————————

Talking About the Parts of the Day

Following are the words for different parts of the day.

早上 zǎoshang   *early morning* (approximately 5–9 A.M.)
早晨 zǎochén   *early morning* (approximately 5–9 A.M.)
上午 shàngwǔ   *morning* (the time before noon)
中午 zhōngwǔ   *the hours around noon* (approximately 11 A.M.–1 P.M.)
下午 xiàwǔ   *afternoon* (the time up to evening)
晚上 wǎnshang   *evening*
半夜 bànyè   *middle of the night* (approximately 1–4 A.M.)

Note that the expressions 中午 zhōngwǔ and 半夜 bànyè, which are sometimes translated into English as *noon* and *midnight,* actually refer to *the middle part of the day* and *the middle part of the night* in Mandarin—not precisely 12 o'clock noon and 12 o'clock midnight. It is acceptable in Mandarin to talk about meeting someone at 中午十二点半 · 中午十二點半 zhōngwǔ shí'èr diǎn bàn or to be awakened at 半夜两点 · 半夜兩點 bànyè liǎng diǎn.

Mandarin does not have words for A.M. and P.M. that denote exact 12-hour periods of the day. Instead, Mandarin requires you to be more precise than English about the part of the day that you are referring to. Six A.M. in Mandarin is 早上六点 · 早上六點 zǎoshang liù diǎn or 早晨六点 · 早晨六點 zǎochén liù diǎn, 10 A.M. is 上午十点 · 上午十點 shàngwǔ shí diǎn, and 2 A.M. is 半夜两点 · 半夜兩點 bànyè liǎng diǎn.

Oral Practice

State the part of the day in Mandarin that each of the following times belongs to.

1. 8 A.M.   → 早上 zǎoshang OR 早晨 zǎochén

2. 5:30 P.M. → 晚上 wǎnshang

3. 4 P.M.   → 下午 xiàwǔ

4. 3 A.M.   → 半夜 bànyè

5. 11 A.M.   → 上午 shàngwǔ

Combining Time Expressions

In Mandarin, time is always recited from the largest unit of time to the smallest. To express clock time, say the part of the day first, the hour second, and the minutes last.

下午三点一刻・下午三點一刻
xiàwǔ sān diǎn yī kè
afternoon 3:15 (i.e., *3:15 in the afternoon* OR *3:15 P.M.*)

早上六点二十分・早上六點二十分
zǎoshang liù diǎn èrshí fēn
morning 6:20 (i.e., *6:20 in the morning* OR *6:20 A.M.*)

中午十二点半・中午十二點半
zhōngwǔ shí'èr diǎn bàn
midday 12:30 (i.e., *12:30 P.M.*)

半夜两点钟・半夜兩點鐘
bànyè liǎng diǎn zhōng
middle of the night 2 o'clock (i.e., *2 o'clock in the morning* OR *2 A.M.*)

Written Practice 19-5

Rearrange each of the following groups of phrases in the correct order to match the time expression in English.

1. 三刻 – 六点 – 晚上・三刻 – 六點 – 晚上・
   sānkè – liù diǎn – wǎnshang
   6:45 P.M.

   _____

2. 八点钟 – 早晨・八點鐘 – 早晨
   bā diǎn zhōng – zǎochen
   8 A.M.

   _____

3. 三点 – 下午 – 二十分 · 三點 – 下午 – 二十分
   sān diǎn – xiàwǔ – èrshí fēn
   3:20 P.M.

_____

4. 上午 – 一刻 – 十点 · 上午 – 一刻 – 十點
   shàngwǔ – yī kè – shí diǎn
   10:15 A.M.

_____

Talking About Weeks and the Days of the Week

Mandarin has two words for *week*: 礼拜 · 禮拜 lǐbài and 星期 xīngqī. These words are identical in meaning, but individual speakers vary in their preference for one or the other. Weeks are counted with the classifier 个 · 個 gè.

一个星期 · 一個星期	yī gè xīngqī	*one week*
两个星期 · 兩個星期	liǎng gè xīngqī	*two weeks*
三个礼拜 · 三個禮拜	sān gè lǐbài	*three weeks*
四个礼拜 · 四個禮拜	sì gè lǐbài	*four weeks*

THE DAYS OF THE WEEK

礼拜 · 禮拜 lǐbài and 星期 xīngqī are used in the names of the days of the week. Note that when you recite the days of the week in Chinese, the first day of the week is Monday. Chinese calendars also begin with Monday.

The Days of the Week Using 礼拜 · 禮拜 lǐbài

礼拜一 · 禮拜一	lǐbàiyī	*Monday*
礼拜二 · 禮拜二	lǐbài'èr	*Tuesday*
礼拜三 · 禮拜三	lǐbàisān	*Wednesday*
礼拜四 · 禮拜四	lǐbàisì	*Thursday*
礼拜五 · 禮拜五	lǐbàiwǔ	*Friday*
礼拜六 · 禮拜六	lǐbàiliù	*Saturday*
礼拜天 · 禮拜天	lǐbàitiān	*Sunday*
礼拜日 · 禮拜日	lǐbàirì	*Sunday*

The Days of the Week Using 星期 xīngqī

星期一	xīngqīyī	*Monday*
星期二	xīngqī'èr	*Tuesday*
星期三	xīngqīsān	*Wednesday*
星期四	xīngqīsì	*Thursday*
星期五	xīngqīwǔ	*Friday*
星期六	xīngqīliù	*Saturday*
星期天	xīngqītiān	*Sunday*
星期日	xīngqīrì	*Sunday*

As you can see, there are two words for *Sunday* in each set of names. 礼拜天 ·
禮拜天 lǐbàitiān and 星期天 xīngqītiān are more common in informal speech and
writing, while 礼拜日 · 禮拜日 lǐbàirì and 星期日 xīngqīrì are more common in
formal speech and writing.

To ask *which day of the week it is,* use the question word 几 · 幾 jǐ.

礼拜几? · 禮拜幾? Lǐbàijǐ?
星期几? · 星期幾? Xīngqījǐ?

Oral Practice

Read each of the following questions aloud, then answer it in Mandarin, using
the information in parentheses.

1. 星期几? · 星期幾? Xīngqījǐ? (Saturday)   → 星期六 xīngqīliù

2. 礼拜几? · 禮拜幾? Lǐbàijǐ? (Tuesday)   → 礼拜二 · 禮拜二 lǐbài'èr

3. 星期几? · 星期幾? Xīngqījǐ? (Thursday)   → 星期四 xīngqīsì

4. 星期几? · 星期幾? Xīngqījǐ? (Friday)   → 星期五 xīngqīwǔ

SAYING *LAST WEEK, THIS WEEK,* AND *NEXT WEEK*

Following are the expressions for *last week, this week,* and *next week.*

上个星期·上個星期	shàng gè xīngqī	*last week*
上个礼拜·上個禮拜	shàng gè lǐbài	*last week*
这个星期·這個星期	zhège xīngqī	*this week*
这个礼拜·這個禮拜	zhège lǐbài	*this week*
下个星期·下個星期	xià gè xīngqī	*next week*
下个礼拜·下個禮拜	xià gè lǐbài	*next week*

To say *last (Saturday), this (Friday),* or *next (Monday),* use 上个·上個 shàng gè, 这个·這個 zhège, or 下个·下個 xià gè followed by the day of the week.

上个星期六·上個星期六	shàng gè xīngqīliù	*last Saturday*
上个礼拜三·上個禮拜三	shàng gè lǐbàisān	*last Wednesday*
这个星期五·這個星期五	zhège xīngqīwǔ	*this Friday*
这个礼拜二·這個禮拜二	zhège lǐbài'èr	*this Tuesday*
下个星期六·下個星期六	xià gè xīngqīliù	*next Saturday*
下个礼拜一·下個禮拜一	xià gè lǐbàiyī	*next Monday*

Written Practice 19-6

Complete each of the following Mandarin phrases to match the English phrase in parentheses.

1. _____星期

   _____ xīngqī (*this week*)

2. _____星期二

   _____ xīngqī'èr (*next Tuesday*)

3. _____星期三

   _____ xīngqīsān (*last Wednesday*)

4. 这个_____·這個_____

   zhège _____ (*this Sunday*)

Counting Days and Referring to Surrounding Days

The Mandarin word for *day* is 天 tiān. To count the number of days, say the number followed by 天 tiān.

一天	yī tiān	*one day*
两天 · 兩天	liǎng tiān	*two days*
三天	sān tiān	*three days*

To ask *how many days*, use the question word 几 · 幾 jǐ.

几天? · 幾天? Jǐ tiān?

Following are the words that refer to today and the surrounding days.

今天	jīntiān	*today*
昨天	zuótiān	*yesterday*
前天	qiántiān	*the day before yesterday*
明天	míngtiān	*tomorrow*
后天 · 後天	hòutiān	*the day after tomorrow*

You can combine these words with the time expressions presented earlier in this chapter to refer to specific times on specific days. Remember that information in time expressions is ordered from the largest unit of time to the smallest.

Oral Practice

Read each of the following phrases aloud, then translate it into English.

1. 今天晚上九点钟 · 今天晚上九點鐘 → *9 o'clock tonight*
   jīntiān wǎnshang jiǔ diǎn zhōng

2. 明天早上七点一刻 · 明天早上七點一刻 → *7:15 tomorrow morning*
   míngtiān zǎoshang qī diǎn yī kè

3. 前天上午十一点 · 前天上午十一點 → *11 A.M. the day before*
   qiántiān shàngwǔ shíyī diǎn   *yesterday*

4. 昨天下午三点四十五 · 昨天下午三點四十五 → *yesterday afternoon at 3:45*
   zuótiān xiàwǔ sān diǎn sìshí wǔ

Talking About Months and the Dates of the Month

The Mandarin word for *month* is 月 yuè. Months are counted with the classifier 个 · 個 gè.

一个月 · 一個月	yī gè yuè	*one month*
两个月 · 兩個月	liǎng gè yuè	*two months*
三个月 · 三個月	sān gè yuè	*three months*

To ask *how many months*, use the question word 几 · 幾 jǐ.

几个月？· 幾個月？ Jǐ gè yuè?

THE NAMES OF THE MONTHS

The names of the months are formed with the numbers 1 through 12 plus the word 月 yuè *month*.

一月	yīyuè	*January*
二月	èryuè	*February*
三月	sānyuè	*March*
四月	sìyuè	*April*
五月	wǔyuè	*May*
六月	liùyuè	*June*
七月	qīyuè	*July*
八月	bāyuè	*August*
九月	jiǔyuè	*September*
十月	shíyuè	*October*
十一月	shíyīyuè	*November*
十二月	shí'èryuè	*December*

To ask *which month*, use the question word 几 · 幾 jǐ.

几月？· 幾月？ Jǐyuè?

Oral Practice

Read each of the following questions aloud, then answer it in Mandarin, using the information in parentheses.

1. 几月？·幾月？ Jǐyuè? (*March*) → 三月 sānyuè

2. 几月？·幾月？ Jǐyuè? (*June*) → 六月 liùyuè

3. 几月？·幾月？ Jǐyuè? (*November*) → 十一月 shíyīyuè

4. 几月？·幾月？ Jǐyuè? (*May*) → 五月 wǔyuè

Note that the names of the months are very similar to the phrases used to count months. Both involve numbers and the word 月 yuè *month*. However, when *naming* the months, the name consists of Number + 月 yuè. When *counting* months, the phrase consists of Number + 个·個 gè + 月 yuè.

Written Practice 19-7

Translate each of the following Mandarin phrases into English, and each of the English phrases into Mandarin. Be careful to distinguish between the names of months and the number of months.

1. 五个月·五個月 wǔ gè yuè _____

2. 五月 wǔyuè _____

3. *six months* _____

4. *July* _____

5. *September* _____

6. 九个月·九個月 jiǔ gè yuè _____

TALKING ABOUT THE DATE OF THE MONTH

To indicate the date of the month, such as the 1st, 2nd, 3rd, 28th, or 30th, insert the word 号·號 hào or 日 rì after the number. 号·號 hào is used in informal, everyday speech, and 日 rì is used in calendars, invitations, and formal speech and writing.

1st	一号·一號 yī hào	OR	一日 yī rì	
2nd	二号·二號 èr hào	OR	二日 èr rì	
3rd	三号·三號 sān hào	OR	三日 sān rì	
28th	二十八号·二十八號 èrshíbā hào	OR	二十八日 èrshíbā rì	
30th	三十号·三十號 sānshí hào	OR	三十日 sānshí rì	

When referring to a month and date, the order of information is always Month + Date.

August 16	八月十六号·八月十六號	bāyuè shíliù hào
February 5	二月五号·二月五號	èryuè wǔ hào

Written Practice 19-8

Translate each of the following Chinese dates into English, and the English date into Chinese.

1. 十月二十五日 shíyuè èrshíwǔ rì _____

2. 七月四日 qīyuè sì rì _____

3. 四月十四日 sìyuè shísì rì _____

4. 一月一号·一月一號 yīyuè yī hào _____

5. *December 25* _____

When asking for the month and date, use one of the following questions.

几月几号?·幾月幾號? Jǐyuè jǐhào?
几月几日?·幾月幾日? Jǐyuè jǐrì?

Oral Practice

Read each of the following questions aloud, then answer it in Mandarin, using the information in parentheses.

1. 几月几号？·幾月幾號？ Jǐyuè jǐhào? (February 12)
   → 二月十二号·二月十二號 èryuè shí'èr hào

2. 几月几日？·幾月幾日？ Jǐyuè jǐrì? (November 18)
   → 十一月十八日 shíyīyuè shíbā rì

3. 几月几号？·幾月幾號？ Jǐyuè jǐhào? (September 4)
   → 九月四号·九月四號 jiǔyuè sì hào

SAYING *LAST MONTH*, *THIS MONTH*, AND *NEXT MONTH*

Following are the expressions for *last month*, *this month*, and *next month*. Note that months use the same system as weeks.

上个月·上個月	shàng gè yuè	*last month*
这个月·這個月	zhège yuè	*this month*
下个月·下個月	xià gè yuè	*next month*

Talking About Years

The Mandarin word for *year* is 年 nián. In counting years, the number comes before 年 nián.

一年	yī nián	*one year*
两年·兩年	liǎng nián	*two years*
三年	sān nián	*three years*

RECITING YEARS

In reciting a date, the year is recited as a series of numbers followed by the word 年 nián. Zeroes are recited as ○ (or 零) líng, and every zero in the date is recited separately.

1492	一四九二年	yī sì jiǔ èr nián
1985	一九八五年	yī jiǔ bā wǔ nián
1972	一九七二年	yī jiǔ qī èr nián
1999	一九九九年	yī jiǔ jiǔ jiǔ nián
2000	二〇〇〇年	èr líng líng líng nián
2006	二〇〇六年	èr líng líng liù nián

To ask *which year*, use the following question.

哪年? Něi nián? / Nǎ nián?

To ask for the last number in a year, use the question word 几·幾 jǐ.

二〇〇几年? · 二〇〇幾年?
Èr líng líng jǐ nián?
Two thousand and what?

Oral Practice

Read each of the following questions aloud, then state the year in Mandarin, using the information in parentheses.

1. 哪年? Nǎ nián? (2008) → 二〇〇八年 èr líng líng bā nián

2. 哪年? Nǎ nián? (2001) → 二〇〇一年 èr líng líng yī nián

3. 哪年? Nǎ nián? (1998) → 一九九八年 yī jiǔ jiǔ bā nián

4. 哪年? Nǎ nián? (1861) → 一八六一年 yī bā liù yī nián

SAYING *THIS YEAR* AND THE SURROUNDING YEARS

Following are expressions referring to the current, previous, and following years.

前年	qiánnián	*two years ago* (i.e., *the year before last*)
去年	qùnián	*last year*
今年	jīnnián	*this year*
明年	míngnián	*next year*
后年·後年	hòunián	*two years from now* (i.e., *the year after next*)

CULTURE DEMYSTIFIED

Picturing Time in Chinese

Chinese refers to previous and following years with the expressions *in front* and *behind,* respectively, so that *next year* is the year *behind (you)* and *last year* is the year *in front (of you).* To remember this distinction, picture yourself standing in time with your face to the past and your back to the future. You can see what has happened in the past, so those are the 前年 qiánnián *the years in front of you.* You cannot see what is going to happen in the future, so those years are the 后年·後年 hòunián *the years behind you.*

Written Practice 19-9

Translate the sentence in question 1 below into English. Based on the date in that sentence, complete the remaining sentences in Mandarin.

1. 今年是二〇〇〇年。Jīnnián shí'èr líng líng líng nián.

   _____

2. 去年是_____。

   Qùnián shì _____.

3. 后年是_____。·

   後年是_____。

   Hòunián shì _____.

4. 明年是_____。

   Míngnián shì _____.

5. 前年是_____。

   Qiánnián shì _____.

Reciting Complete Dates: Year, Month, and Date

Time is always recited in Mandarin from the largest unit to the smallest. To recite dates, say the year first, the month second, and the date third.

一七七六年七月四号·一七七六年七月四號
yī qī qī liù nián qīyuè sì hào
July 4, 1776

一九六九年七月二十日
yī jiǔ liù jiǔ nián qīyuè èrshí rì
July 20, 1969

二〇〇〇年一月一日
èr líng líng líng nián yīyuè yī rì
January 1, 2000

Written Practice 19-10

Write the following dates in Mandarin, using 日 rì for the date of the month.

1. *February 16, 1952*

   _____

2. *April 14, 1961*

   _____

3. *June 30, 2008*

   _____

QUIZ

Write each of the following times in Mandarin, using the expression in parentheses.

1. 5:18 (过·過 guò)

_____

2. 8:40 (差 chà)

_____

3. 10:30 (半 bàn)

_____

Rewrite each of the following time expressions in Mandarin, using 小时·小時 xiǎoshí. Then translate the expression into English.

4. 三十五个钟头·三十五個鐘頭 sānshí wǔ gè zhōngtóu

_____

5. 两个钟头·兩個鐘頭 liǎng gè zhōngtóu

_____

Answer the following questions using the calendar at the top of page 321. For these questions, assume that the year of the calendar is *this year* and the month is *this month*. Today is the 15th.

6. 今年是哪年?
   Jīnnián shì něi nián?

_____

7. 二月有几个星期?·二月有幾個星期?
   Éryuè yǒu jǐ gè xīngqī?

_____

8. 前天是星期几?·前天是星期幾?
   Qiántiān shì xīngqījǐ?

_____

二〇〇八年二月 èr líng líng bā nián èryuè						
星期一 xīngqīyī	星期二 xīngqī'èr	星期三 xīngqīsān	星期四 xīngqīsì	星期五 xīngqīwǔ	星期六 xīngqīliù	星期日 xīngqīrì
				1	2	3
4	5	6	7	8	9	10
11	12	13	14	15	16	17
18	19	20	21	22	23	24
25	26	27	28	29		

9. 上个礼拜二是几月几号？· 上個禮拜二是幾月幾號？
   Shàng gè lǐbài èr shì jǐyuè jǐhào?

   _____

10. 下个月是几月？· 下個月是幾月？
    Xià gè yuè shì jǐyuè?

    _____

CHAPTER 20

Describing How Actions Are Performed

In this chapter, you will learn about:

In English, manner adverbs are used to describe the way an action is performed. These adverbs are often identifiable by an *-ly* ending. Mandarin does not have manner adverbs; it uses adjectival verbs instead.

Describing an Action When There Is No Object

To describe the general performance of an action (as in *my younger sister eats slowly*) or to evaluate the performance of an action (as in *you sang very well*), use the following construction.

Action Verb + 得 de + Adjectival Verb

跑得快 pǎo de **kuài**	*run **quickly***
说得慢·說得慢 shuō de **màn**	*speak **slowly***
唱得好 chàng de **hǎo**	*sing **well***
写得清楚·寫得清楚 xiě de **qīngchu**	*write **clearly***

Since adjectival verbs in affirmative sentences are generally preceded by an intensifier (see Chapter 7), the intensifier 很 hěn *very* is included in the next two example sentences.

The following sentence says that 张美丽·張美麗 Zhāng Měilì sings well in general (that is, that she is a good singer).

张美丽唱得很好。· 張美麗唱得很好。
Zhāng Měilì chàng de hěn hǎo.
Zhang Meili sings very well.

The following sentence says that 陈明·陳明 Chén Míng runs fast (that is, that he is a fast runner).

陈明跑得很快。· 陳明跑得很快 。
Chén Míng pǎo de hěn kuài.
Chen Ming runs very fast.

To say that 张美丽·張美麗 Zhāng Měilì does not sing well (that is, that she is not a good singer), or that 陈明·陳明 Chén Míng does not run fast (that is, that he is not a fast runner), insert 不 bù before the adjectival verb.

张美丽唱得**不好**。· 張美麗唱得**不好**。
Zhāng Měilì chàng de **bù hǎo**.
Zhang Meili doesn't sing well. (lit., *Zhang Meili sings **not well**.*)

陈明跑得**不快**。· 陳明跑得**不快**。
Chén Míng pǎo de **bù kuài**.
Chen Ming doesn't run fast. (lit., *Cheng Ming runs **not fast**.*)

Oral Practice

Read aloud the following statements of 小王 Xiǎo Wáng about 小李 Xiǎo Lǐ, then say the opposite.

EXAMPLE   小王   小李跑得不快。
                Xiǎo Lǐ pǎo de bù kuài.
                Xiao Li does not run quickly.
       You   小李跑得很快。
                Xiǎo Lǐ pǎo de hěn kuài.
                Xiao Li runs quickly.

小王	You
1. 小李学得很好。 小李學得很好。 Xiǎo Lǐ xué de hěn hǎo. *Little Li studies very well.*	→ 小李学得不好。 小李學得不好。 Xiǎo Lǐ xué de bù hǎo. *Little Li doesn't study well.* (lit., *studies not well*)
2. 小李唱得不好听。 小李唱得不好聽。 Xiǎo Lǐ chàng de bù hǎo tīng. *Little Li sings unpleasantly.*	→ 小李唱得很好听。 小李唱得很好聽。 Xiǎo Lǐ chàng de hěn hǎo tīng. *Little Li sings very pleasantly.*
3. 小李说得很准。 小李說得很準。 Xiǎo Lǐ shuō de hěn zhǔn. *Little Li speaks very accurately.*	→ 小李说得不准。 小李說得不準。 Xiǎo Lǐ shuō de bù zhǔn. *Little Li speaks inaccurately.*
4. 小李走得不快。 Xiǎo Lǐ zǒu de bù kuài. *Little Li doesn't walk quickly.* (lit., *walks not quickly*)	→ 小李走得很快。 Xiǎo Lǐ zǒu de hěn kuài. *Little Li walks very quickly.*

Written Practice 20-1

Write a complete Mandarin sentence, using each of the following pairs of words to indicate how 小白 Xiǎo Bái generally performs an activity.

1. 说·說 shuō *talk* – 慢 màn *slowly*

_____

2. 吃 chī *eat* – 快 kuài *fast*

_____

3. 写·寫 xiě *write* – 清楚 qīngchu *clearly*

_____

4. 画·畫 huà *paint* – 好 hǎo *well*

_____

5. 睡 shuì *sleep* – 多 duō *a lot*

_____

Describing an Action When There Is an Object Noun Phrase

To include an object noun phrase in a description (as in *my younger sister eats cookies very fast*), add the phrase to the sentence by using the action verb twice, once followed by the object and once followed by 得 de + Adjectival Verb.

[Action Verb + Object] + [Action Verb + 得 de] + Adjectival Verb

张美丽唱歌唱得很好。· 張美麗唱歌唱得很好。
Zhāng Měilì **chàng** gē **chàng** de hěn hǎo.
Zhang Meili sings songs very well.

陈明说法国话说得很慢。· 陳明說法國話說得很慢。
Chén Míng **shuō** Fǎguó huà **shuō** de hěn màn.
Chen Ming speaks French very slowly.

Written Practice 20-2

Rewrite each of the following sentences, adding the description in parentheses to indicate how the action is performed, and matching the English sentence.

1. 小陈跑步。(慢) · 小陳跑步。(慢)
   Xiǎo Chén pǎo bù. (màn)
   Little Chen runs very slowly.

   _____

2. 小陈唱歌。(好听) · 小陳唱歌。(好聽)
   Xiǎo Chén chàng gē. (hǎotīng)
   Little Chen sings prettily.

   _____

3. 小陈跳舞。(很好) · 小陳跳舞。(很好)
   Xiǎo Chén tiào wǔ. (hěn hǎo)
   Little Chen dances well.

   _____

4. 小陈写汉字。(很快) · 小陳寫漢字。(很快)
   Xiǎo Chén xiě Hànzì. (hěn kuài)
   Little Chen writes Chinese characters quickly.

   _____

5. 小陈打球。(很多) · 小陳打球。(很多)
   Xiǎo Chén dǎ qiú. (hěn duō)
   Little Chen plays ball a lot.

   _____

Negation words always come before the adjectival verb. To say that 张美丽 · 張美麗 Zhāng Měilì does not sing songs well, or that 陈明 · 陳明 Chén Míng does not speak French slowly, use the following sentences.

张美丽唱歌唱得**不好**。· 張美麗唱歌唱得**不好**。
Zhāng Měilì chàng gē chàng de **bù hǎo**.
Zhang Meili does not sing songs well. (lit., *sings songs **not well***)

陈明说法国话说得**不慢**。· 陳明說法國話說得**不慢**。
Chén Míng shuō Fǎguó huà shuō de **bù màn**.
Chen Ming does not speak French slowly. (lit., *speaks French **not slowly***)

Oral Practice

In Chinese culture, you do not thank someone who compliments you. Instead, you find a way to reject or deflect the praise. Read each of the following compliments aloud. Then deflect the praise by saying that you do not have that quality. In your reply, omit the object, which is in bold type.

1. 你说**中文**说得很好。   → 我说得不好。
   你說**中文**說得很好。   我說得不好。
   Nǐ shuō **Zhōngwén** shuō de hěn hǎo. Wǒ shuō de bù hǎo.
   *You speak **Chinese** very well.*

2. 你写**字**写得很好看。   → 我写得不好看。
   你寫**字**寫得很好看。   我寫得不好看。
   Nǐ xiě **zì** xiě de hěn hǎokàn.   Wǒ xiě de bù hǎokàn.
   *You write **characters** nicely.*

3. 你唱**歌**唱得很好听。   → 我唱得不好听。
   你唱**歌**唱得很好聽。   我唱得不好聽。
   Nǐ chàng **gē** chàng de hěn hǎotīng. Wǒ chàng de bù hǎotīng.
   You sing very pleasantly.

4. 你做**饭**做得很好吃。   → 我做得不好吃。
   你做**飯**做得很好吃。
   Nǐ zuò **fàn** zuò de hěn hǎo chī. Wǒ zuò de bù hǎo chī.
   You cook deliciously.
      (i.e., *You cook delicious **food**.*)

5. 你打**球**打得很好。   → 我打得不好。
   Nǐ dǎ **qiú** dǎ de hěn hǎo. Wǒ dǎ de bù hǎo.
   *You play **ball** very well.*

Asking How Someone Performs an Action

If you want to know how someone performs an action and you have no expectations about the answer, use the question phrase 怎么样·怎麼樣 zěnmeyàng *how about it* (see Chapter 15).

他做饭做得怎么样？· 他做飯做得怎麼樣？
Tā zuò fàn zuò de zěnmeyàng?
How does he cook?

她打球打得怎么样？· 她打球打得怎麼樣？
Tā dǎ qiú dǎ de zěnmeyàng?
How does she play ball?

她唱歌唱得怎么样？· 她唱歌唱得怎麼樣？
Tā chàng gē chàng de zěnmeyàng?
How does she sing?

Oral Practice

For each of the following activities, compose a Mandarin sentence asking how 小王 Xiǎo Wáng performs the activity. Then read the question aloud.

1. 说英文
   說英文
   shuō Yīngwén
   speak English
   → 小王说英文说得怎么样？
   小王說英文說得怎麼樣？
   Xiǎo Wáng shuō Yīngwén shuō de zěnmeyàng?

2. 打球
   dǎ qiú
   play ball
   → 小王打球打得怎么样？
   小王打球打得怎麼樣？
   Xiǎo Wáng dǎ qiú dǎ de zěnmeyàng?

3. 写字
   寫字
   xiě zì
   write characters
   → 小王写字写得怎么样？
   小王寫字寫得怎麼樣？
   Xiǎo Wáng xiě zì xiě de zěnmeyàng?

4. 跳舞
   tiào wǔ
   dance
   → 小王跳舞跳得怎么样？
   小王跳舞跳得怎麼樣？
   Xiǎo Wáng tiào wǔ tiào de zěnmeyàng?

To ask if someone performs an action *fast/well*/etc. or not, use one of the following constructions. (To review yes-no questions in Mandarin, see Chapter 14.)

Verb-Not-Verb Question

Subject (+ Verb + Object) + Verb + 得 de + Adjectival Verb + 不 bù + Adjectival Verb

他画画儿画得**好不好**？·他畫畫兒畫得**好不好**？

Tā huà huàr huà de **hǎo bù hǎo**?

Does he paint well?

吗·嗎 ma Question

Subject (+ Verb + Object) + Verb + 得 de + Adjectival Verb + 吗·嗎 ma

她说中文说得**准吗**？·她說中文說得**準嗎**？

Tā shuō Zhōngwén shuō de **zhǔn ma**?

Does she speak Chinese accurately?

Written Practice 20-3

Write a Mandarin question from each of the following groups of phrases, using the question form in parentheses to match the English question.

1. 他 – 开车 – 慢·他 – 開車 – 慢 (吗·嗎 ma question)

   tā – kāi chē – màn

   Does he drive slowly?

   _____

2. 你 – 考试 – 好·你 – 考試 – 好 (吗·嗎 ma question)

   nǐ – kǎo shì – hǎo

   Did you do well on the test?

   _____

3. 她 – 喝咖啡 – 多 (Verb-Not-Verb question)

   tā – hē kāfēi – duō

   Does she drink a lot of coffee?

   _____

4. 她 – 睡觉 – 少 · 她 – 睡覺 – 少 (吗 · 嗎 ma question)
   tā – shuì jiào – shǎo
   Does she sleep a small amount?

   _____

5. 你 – 跑步 – 快 (Verb-Not-Verb question)
   nǐ – pǎo bù – kuài
   Do you jog fast?

   _____

Describing How Someone Performs a Specific Action

In describing the performance of a specific action at a specific time, the adjectival verb comes before the action verb. In this construction, note that the particle that follows the adjectival verb is written 地 and pronounced de.

Adjectival Verb + 地 de + Action Verb

   This construction is used to describe a specific event in the past.

他不停地说话。· 他不停地說話。
Tā bùtíng de shuō huà.
He talked continuously.

It may also be used to give advice or a suggestion.

你得很努力地学习。· 你得很努力地學習。
Nǐ děi hěn nǔlì de xuéxí.
You should study hard.

It may also be used to give a command.

认真地回答每一个问题！· 認真地回答每一個問題！
Rènzhēn de huídá měi yī gè wèntí!
Conscientiously answer every question!

When used in this construction, the adjectival verb typically has two or more syllables, as in the examples above. Additional examples follow.

仔细·仔細 zǐxì   *meticulously, in detail*
安静 ānjìng   *quietly, peacefully*
用心 yòngxīn   *attentively, carefully*
不知不觉·不知不覺 bùzhī bùjué   *unaware, without thinking about it*
无意·無意 wúyì   *unintentionally*

Oral Practice

For each of the following sentences, add the adverbial word or phrase in parentheses to match the English sentence, then read the new sentence aloud.

1. 学生听老师说话。(用心)   → 学生用心地听老师说话。
   学生聽老師說話。(用心)   學生用心地聽老師說話。
   Xuésheng tīng lǎoshī shuō huà.   Xuésheng yòngxīn de tīng lǎoshī shuō
   (yòngxīn)   huà.
                                The students attentively listened to
                                  the teacher talking.

2. 孩子听了音乐。(安静)   → 孩子安静地听了音乐。
   孩子聽了音樂。(安靜)   孩子安靜地聽了音樂。
   Háizi tīng le yīnyuè. (ānjìng)   Háizi ānjìng de tīng le yīnyuè.
                                    The children quietly listened to
                                  music.

3. 他哭起来了。(不知不觉)   → 他不知不觉地哭起来了。
   他哭起來了。(不知不覺)   他不知不覺地哭起來了。
   Tā kū qǐlái le. (bùzhī bùjué)   Tā bùzhī bùjué de kūqǐlái le.
                                    He began to cry without being
                                  aware of it.

When used in this construction, one-syllable adjectival verbs must be *reduplicated* (repeated), sometimes with a tone change, sometimes with the addition of a final *r*. Since reduplicated adjectival verbs are always followed by 地 de, we present them with 地 de in the following list.

好 hǎo → 好好地·好好地 hǎohāo de *carefully, well*
好好地听老师吧！·好好兒地聽老師吧！
Hǎohāo de tīng lǎoshī ba!
Listen carefully to the teacher!

偷 tōu → 偷偷地 tōutou de *secretly*
他偷偷地走出去了。
Tā tōutou de zǒuchūqu le.
He secretly snuck out.

慢 màn → 慢慢儿地·慢慢兒地 mànmān(r) de *slowly*
她慢慢儿地把她的名字写下来了。·
她慢慢兒地把她的名字寫下來了。
Tā mànmān(r) de bǎ tā de míngzi xiě xiàlai le.
She slowly wrote her name.

快 kuài → 快快地 kuàikuāi de *quickly*
他快快地跑进来了。·他快快地跑進來了。
Tā kuàikuāi de pǎo jìnlái le.
He ran in quickly.

Oral Practice

For each of the following sentences, add the adverbial phrase in parentheses to match the English sentence, then read the new sentence aloud.

1. 他们走回家了。(慢慢地)   → 他们慢慢地走回家了。
   他們走回家了。(慢慢地)   他們慢慢地走回家了。
   Tāmen zǒu huí jiā le. (mànmān de)   Tāmen mànmān de zǒu huí jiā le.
                                        They slowly walked home.

2. 他看了那本书。(偷偷地)   → 他偷偷地看了那本书。
   他看了那本書。(偷偷地)   他偷偷地看了那本書。
   Tā kàn le nà běn shū. (tōutōu de)   Tā tōutōu de kàn le nà běn shū.
                                        He secretly read that book.

3. 他们吃了晚饭。(快快地)   → 他们快快地吃了晚饭。
   他們吃了晚飯。(快快地)   他們快快地吃了晚飯。
   Tāmen chī le wǎnfàn. (kuàikuāi de) Tāmen kuàikuāi de chī le wǎnfàn.
                                        They quickly ate dinner.

Some two-syllable adjectival verbs have special reduplicated forms.

高兴 · 高興 gāoxìng → 高高兴兴 · 高高興興 gāogāo xìngxìng *happy*
他们高高兴兴地玩儿了一天。·
他們高高興興地玩兒了一天。
Tāmen gāogāo xìngxìng de wár le yītiān.
They played happily the entire day.

清楚 qīngchu → 清清楚楚 qīngqīng chǔchǔ *clearly*
请把你的意见清清楚楚地说出来。·
請把你的意見清清楚楚地說出來。
Qǐng bǎ nǐ de yìjian qīngqīng chǔchǔ de shuōchulai.
Please state your opinions clearly.

Written Practice 20-4

For each of the following actions, write a Mandarin sentence about 小张 · 小張 Xiǎo Zhāng, using the appropriate adverbial phrase to match the English sentence.

1. 听音乐 · 聽音樂 tīng yīnyuè
*Little Zhang listens to music **nonstop**.*

   _____

2. 准备功课 · 準備功課 zhǔnbèi gōngkè
*Little Zhang **diligently** prepared the lesson.*

   _____

3. 喝酒 hē jiǔ
*Little Zhang **secretly** drank alcohol.*

   _____

4. 做作业 · 做作業 zuò zuòyè
*Little Zhang did his homework **carefully**.*

   _____

5. 睡觉 · 睡覺 shuì jiào
*Little Zhang fell asleep **without being aware of it**.*

   _____

QUIZ

Rewrite each of the following sentences, adding the phrase in parentheses to match the English sentence.

1. 她写汉字。(很美) · 她寫漢字。(很美)
   Tā xiě Hànzì. (hěn měi)
   She writes Chinese characters very beautifully.

   _____

2. 他开车。(很慢) · 他開車。(很慢)
   Tā kāi chē. (hěn màn)
   He drives very slowly.

   _____

3. 我弟弟吃饭。(太快) · 我弟弟吃飯。(太快)
   Wǒ dìdi chī fàn. (tài kuài)
   My younger brother eats too fast.

   _____

Reply to each of the following compliments, saying that you do not have that quality.

4. 你做饭做得很好。· 你做飯做得很好。
   Nǐ zuò fàn zuò de hěn hǎo.
   You cook very well.

   _____

5. 你跑步跑得很快。
   Nǐ pǎo bù pǎo de hěn kuài.
   You run very fast.

   _____

6. 你唱歌唱得很好听。· 你唱歌唱得很好聽。
   Nǐ chàng gē chàng de hěn hǎotīng.
   You sing very well.

   _____

Rearrange each of the following groups of phrases into a complete Mandarin sentence, matching the English sentence.

7. 快快地 – 孩子 – 跑 – 去 – 到公园 – 了
   快快地 – 孩子 – 跑 – 去 – 到公園 – 了
   kuàikuāi de – háizi – pǎo – qù – dào gōngyuán – le
   The children quickly ran to the park.

   _____

8. 说 – 说话 – 小孩子 – 很快 – 得
   說 – 說話 – 小孩子 – 很快 – 得
   shuō – shuō huà – xiǎo háizi – hěn kuài – de
   Children speak very quickly.

   _____

9. 写信 – 给 – 他 – 他的女朋友 – 偷偷地
   寫信 – 給 – 他 – 他的女朋友 – 偷偷地
   xiě xìn – gěi – tā – tā de nǚ péngyou – tōutōu de
   He secretly writes letters to his girlfriend.

   _____

10. 高高兴兴地 – 她 – 看了 – 信 – 的 – 男朋友
    高高興興地 – 她 – 看了 – 信 – 的 – 男朋友
    gāogāoxìngxìng de – tā – kàn le – xìn – de – nán péngyou
    She happily read her boyfriend's letter.

    _____

CHAPTER 21

Making Comparisons

In this chapter, you will learn about:

Indicating More Than: *Comparison with* 比 bǐ

Indicating Less Than: *Comparison with* 没有 méi yǒu

Indicating The Same As: *Comparison with* 一样·一樣 yīyàng

There are three types of comparison.

- **More than.** Something is *better/faster/more numerous/etc. than* something else, or some action is performed *better/faster/etc. than* some other action.

- **Less than.** Something is *not as good/fast/much/etc. as* something else, or some action is *not* performed *as well/fast/much/etc. as* some other action.

- **The same as.** Something is *the same as* something else, or two actions are performed *in the same way*.

Indicating *More Than*: Comparison with 比 bǐ

The comparison word 比 bǐ *compared to* is used to indicate the relationship *more than*. Following is the basic structure of a comparison sentence with 比 bǐ.

A 比 bǐ B AV

In this construction and throughout the chapter, **A** and **B** are nouns or noun phrases that are being compared. Note that comparisons with 比 bǐ always end in an adjectival verb (AV). Also note that Mandarin has no distinct *comparative* forms for adjectival verbs, unlike English, which has comparative forms like *good*:**better**, *fast*:**faster**, *big*:**bigger**. In Mandarin, the construction of the sentence—not the form of the words—conveys the comparison.

To compare two people, places, or things—Noun Phrase₁ (NP₁) and Noun Phrase₂ (NP₂)—indicating that the first one has *more* of some quality than the second one, use the following construction.

NP₁ 比 bǐ NP₂ AV
我比你高。
Wǒ bǐ nǐ gāo.
I am taller than you.
　　(lit., *I compared to you tall.*)
中国比日本大。· 中國比日本大。
Zhōngguó bǐ Rìběn dà.
China is bigger than Japan.
　　(lit., *China compared to Japan big.*)

电视比电脑贵。· 電視比電腦貴。
Diànshì bǐ diànnǎo guì.
Televisions are more expensive than computers.
   (lit., *Television compared to computer expensive.*)

Written Practice 21-1

Translate the following sentences into Mandarin, using the construction above.

1. 小高 Xiǎo Gāo *is smarter than* 小王 Xiǎo Wáng.

   _____

2. 小高 Xiǎo Gāo *is more hardworking than* 小王 Xiǎo Wáng.

   _____

3. 小高 Xiǎo Gāo *is happier than* 小王 Xiǎo Wáng.

   _____

4. 小高 Xiǎo Gāo *is more tired than* 小王 Xiǎo Wáng.

   _____

INDICATING *A LOT MORE*

In comparison constructions, the adjectival verb is never preceded by the intensifier 很 hěn (see Chapter 7). To indicate that one person, place, or thing has *a lot more* of the quality of the adjectival verb than another, insert 得多 de duō *a lot* after the adjectival verb.

中文比法文难得多。· 中文比法文難的多。
Zhōngwén bǐ Fǎwén nán de duō.
Chinese is a lot more difficult than French.

中国比日本大得多。· 中國比日本大得多。
Zhōngguó bǐ Rìběn dà de duō.
China is a lot bigger than Japan.

Oral Practice

Read each of the following sentences aloud, then translate the phrase in bold type into English.

1. 小王比小高**高得多**。 → *a lot taller*
   Xiǎo Wáng bǐ Xiǎo Gāo **gāo de duō**.

2. 你的字典比我的字典**大得多**。 → *a lot bigger*
   Nǐ de zìdiǎn bǐ wǒ de zìdiǎn **dà de duō**.

3. 王老师的考试比高老师的考试**难得多**。 → *a lot harder*
   王老師的考試比高老師的考試**難得多**。
   Wáng lǎoshī de kǎoshì bǐ Gāo lǎoshī
        de kǎoshì **nán de duō**.

4. 小高比小王**快得多**。 → *a lot faster*
   Xiǎo Gāo bǐ Xiǎo Wáng **kuài de duō**.

INDICATING *A LITTLE MORE*

To indicate that one person, place, or thing has *a little more* of the quality of the adjectival verb than another, insert 一点 · 一點 yīdiǎn *a little* after the adjectival verb.

我比你高一点。 · 我比你高一點。
Wǒ bǐ nǐ gāo yīdiǎn.
I am a little taller than you.

电视比电脑贵一点。 · 電視比電腦貴一點。
Diànshì bǐ diànnǎo guì yīdiǎn.
Televisions are a little more expensive than computers.

Written Practice 21-2

Translate the following sentences into Mandarin. Be sure to put the adjectival verb followed by 一点 · 一點 yīdiǎn at the end of the sentence.

1. 小王 Xiǎo Wáng *is a little taller than* 小高 Xiǎo Gāo.

   _____

2. 小王 Xiǎo Wáng *is a little faster than* 小高 Xiǎo Gāo.

   _____

3. 小王 Xiǎo Wáng *is a little happier than* 小高 Xiǎo Gāo.

   _____

4. 小王 Xiǎo Wáng *is a little busier than* 小高 Xiǎo Gāo.

   _____

INDICATING *EVEN MORE* WITH 更 gèng

The intensifier 更 gèng *even more* is inserted before the adjectival verb to add the meaning *even more* to a comparison.

哥哥比弟弟高。爸爸更高。
Gēge bǐ dìdi gāo. Bàba gèng gāo.
Older brother is taller than younger brother. Dad is even taller.

更 gèng can produce a comparison when it occurs in a sentence that follows a simple statement of fact. In the following example, the first sentence is such a statement of fact.

公共汽车快。地铁更快。· 公共汽車快。地鐵更快。
Gōnggòng qìchē kuài. Dìtiě gèng kuài.
Buses are fast. Subways are even faster.

Written Practice 21-3

Translate the English sentences in bold italic type into Mandarin, thereby completing the comparisons.

1. 小王的朋友很多。
   Xiǎo Wáng de péngyou hěn duō.
   Little Wang has a lot of friends. ***Little Li has even more friends.***

   _____

2. 林老师的考试比王老师的考试难。· 林老師的考試比王老師的考試難。
   Lín lǎoshī de kǎoshì bǐ Wáng lǎoshī de kǎoshì nán.
   Professor Lin's tests are harder than Professor Wang's tests.
        Professor Zhang's tests are even harder.

   _____

3. 小白很漂亮。
   Xiǎo Bái hěn piàoliang.
   Little Bai is very pretty. ***Little Li is even prettier.***

   _____

4. 这本书很长。· 這本書很長。
   Zhè běn shū hěn cháng.
   This book is very long. ***That book is even longer.***

   _____

INDICATING *MORE THAN* WITH ACTIONS

When comparing actions, the construction used has a number of variations, as follows.

Comparing the Performance of Actions Without the Object Included

To indicate that someone (some NP) performs one action (V_1) *better/faster/more/etc.* *than* another action (V_2), use the following construction.

NP [V₁ 得 de] 比 bǐ [V₂ 得 de] AV
她 [写得] 比 [说得] 好。· 她 [寫得] 比 [說得] 好。
Tā [xiě de] bǐ [shuō de] hǎo.
She writes better than she speaks.

To indicate that one person (NP₁) performs an action *better/faster/more/etc. than* another person (NP₂), use the following construction.

NP₁ 比 bǐ NP₂ [V 得 de] AV

她比我 [吃得] 多。
Tā bǐ wǒ [chī de] duō.
She eats more than I do.

Comparing the Performance of Actions with the Object Included

If the object of the verb is included in the comparison, the verb is stated twice, once followed by the object and once followed by 得 de.

NP [V O] [V 得 de] AV

O here designates the object. For a detailed discussion of this construction, see Chapter 20.

To indicate that a person (NP) performs one action (V₁) *better/faster/more/ etc. than* another action (V₂), use the following construction.

NP [V₁ O] [V₁ 得 de] 比 bǐ [V₂ O] [V₂ 得 de] AV

她 [写中文] [写得] 比 [说中国话] [说得] 好。 ·
她 [寫中文] [寫得] 比 [說中國話] [說得] 好。
Tā [xiě Zhōngwén] [xiě de] bǐ [shuō Zhōngguó huà] [shuō de] hǎo.
She writes Chinese better than she speaks Chinese.

To compare two different objects, use the following construction.

NP O₁ 比 bǐ O₂ [V 得 de] AV

他 [中国电影] 比 [美国电影] 看得多。 ·
他 [中國電影] 比 [美國電影] 看得多。
Tā [Zhōngguó diànyǐng] bǐ [Měiguó diànyǐng] kàn de duō.
He watches Chinese movies more than American movies.

To indicate that one person (NP₁) performs some action (V) *better/faster/ more*/etc. *than* another person (NP₂), use the following construction.

NP₁ 比 bǐ NP₂ [V O] [V 得 de] AV

他比我吃中国饭吃得多。· 他比我吃中國飯吃得多。

Tā bǐ wǒ chī Zhōngguó fàn chī de duō.

She eats more Chinese food than I do.

The [V O V 得 de] phrase may also come before 比 bǐ.

他吃中国饭吃得比我多。· 他吃中國飯吃得比我多。

Tā chī Zhōngguó fàn chī de bǐ wǒ duō.

She eats more Chinese food than I do.

Written Practice 21-4

Write a comparison sentence from each of the following groups of phrases to match the English sentence. For questions 1, 2, and 4, objects can be compared in a shortened version.

1. 做意大利菜 zuò Yìdàlì cài *cook Italian food*
   做中国菜·做中國菜 zuò Zhōngguó cài *cook Chinese food*
   好 hǎo *well*
   He cooks Italian food better than he cooks Chinese food.

   _____

2. 学中文·學中文 xué Zhōngwén *study Chinese*
   学日文·學日文 xué Rìwén *study Japanese*
   多 duō *a lot*
   She has studied Chinese more than she has studied Japanese.

   _____

3. 吃饺子·吃餃子 chī jiǎozi *eat dumplings*
   包饺子·包餃子 bāo jiǎozi *make dumplings*
   快 kuài *fast*
   He eats dumplings faster than he makes them.

   _____

4. 喝可乐·喝可樂 hē kělè *drink cola*
   喝水 hē shuǐ *drink water*
   多 duō *a lot*
   She drinks more cola than water.

---

5. 写字·寫字 xiě zì *write*
   说话·說話 shuō huà *speak*
   慢 màn *slowly*
   She writes more slowly than she speaks.

Indicating *Less Than*: Comparison with 没有méi yǒu

没有méi yǒu, like 比 bǐ, can be used to compare noun phrases (people, places, and things) or verb phrases (actions).

COMPARING NOUN PHRASES

To compare two people, places, or things—Noun Phrase₁ (NP₁) and Noun Phrase₂ (NP₂)—indicating that the first one *does not have as much* of some quality as the second one, use the following construction.

NP₁ 没有 méi yǒu NP₂ AV
你没有我高。
Nǐ méi yǒu wǒ gāo.
You are not as tall as I am.
   (lit., *You not as I tall.*)
日本没有中国大。· 日本沒有中國大。
Rìběn méi yǒu Zhōngguó dà.
Japan is not as big as China.
   (lit., *Japan not as China big.*)

电脑没有电视贵。· 電腦沒有電視貴。
Diànnǎo méi yǒu diànshì guì.
Computers are not as expensive as televisions.
  (lit., *Computer not as television expensive.*)

Written Practice 21-5

Translate the following sentences into Mandarin.

1. 小高 Xiǎo Gāo *is not as lazy as* 小王 Xiǎo Wáng.

   _____

2. 小高 Xiǎo Gāo *is not as slow as* 小王 Xiǎo Wáng.

   _____

3. 小王 Xiǎo Wáng *is not as short as* 小高 Xiǎo Gāo.

   _____

4. 小王 Xiǎo Wáng *is not as smart as* 小高 Xiǎo Gāo.

   _____

USING 这么·這麽 zhème AND 那么·那麽 nàme IN COMPARISONS

The expressions 这么·這麽 zhème *this* and 那么·那麽 nàme *that* often occur in 没有 méi yǒu comparison sentences, right before the adjectival verb. They are used to compare both noun phrases and actions.

这么·這麽 zhème is used when the second item that you are comparing is present at the time you are speaking. For example, if you are eating Chinese food, you could say the following sentence.

美国饭没有中国饭这么好吃。· 美國飯沒有中國飯這麽好吃。
Měiguó fàn méi yǒu Zhōngguó fàn zhème hǎo chī.
American food is not as delicious as Chinese food.

Think of this sentence as *American food is not, compared to Chinese food,* this *good.*

If you are traveling in Shanghai, you could say the following sentence.

北京没有上海这么贵。· 北京没有上海這麼貴。
Běijīng méi yǒu Shànghǎi zhème guì.
Beijing is not as expensive as Shanghai.

Think of this sentence as *Beijing is not, compared to Shanghai,* this *expensive.*

那么·那麼 nàme is used when neither of the items that you are comparing is present at the time you are speaking. For example, if you are comparing 小王 Xiǎo Wáng and 小白 Xiǎo Bái and neither of them is with you, you could say the following sentence.

小王没有小白那么聪明。· 小王没有小白那麼聰明。
Xiǎo Wáng méi yǒu Xiǎo Bái nàme cōngming.
Little Wang is not as smart as Little Bai.

Written Practice 21-6

Rewrite each of the following sentences, adding the expression 这么·這麼 zhème or 那么·那麼 nàme, as indicated. Then translate the sentence into English.

1. 自行车没有公共汽车快。(那么) · 自行車没有公共汽車快。(那麼)
   Zìxíngchē méi yǒu gōnggòng qìchē kuài. (nàme)

   _____

2. 小高没有小王用功。(那么) · 小高没有小王用功。(那麼)
   Xiǎo Gāo méi yǒu Xiǎo Wáng yònggōng. (nàme)

   _____

3. 那个电影没有这个电影有意思。(这么) ·
   那個電影没有這個電影有意思。(這麼)
   Nàge diànyǐng méi yǒu zhège diànyǐng yǒu yìsi. (zhème)

   _____

4. 茶没有咖啡贵。(那么) · 茶没有咖啡貴。(那麼)
   Chá méi yǒu kāfēi guì. (nàme)

   _____

INDICATING *LESS THAN* WITH ACTIONS

As is the case with 比 bǐ, the construction used in comparisons with 没有 méi yǒu differs, depending on whether an object is included or not.

Comparisons with 没有 méi yǒu Without the Object Included

To indicate that someone (some NP) does *not* perform one action (V_1) *as well/fast/much/etc. as* another action (V_2), use the following construction.

NP [V_1 得 de] 没有 méi yǒu [V_2 得 de] AV

她写得没有说得好。· 她寫得沒有說得好。
Tā xiě de méi yǒu shuō de hǎo.
She does not write as well as she speaks.
  (lit., *She writes not as well as she speaks.*)

To indicate that one person (NP_1) does *not* perform an action *as well/fast/much/etc. as* another person (NP_2), use the following construction.

NP_1 没有 méi yǒu NP_2 [V 得 de] AV

她没有她妹妹说得快。· 她沒有她妹妹說得快。
Tā méi yǒu tā mèimei shuō de kuài.
She does not speak as fast as her younger sister.

Comparisons with 没有 méi yǒu with the Object Included

As is the case with 比 bǐ, when the object is included in a comparison with 没有 méi yǒu, the verb is stated twice, once followed by the object and once followed by 得 de.

To indicate that someone (some NP) does *not* perform one action (V_1) *as well/fast/much/etc. as* another action (V_2), use the following construction.

NP [V_1 O] [V_1 得 de] 没有 méi yǒu [V_2 O] [V_2 得 de] AV

她 [写中文] [写得] 没有 [说中国话] [说得] 好。·
她 [寫中文] [寫得] 沒有 [說中國話] [說得] 好。
Tā [xiě Zhōngwén] [xiě de] méi yǒu [shuō Zhōngguó huà] [shuō de] hǎo.
She doesn't write Chinese as well as she speaks Chinese.
  (lit., *She writes Chinese not as well as she speaks Chinese.*)

To indicate that one person (NP₁) does not perform an action (V) *as well/fast/much/etc. as* another person (NP₂), use the following construction.

NP₁ 没有 méi yǒu NP₂ [V O] [V 得 de] AV

她没有她妹妹说中国话说得快。· 她没有她妹妹說中國話說得快。
Tā méi yǒu tā mèimei shuō Zhōngguó huà shuō de kuài.
She does not speak Chinese as fast as her younger sister.

As is the case when comparing people, places, and things, it is possible to insert 这么·這麼 zhème or 那么·那麼 nàme before the adjectival verb (see Chapter 7).

他吃中国饭没有吃美国饭吃得**这么**快。·
他吃中國飯沒有吃美國飯吃得**這麼**快。
Tā chī Zhōngguó fàn méi yǒu chī Měiguó fàn chī de **zhème** kuài.
He doesn't eat Chinese food as fast (like this) as American food.

她写中文写得没有说中国话说得**那么**好。·
她寫中文寫得沒有說中國話說得**那麼**好。
Tā xiě Zhōngwén xiě de méi yǒu shuō Zhōngguó huà shuō de **nàme** hǎo.
She doesn't write Chinese as well as she speaks Chinese.

她没有她妹妹喝咖啡喝得**那么**多。· 她沒有她妹妹喝咖啡喝得**那麼**多。
Tā méi yǒu tā mèimei hē kāfēi hē de **nàme** duō.
She doesn't drink as much coffee as her younger sister.

Written Practice 21-7

Write a comparison sentence with 没有 méi yǒu from each of the following groups of phrases, matching the English sentence. Include 那么·那麼 nàme in each sentence. The answers in the Answer Key show the construction in which the entire actions are compared.

1. 看中国电影·看中國電影 kàn Zhōngguó diànyǐng *watch Chinese movies*
   看美国电影·看美國電影 kàn Měiguó diànyǐng *watch American movies*
   多 duō *a lot, much*
   She doesn't watch Chinese movies as much as American movies.

   _____

2. 吃中国饭·吃中國飯 chī Zhōngguó fàn *eat Chinese food*
   吃美国饭·吃美國飯 chī Měiguó fàn *eat American food*
   多 duō *a lot, much*
   They don't eat Chinese food as much as they eat American food.

---

3. 喝茶 hē chá *drink tea*
   喝咖啡 hē kāfēi *drink coffee*
   多 duō *a lot, much*
   He doesn't drink tea as much as he drinks coffee.

---

4. 看电视·看電視 kàn diànshì *watch televison*
   听音乐·聽音樂 tīng yīnyuè *listen to music*
   多 duō *a lot, much*
   I don't watch television as much as I listen to music.

---

5. 说中文·說中文 shuō Zhōngwén *speak Chinese*
   说英文·說英文 shuō Yīngwén *speak English*
   快 kuài *fast*
   He doesn't speak Chinese as fast as he speaks English.

Indicating *The Same As*: Comparison with 一样·一樣 yīyàng

The comparison word 一样·一樣 yīyàng is used to indicate the relationship *the same as*. Following are the basic structures of comparison sentences with 一样·一樣 yīyàng.

A 跟 gēn / 和 hé *B* 一样·一樣 yīyàng
A and B are the same.

A 跟 gēn / 和 hé *B* 一样·一樣 yīyàng AV
A and B have the same quality.

Either 跟 gēn or 和 hé may be used in this construction; they are equivalent in meaning.

INDICATING THAT TWO THINGS ARE THE SAME

To indicate that two people, places, or things are the same, use one of the following constructions.

NP₁ 跟 gēn NP₂ 一样·一樣 yīyàng
NP₁ 和 hé NP₂ 一样·一樣 yīyàng

这本书跟那本书 一样。· 這本書 跟那本書一樣。
Zhè běn shū gēn nà běn shū yīyàng.
This book and that book are the same.

我的鞋子和你的鞋子一样。· 我的鞋子和你的鞋子一樣。
Wǒ de xiézi hé nǐ de xiézi yīyàng.
My shoes and your shoes are the same.

Oral Practice

For each of the following pairs of items, write a Mandarin sentence stating that the items in the pair are the same.

1. 五十分 wǔshí fēn *50 pennies*
   五毛 wǔ máo *5 dimes*
   → 五十分跟五毛一样。· 五十分跟五毛一樣。
      Wǔshí fēn gēn wǔ máo yīyàng.

2. 半个小时·半個小時 bàn ge xiǎoshí *half an hour*
   半个钟头·半個鐘頭 bàn ge zhōngtóu *half an hour*
   → 半个小时和半个钟头一样。· 半個小時和半個鐘頭一樣。
      Bàn ge xiǎoshí hé bàn ge zhōngtóu yīyàng.

3. 上午九点钟·上午九點鐘 shàngwǔ jiǔ diǎn zhōng *9 A.M.*
   早上九点钟·早上九點鐘 zǎoshang jiǔ diǎn zhōng *9 o'clock in the morning*
   → 上午九点钟跟早上九点钟一样。· 上午九點鐘跟早上九點鐘一樣。
      Shàngwǔ jiǔ diǎn zhōng gēn zǎoshang jiǔ diǎn zhōng yīyàng.

To indicate that two things are not the same, use 不一样·不一樣 bù yīyàng.

我的鞋子和你的鞋子不一样。· 我的鞋子和你的鞋子不一樣。
Wǒ de xiézi hé nǐ de xiézi bù yīyàng.
My shoes and your shoes are not the same.

Written Practice 21-8

For each of the following pairs of items, write a Mandarin sentence stating that the items are not the same.

1. 日本饭·日本飯 Rìběn fàn *Japanese food*
   中国饭·中國飯 Zhōngguó fàn *Chinese food*

   _____

2. 棒球 bàngqiú *baseball*
   足球 zúqiú *football*

   _____

3. 北京 Běijīng *Beijing*
   南京 Nánjīng *Nanjing*

   _____

INDICATING THAT TWO THINGS ARE THE SAME IN A SPECIFIC WAY

To indicate that two people, places, or things are the same in a specific way, use one of the following constructions. Note that the shared quality is always expressed as an adjectival verb.

NP₁ 跟 gēn NP₂ 一样·一樣 yīyàng AV
NP₁ 和 hé NP₂ 一样·一樣 yīyàng AV

公共汽车票跟地铁票一样贵。· 公共汽車票跟地鐵票一樣貴。
Gōnggòng qìchē piào gēn dìtiě piào yīyàng guì.
Bus tickets and subway tickets are equally expensive.

我妹妹和我姐姐一样漂亮。· 我妹妹和我姐姐一樣漂亮。

Wǒ mèimei hé wǒ jiějie yīyàng piàoliang.

My younger sister and my older sister are equally beautiful.

台北跟北京一样有名。· 台北跟北京一樣有名。

Táiběi gēn Běijīng yīyàng yǒu míng.

Taipei and Beijing are equally famous.

Written Practice 21-9

For each of the following groups of phrases, write a Mandarin sentence stating that (a) and (b) share the quality (c).

1. a. 杭州 Hángzhōu
    b. 苏州 · 蘇州 Sūzhōu
    c. 漂亮 piàoliang *beautiful*

    _____

2. a. 这本字典 · 這本字典 zhè běn zìdiǎn *this dictionary*
    b. 那本字典 · 那本字典 nà běn zìdiǎn *that dictionary*
    c. 贵 · 貴 guì *expensive*

    _____

3. a. 我的弟弟 wǒ de dìdi *my younger brother*
    b. 我的哥哥 wǒ de gēge *my older brother*
    c. 高 gāo *tall*

    _____

INDICATING *ALMOST THE SAME* WITH 差不多 chàbuduō *ALMOST*

To indicate that two people, places, or things are *almost the same*, use 差不多一样·差不多一樣 chàbuduō yīyàng *almost the same*.

NP₁ 跟/和 NP₂ 差不多一样·差不多一樣 AV
NP₁ gēn/hé NP₂ chàbuduō yīyàng AV

我弟弟和我哥哥差不多一样高。· 我弟弟和我哥哥差不多一樣高。
Wǒ dìdi hé wǒ gēge chàbuduō yīyàng gāo.
My younger brother and my older brother are almost the same height.

Written Practice 21-10

For each of the following groups of phrases, write a Mandarin sentence stating that (a) shares the quality (c) with (b) to almost the same degree.

1. a. 王老师·王老師 Wáng lǎoshī
   b. 高老师·高老師 Gāo lǎoshī
   c. 有名 yǒu míng *famous*

   _____

2. a. 我的车·我的車 wǒ de chē *my car*
   b. 他的车·他的車 tā de chē *his car*
   c. 慢 màn *slow*

   _____

3. a. 公共汽车票·公共汽車票 gōnggòng qìchē piào *bus ticket*
   b. 地铁票·地鐵票 dìtiě piào *subway ticket*
   c. 贵·貴 guì *expensive*

   _____

INDICATING *THE SAME AS* WITH ACTIONS

Comparisons with 一样 · 一樣 yīyàng Without the Object Included

To indicate that someone (some NP) performs one action (V₁) *in the same way as* another action (V₂), use the following construction.

NP [V₁ 得 de] 跟 gēn [V₂ 得 de] 一样 · 一樣 yīyàng

他 [写得] 跟 [说得] 一样。 · 他 [寫得] 跟 [說得] 一樣。
Tā [xiě de] gēn [shuō de] yīyàng.
He writes and speaks in the same way.

To indicate that two people (NP₁ and NP₂) perform an action (V) in the same way, use the following construction.

NP₁ 跟 gēn NP₂ [V 得 de] 一样 · 一樣 yīyàng

他跟他弟弟 [写得] 一样。 · 他跟他弟弟 [寫得] 一樣。
Tā gēn tā dìdi [xiě de] yīyàng.
He and his younger brother write the same way.

他跟他弟弟 [长得] 一样。 · 他跟他弟弟 [長得] 一樣。
Tā gēn tā dìdi [zhǎng de] yīyàng.
He and his younger brother have grown (to look) identical.

Oral Practice

Following are ways in which 小王 Xiǎo Wáng and 小白 Xiǎo Bái are the same. Read the sentences aloud, then translate them into English.

1. 小王跟小白考得一样。 · 小王跟小白考得一樣。
   Xiǎo Wáng gēn Xiǎo Bái kǎo de yīyàng.
   → *Little Wang and Little Bai do the same on tests.*

2. 小王跟小白吃得一样。 · 小王跟小白吃得一樣。
   Xiǎo Wáng gēn Xiǎo Bái chī de yīyàng.
   → *Little Wang and Little Bai eat the same way.*

3. 小王跟小白唱得一样。 · 小王跟小白唱得一樣。
   Xiǎo Wáng gēn Xiǎo Bái chàng de yīyàng.
   → *Little Wang and Little Bai sing the same way.*

4. 小王跟小白穿得一样。· 小王跟小白穿得一樣。
   Xiǎo Wáng gēn Xiǎo Bái chuān de yīyàng.
   → *Little Wang and Little Bai dress the same.*

INDICATING *THE SAME AS* WITH SPECIFIC ACTIONS

Comparisons with 一样·一樣 yīyàng Without the Object Included

To indicate that someone (some NP) performs one action (V_1) *in the same specific way as* another action (V_2), use the following construction.

NP [V_1 得 de] 跟 gēn [V_2 得 de] 一样·一樣 yīyàng AV

他 [写得] 跟 [说得] 一样好。· 他 [寫得] 跟 [說得] 一樣好。
Tā [xiě de] gēn [shuō de] yīyàng hǎo.
He writes and speaks equally well.

To indicate that two people (NP_1 and NP_2) perform an action (V) in the same specific way, use the following construction.

NP_1 跟 gēn NP_2 [V 得 de] 一样·一樣 yīyàng AV

他跟他弟弟 [说得] 一样快。· 他跟他弟弟 [說得] 一樣快。
Tā gēn tā dìdi [shuō de] yīyàng kuài.
He and his younger brother speak equally fast.

他跟他弟弟 [长得] 一样高。· 他跟他弟弟 [長得] 一樣高。
Tā gēn tā dìdi [zhǎng de] yīyàng gāo.
He and his younger brother have grown equally tall.

Written Practice 21-11

For each of the following groups of phrases, write a Mandarin sentence stating that 小白 Xiǎo Bái performs both actions in the same specific way, matching the English sentence.

1. 唱 chàng *sing*
   跳 tiào *dance*
   好 hǎo *well*
   Little Bai sings and dances equally well.

2. 走 zǒu *walk*
   说·說 shuō *talk*
   快 kuài *fast*
   Little Bai walks and talks equally fast.

   _____

3. 吃 chī *eat*
   喝 hē *drink*
   多 duō *much*
   Little Bai eats and drinks the same amount.

   _____

4. 走 zǒu *walk*
   说·說 shuō *talk*
   慢 màn *slowly*
   Little Bai walks and talks equally slowly.

   _____

5. 吃 chī *eat*
   喝 hē *drink*
   快 kuài *fast*
   Little Bai eats and drinks equally fast.

   _____

Comparisons with 一样·一樣 yīyàng with the Object Included

To indicate that someone (some NP) performs two different actions (V₁ and V₂) in the same specific way, use the following construction.

NP [V₁ O] [V₁ 得 de] 跟 gēn [V₂ O] [V₂ 得 de] 一样·一樣 yīyàng AV

他 [写中文] [写得] 跟 [说中国话] [说得] 一样好。·
他 [寫中文] [寫得] 跟 [說中國話] [說得] 一樣好。
Tā [xiě Zhōngwén] [xiě de] gēn [shuō Zhōngguó huà] [shuō de] yīyàng hǎo.
He writes Chinese and speaks Chinese equally well.

To indicate that two people (NP₁ and NP₂) perform an action (V) in the same specific way, use the following construction.

NP₁ 跟 gēn NP₂ [V O] [V 得 de] 一样·一樣 yīyàng AV

他跟他弟弟 [吃中国饭] [吃得] 一样多。· 他跟他弟弟 [吃中國飯] [吃得] 一樣多。
Tā gēn tā dìdi [chī Zhōngguó fàn] [chī de] yīyàng duō.
He and his younger brother eat the same amount of Chinese food.

Note that the verb is stated twice, once followed by its object and once followed by 得 de.

Written Practice 21-12

For each of the following groups of phrases, write a Mandarin sentence to match the English sentence. In questions 1–3, a third-person singular pronoun is the subject; in questions 4–6, 小白 Xiǎo Bái and his younger brother are compared.

1. 做中国菜·做中國菜 zuò Zhōngguó cài *cook Chinese food*
   做意大利菜 zuò Yìdàlì cài *cook Italian food*
   好 hǎo *well*
   He cooks Chinese food and Italian food equally well.

   _____

2. 读书·讀書 dú shū *study*
   做事 zuò shì *work*
   用功 yònggōng *hardworking*
   She studies and works equally hard.

   _____

3. 学中文·學中文 xué Zhōngwén *study Chinese*
   学日文·學日文 xué Rìwén *study Japanese*
   多 duō *a lot, much*
   She has studied Chinese and Japanese for the same amount of time.

   _____

4. 吃饭·吃飯 chī fàn *eat*
   多 duō *a lot, much*
   Little Bai and his younger brother both eat a lot.

   _____

5. 说中国话·說中國話 shuō Zhōngguó huà *speak Chinese*
   好 hǎo *well*
   Little Bai and his younger brother speak Chinese equally well.

   _____

6. 写汉字·寫漢字 xiě Hànzì *write Chinese characters*
   好看 hǎokàn *attractive*
   Little Bai and his younger brother write Chinese characters equally attractively.

   _____

Comparing Two Actions Performed by the Same Subject

In comparing two actions performed by the same subject, the object of the verb may come before the verb, either at the beginning of the sentence or right after the subject.

In the following sentence, the two verbs have the same object.

中文，他写得跟说得一样好。· 中文，他寫得跟說得一樣好。
Zhōngwén, tā xiě de gēn shuō de yīyàng hǎo.
As for Chinese, he writes it and speaks it equally well.

In the following sentences, a single verb has two different objects.

他说英文说得跟说中文说得一样快。· 他說英文說得跟說中文說得一樣快。
Tā shuō Yīngwén shuō de gēn shuō Zhōngwén shuō de yīyàng kuài.
He speaks English and Chinese equally fast.

他 [英文跟中文] 说得一样快。· 他 [英文跟中文] 說得一樣快。
Tā [Yīngwén gēn Zhōngwén] shuō de yīyàng kuài.
As for English and Chinese, he speaks them equally fast.

Written Practice 21-13

Rewrite each of the following sentences, stating the object first.

1. 他做中国菜做的跟做意大利菜做得一样好。·
   他做中國菜做的跟做意大利菜做得一樣好。
   Tā zuò Zhōngguó cài zuò de gēn zuò Yìdàlì cài zuò de yīyàng hǎo.
   He cooks Chinese food as well as he cooks Italian food.

   _____

2. 她学中文学得跟学日文学得一样多。·
   她學中文學得跟學日文學得一樣多。
   Tā xué Zhōngwén xué de gēn xué Rìwén xué de yīyàng duō.
   She has studied Chinese and Japanese for the same amount of time.

   _____

3. 她喝可乐喝得跟喝水喝得一样多。·
   她喝可樂喝得跟喝水喝得一樣多。
   Tā hē kělè hē de gēn hē shuǐ hē de yīyàng duō.
   She drinks as much cola as water.

   _____

4. 他们卖牛肉卖的跟卖猪肉卖的一样贵。·
   他們賣牛肉賣的跟賣豬肉賣的一樣貴。
   Tāmen mài niúròu mài de gēn mài zhūròu mài de yīyàng guì.
   They sell beef and pork at the same price (equally expensive).

   _____

QUIZ

Rewrite the following sentence, adding the word in parentheses. Then identify the object of comparison.

1. 昨天的考试没有今天的考试难。(这么) ·
   昨天的考試沒有今天的考試難。(這麼)
   Zuótiān de kǎoshì méi yǒu jīntiān de kǎoshì nán. (zhème)

   _____

Select the correct pair of words or phrases to complete each of the following sentences, matching the English sentence.

2. 哥哥＿＿＿＿＿＿姐姐＿＿＿＿＿＿用功。

   Gēge ＿＿＿＿＿＿＿＿ jiějie ＿＿＿＿＿＿＿＿ yònggōng.

   Older brother is not as hardworking as older sister.

   a. 跟　gēn，那么·那麼　nàme
   b. 比　bǐ，不　bù
   c. 没有　méi yǒu，那么·那麼　nàme

3. 王老师的学生＿＿＿＿＿＿陈老师的学生＿＿＿＿＿＿忙。·

   王老師的學生＿＿＿＿＿＿陳老師的學生＿＿＿＿＿＿忙。

   Wáng lǎoshī de xuésheng ＿＿＿＿＿＿＿＿ Chén lǎoshī de xuésheng

   ＿＿＿＿＿＿＿＿ máng.

   Professor Wang's students are as busy as Professor Chen's students.

   a. 跟　gēn，一样·一樣　yīyàng
   b. 比　bǐ，—
   c. 没有　méi yǒu，那么·那麼　nàme

4. 美国的电影＿＿＿＿＿＿中国的电影＿＿＿＿＿＿有名。·

   美國的電影＿＿＿＿＿＿中國的電影＿＿＿＿＿＿有名。

   Měiguó de diànyǐng ＿＿＿＿＿＿＿＿ Zhōngguó de diànyǐng

   ＿＿＿＿＿＿＿＿ yǒu míng.

   American movies are more famous than Chinese movies.

   a. 跟　gēn，一样·一樣　yīyàng
   b. 比　bǐ，—
   c. 没有　méi yǒu，那么·那麼　nàme

Rewrite each of the following sentences, adding the appropriate expression from the list in parentheses to match the English sentence.

5. 地铁票比公共汽车票贵。(一點，更，得多) ·
   地鐵票比公共汽車票貴。(一點，更，得多)
   Dìtiě piào bǐ gōnggòng qìchē piào guì. (yìdiǎn, gèng, de duō)
   Subway tickets are a lot more expensive than bus tickets.

   _____

6. 王老师的书比张老师的书多。(一点，更，得多) ·
   王老師的書比張老師的書多。(一點，更，得多)
   Wáng lǎoshī de shū bǐ Zhāng lǎoshī de shū duō. (yìdiǎn, gèng, de duō)
   Professor Wang has even more books than Professor Zhang.

   _____

7. 你的哥哥比我的哥哥高。(一点，更，得多) ·
   你的哥哥比我的哥哥高。(一點，更，得多)
   Nǐ de gēge bǐ wǒ de gēge gāo. (yìdiǎn, gèng, de duō)
   Your older brother is a little taller than my older brother.

   _____

Translate the following sentences into Mandarin.

8. 小王 Xiǎo Wáng *is a lot more hardworking than* 小高 Xiǎo Gāo.

   _____

9. 小王 Xiǎo Wáng *is almost as fast as* 小高 Xiǎo Gāo.

   _____

10. 小高 Xiǎo Gāo *is a little smarter than* 小王 Xiǎo Wáng.

   _____

1. Identify the subject and the verb in the following sentence.

   中国人都会说中国话吗？ · 中國人都會說中國話嗎？
   Zhōngguó rén dōu huì shuō Zhōngguó huà ma?
   Can all Chinese people speak Chinese?

   Subject _____

   Verb _____

2. Rewrite the following sentence, adding the location phrase in parentheses to match the English sentence.

   我每个周末听音乐。(在学生中心) ·
   我每個週末聽音樂。(在學生中心)
   Wǒ měi gè zhōumò tīng yīnyuè. (zài xuésheng zhōngxīn)
   I listen to music every weekend at the student center.

   _____

3. Rewrite the following sentence, adding the *time when* phrase in parentheses to match the English sentence.

   我的朋友给我打电话了。(昨天晚上) ·
   我的朋友給我打電話了。(昨天晚上)
   Wǒ de péngyou gěi wǒ dǎ diànhuà le. (zuótiān wǎnshang)
   My friend phoned me last night.

   _____

4. Rearrange the following names and titles in the correct Chinese order. The family name is in bold type.

   a. xiǎojie **Mǎ** Jiāměi _____

   b. lǎoshī Xìngróng **Ráo** _____

5. Rearrange the following names and titles in the correct Chinese order, using the pinyin form of the title. The family name is in bold type.

   a. Dr. Xiǎoyīng **Lín** _____

   b. Professor Píng **Zhāng** _____

6. Lili Wang is 17 years old. She has two sisters, 14 and 16.

   a. How many 姐姐 jiějie does she have? _____

   b. How many 妹妹 mèimei does she have? _____

7. Dr. Wang's children have three 叔叔 shūshu and two 姑姑 gūgu.

     a. How many brothers does Dr. Wang have? _____

     b. How many sisters does Dr. Wang have? _____

8. Write the following numbers in Arabic numerals (1, 2, 3, and so on).

     a. 七十八 qīshíbā _____

     b. 九百五十六 jiǔbǎi wǔshíliù _____

9. Write the following numbers in Mandarin.

     a. 413 _____

     b. 2,020 _____

     c. 64,888 _____

10. Write the following phone number in pinyin: 011-8610-7226-8389.

     _____

11. Write the following number in Chinese: 902,305.

     _____

12. Write the following ordinal numbers in Chinese.

     a. 7th _____

     b. 20th _____

13. Fill in the blanks with the correct pronouns to match the English sentence.

     _____喜欢_____。· _____喜歡_____。

     _____ xǐhuan _____.

     They like you.

14. Rewrite the following sentence, adding 都 dōu to match the English sentence.

     飞机票很贵。· 飛機票很貴。

     Fēijī piào hěn guì.

     Airplane tickets are all expensive.

     _____

15. Rewrite the following sentence, adding 都 dōu to match the English sentence.

    王老师跟白老师会说法国话。· 王老師跟白老師會說法國話。
    Wáng lǎoshī gēn Bái lǎoshī huì shuō Fǎguó huà.
    Professor Wang and Professor Bai can both speak French.

    _____

16. Write the following Mandarin phrase in the correct order.

    四鞋子这双 · 四鞋子這雙
    sì xiézi zhè shuāng
    these four pairs of shoes

    _____

17. Answer the following question in Mandarin, using only the number and classifier for the information in parentheses.

    How many books did you read? (5) _____

18. Write a complete Mandarin sentence from each of the following phrases, adding 是 shì to match the English sentence.

    a. 他 … 我哥哥
       tā … wǒ gēge
       He is my older brother.

       _____

    b. 我的朋友 … 大学生 · 我的朋友 … 大學生
       wǒ de péngyou … dàxuéshēng
       My friend is a college student.

       _____

19. Negate the following sentence to match the English sentence.

    那个学生是中国人。· 那個學生是中國人。
    Nàge xuésheng shì Zhōngguó rén.
    That student is not Chinese.

    _____

20. Rewrite each of the following sentences, adding 不都 bù dōu or 都不 dōu bù to match the English sentence.

    a. 他们是老师。· 他們是老師。
       Tāmen shì lǎoshī.
       They are all not teachers. (i.e., *None of them is a teacher.*)

    _____

    b. 我们认识他。· 我們認識他。
       Wǒmen rènshi tā.
       We don't all know him.

    _____

21. Rewrite the following 吗 · 嗎 ma question as a 是不是 shì bù shì question.

    她是你的妹妹吗? · 她是你的妹妹嗎?
    Tā shì nǐ de mèimei ma?
    Is she your younger sister?

    _____

22. You have just met a stranger.

    a. Ask him what his name is.

    _____

    b. Tell him your family name and given name.

    _____

23. Write a Mandarin sentence, putting the following phrases in the correct order to match the English sentence.

    太多 – 鞋子 – 你的
    tài duō – xiézi – nǐ de
    You have too many shoes.

    _____

24. Write a Mandarin sentence, putting the following phrases in the correct order to match the English sentence.

不 – 睡觉 – 我 – 想 · 不 – 睡覺 – 我 – 想

bù – shuì jiào – wǒ – xiǎng

I do not want to go to sleep.

_____

25. Fill in the blank in each of the following sentences with 想 xiǎng or 喜欢 · 喜歡 xǐhuan.

a. 我不_____那双鞋子。· 我不_____那雙鞋子。

Wǒ bù _____ nà shuāng xiézi.

I do not like that pair of shoes.

b. 我不_____买那双鞋子。· 我不_____買那雙鞋子。

Wǒ bù _____ mǎi nà shuāng xiézi.

I do not want to buy that pair of shoes.

26. Rewrite each of the following sentences, adding the appropriate intensifier to match the English sentence.

a. 这个菜好吃。· 這個菜好吃。

Zhège cài hǎo chī.

This dish is especially delicious.

_____

b. 这双鞋子贵。· 這雙鞋子貴。

Zhè shuāng xiézi guì.

These shoes are a little expensive.

_____

27. Rewrite the following sentence, replacing the placeholder object in bold type with the object in parentheses. Then translate the new sentence into English.

他们会唱**歌**。(京剧) · 他們會唱**歌**。(京劇)

Tāmen huì chàng **gē**. (Jīngjù)

They can sing. (*Beijing opera*)

_____

28. Rewrite the following sentence, replacing the placeholder object in bold type with the object in parentheses. Then translate the new sentence into English.

我们吃**饭**吧! (烤鸭) · 我們吃**飯**吧! (烤鴨)

Wǒmen chī **fàn** ba! (kǎoyā)

Let's eat! (*roast duck*)

_____

29. Rewrite the following sentence, replacing the placeholder object in bold type with the object in parentheses. Then translate the new sentence into English.

她每天晚上看**书**。(小说) · 她每天晚上看**書**。(小說)

Tā měitiān wǎnshang kàn **shū**. (xiǎoshuō)

She reads every night. (*novels*)

_____

30. Rewrite the following sentence, adding the expressions in parentheses to match the English sentence.

我的朋友打球。(每个周末，都) · 我的朋友打球。(每個週末，都)

Wǒ de péngyou dǎ qiú. (měi gè zhōumò, dōu)

My friends play ball every weekend.

_____

31. Write a Mandarin sentence, putting the following phrases in the correct order to match the English sentence.

会 – 下雪 – 一定 – 今天晚上 · 會 – 下雪 – 一定 – 今天晚上

huì – xià xuě – yīdìng – jīntiān wǎnshang

It is definitely going to snow tonight.

_____

32. Rewrite the following sentence to emphasize the ongoing action, adding the words in parentheses.

她写信。· 她寫信。(在，着，呢)

Tā xiě xìn. (zài, zhe, ne)

She is writing a letter right now.

_____

33. Rewrite each of the following sentences, indicating that the action is complete, as in the English sentence.

a. 她在书店买书。· 她在書店買書。
Tā zài shūdiàn mǎi shū.
She bought books at the bookstore.

_____

b. 她在书店买三本书。· 她在書店買三本書。
Tā zài shūdiàn mǎi sān běn shū.
She bought three books at the bookstore.

_____

c. 她在餐厅吃午饭。· 她在餐廳吃午飯。
Tā zài cāntīng chī wǔfàn.
She ate lunch in the cafeteria.

_____

34. Rewrite the following sentence, indicating that the action has already happened, as in the English sentence.

我的同屋睡觉了。· 我的同屋睡覺了。
Wǒ de tóngwū shuì jiào le.
My roommate is already asleep.

_____

35. Answer the following question, saying that you haven't performed the action yet.

你已经买课本了吗？· 你已經買課本了嗎？
Nǐ yǐjing mǎi kèběn le ma?
Have you already bought the textbook?

_____

36. Answer the following question, saying that you haven't performed the action yet.

你已经考试了吗？· 你已經考試了嗎？
Nǐ yǐjing kǎoshì le ma?
Have you already taken the test?

_____

37. You are e-mailing a classmate in Mandarin. Write that you have eaten Chinese food before, but you haven't been to China yet. Use 过·過 guo to express both ideas.

   _____

38. Ask your classmate in Mandarin if she has been to China before.

   _____

39. a. Ask your mother in Mandarin if you can go to see a movie tonight.

   _____

   b. Your mother gives you the short answer *no*. What does she say?

   _____

40. a. Ask your roommate in Mandarin if he can write this character (*if he knows how to write it*).

   _____

   b. Your roommate gives you the short answer *yes*. What does he say?

   _____

41. Write a complete Mandarin sentence, naming one thing you cannot do in the library.

   _____

42. Write a Mandarin sentence, putting the following phrases in the correct order to match the English sentence.

   能 – 你 – 帮助 – 我 – 作业 – 不能 – 做 ·
   能 – 你 – 幫助 – 我 – 作業 – 不能 – 做
   néng – nǐ – bāngzhù – wǒ – zuòyè – bù néng – zuò
   Can you help me do the homework?

   _____

Your younger brother is going away to school. You have made a list of things that he should do, must do, shouldn't do, or doesn't have to do. For questions 43–47 below, write a complete Mandarin sentence, expressing an item on your list. The actions are given in parentheses.

43. You should call Mom every day.
    (给妈妈打电话 · 給媽媽打電話 gěi māma dǎ diànhuà)

    _____

44. You have to go to class every day.
    (上课 · 上課 shàng kè)

    _____

45. You don't have to bathe every day.
    (洗澡 xǐzǎo)

    _____

46. You shouldn't smoke.
    (抽烟 · 抽煙 chōu yān)

    _____

47. You'd best not drink beer with your classmates.
    (喝啤酒 hē píjiǔ)

    _____

48. Li-li is getting ready for the new school year.

    a. Write a complete Mandarin sentence saying that Li-li has these two
       items: 本子 běnzi _notebooks_ and 书包 · 書包 shūbāo _a book bag_.

       _____

    b. Write a complete Mandarin sentence saying that Li-li does not have
       these two items: 电脑 · 電腦 diànnǎo _a computer_ and 手机 · 手機 shǒujī
       a cell phone.

       _____

49. Translate the following sentence into English.

    这双鞋子是我姐姐的。· 這雙鞋子是我姐姐的。
    (一双鞋子 · 一雙鞋子 yī shuāng xiézi _one pair of shoes_)
    Zhè shuāng xiézi shì wǒ jiějie de.

    _____

50. Write the phrase _my roommate's cellphone_ in Mandarin.
    (同屋 tóngwū _roommate_; 手机 · 手機 shǒujī _cell phone_)

    _____

51. Write a Mandarin sentence, putting the following phrases in the correct order to match the English sentence.

    是 – 哥哥 – 你 – 姐姐 – 同学 – 的 – 我．
    是 – 哥哥 – 你 – 姐姐 – 同學 – 的 – 我
    shì – gēge – nǐ – jiějie – tóngxué – de – wǒ
    Your older brother is my older sister's classmate.

    _____

52. Write a Mandarin sentence, putting the following phrases in the correct order to match the English sentence.

    我 – 是 – 那个 – 不 – 的 – 书包．
    我 – 是 – 那個 – 不 – 的 – 書包
    wǒ – shì – nàge – bù – de – shūbāo
    That book bag is not mine.

    _____

53. Identify the description clause in each of the following noun phrases.

    a. 她今天穿的衣服 tā jīntiān chuān de yīfu

    _____

    b. 我昨天看的电影．我昨天看的電影 wǒ zuótiān kàn de diànyǐng

    _____

54. Rewrite each of the following Mandarin phrases, adding the intensifier in parentheses. Then translate the phrase into English.

    a. 有意思的书．有意思的書 yǒu yìsi de shū (*very*)

    _____

    b. 难的考试．難的考試 nán de kǎoshì (*especially*)

    _____

55. Fill in the missing noun in the second sentence below. Then translate the sentences into English.

    你的哥哥很高。我的_____不高。

    Nǐ de gēge hěn gāo. Wǒ de _____ bù gāo.

    _____

56. Negate the following phrase to match the English phrase.

    很有意思的电影 · 很有意思的電影

    hěn yǒu yìsi de diànyǐng

    an uninteresting movie

    _____

57. Rearrange the following Mandarin words to create a noun phrase with a description clause, matching the English phrase.

    老师 – 的 – 拍 – 照片 · 老師 – 的 – 拍 – 照片

    lǎoshī – de – pāi – zhàopiàn

    the photograph that the teacher took

    _____

58. Write the question that elicits the following statement, using the question form in parentheses.

    我很喜欢跳舞。· 我很喜歡跳舞。(吗 · 嗎 ma)

    Wǒ hěn xǐhuan tiào wǔ.

    _____

59. Write the question that elicits the following statement, using the question form in parentheses.

    我不会说日本话。· 我不會說日本話。(Verb-Not-Verb)

    Wǒ bù huì shuō Rìběn huà.

    _____

60. Write the question that elicits the following statement, using the question form in parentheses.

    我也学中文。· 我也學中文。(呢 ne)

    Wǒ yě xué Zhōngwén.

    _____

61. Rewrite the following 吗 · 嗎 ma question as a Verb-Not-Verb question.

    她有男朋友吗？· 她有男朋友嗎？(男朋友 nán péngyou *boyfriend*)

    Tā yǒu nán péngyou ma?

    _____

62. Write the short answer *yes* to the following question.

你想看电视吗？· 你想看電視嗎？

Nǐ xiǎng kàn diànshì ma?

_____

63. Write the question that elicits the following statement, using the question word in parentheses.

我的同屋跟我一起去吃晚饭。· 我的同屋跟我一起去吃晚飯。
(谁 · 誰 shéi)

Wǒ de tóngwū gēn wǒ yīqǐ qù chī wǎnfàn.

My roommate is going with me to eat dinner. (Q: Who is going with you to eat dinner?)

_____

64. Write the question that elicits the following statement, using the question word in parentheses.

我们在宿舍看电视。· 我們在宿舍看電視。(哪儿 · 哪兒 nǎr)

Wǒmen zài sùshè kàn diànshì.

We watch television in the dorm.

_____

65. Write the question that elicits the following statement, using the question word in parentheses.

我昨天买飞机票了。· 我昨天買飛機票了。(什么 · 甚麼 shénme)

Wǒ zuótiān mǎi fēijī piào le.

I bought an airplane ticket yesterday.

_____

66. Write the question that elicits the following statement, using the question word in parentheses.

我觉得那件衣服最好看。· 我覺得那件衣服最好看。(哪 nǎ)

Wǒ juéde nà jiàn yīfu zuì hǎokàn.

I think that that article of clothing is the best-looking.

_____

67. Write the question that elicits the following statement, using the question word in parentheses.

我们九点钟考试。· 我們九點鐘考試。(几·幾 jǐ)
Wǒmen jiǔ diǎn zhōng kǎo shì.
We take a test at 9 o'clock.

_____

68. Rewrite the following sentence, adding 都 dōu to match the English sentence.

我的朋友很喜欢唱卡拉OK。· 我的朋友很喜歡唱卡拉OK。
Wǒ de péngyou hěn xǐhuan chàng kǎlāOK.
All of my friends like to sing karaoke.

_____

69. Rewrite the following sentence, adding 都 dōu to match the English sentence.

他每天给他的女朋友打电话。· 他每天給他的女朋友打電話。
Tā měitiān gěi tā de nǚ péngyou dǎ diànhuà.
He phones his girlfriend every day.

_____

70. Rewrite the following sentence, adding 所有的 suóyǒu de and 都 dōu to match the English sentence.

美国人会开车吗？· 美國人會開車嗎？
Měiguó rén huì kāi chē ma?
Can all Americans drive?

_____

71. Rewrite the following sentence, adding 都 dōu to match the English sentence.

他们不会说英文。· 他們不會說英文。
Tāmen bù huì shuō Yīngwén.
None of them can speak English.

_____

72. Answer the following question with a complete Mandarin sentence, saying that she can't even speak a little Chinese.

    她会说中文吗？· 她會說中文嗎？ Tā huì shuō Zhōngwén ma?

    _____

For questions 73–76, write a complete Mandarin sentence from each set of phrases to match the English sentence, using a connecting word from the following list.

和 hé   也 yě   又 … 又 yòu … yòu
跟 gēn   还·還 hái

73. 去过·去過 qùguo
    中国·中國 Zhōngguó
    越南 Yuènán
    My older sister has been to China, and she has also been to Vietnam.

    _____

74. 高中生 gāozhōng shēng _high school student_
    My younger brother and my younger sister are both high school students.

    _____

75. 新的鞋子 xīn de xiézi
    新的大衣 xīn de dàyī
    I bought a new pair of shoes, and I also bought a new coat.

    _____

76. 漂亮 piàoliang
    便宜 piányi
    The shoes were beautiful and cheap.

    _____

77. Write a Mandarin sentence, putting the following phrases in the correct order to match the English sentence.

    只 – 弟弟 – 唱 – 会 – 中国 – 歌 – 我 ·
    只 – 弟弟 – 唱 – 會 – 中國 – 歌 – 我
    zhǐ – dìdi – chàng – huì – Zhōngguó – gē – wǒ
    My little brother only knows how to sing Chinese songs.

    _____

The answers to questions 78–82 are based on the following chart, which shows the relative position of several locations in a city. Answer each question with a complete Mandarin sentence.

School 学校·學校 xuéxiào	Restaurant 饭馆·飯館 fànguǎn	Library (studying) 图书馆·圖書館 túshūguǎn
Bank 银行·銀行 yínháng	Train station 火车站·火車站 huǒchēzhàn	Movie theater 电影院·電影院 diànyǐngyuàn
Bookstore 书店·書店 shūdiàn	Park (playing ball) 公园·公園 gōngyuán (打球 dǎ qiú)	Hospital 医院·醫院 yīyuàn

78. 火车站在银行的哪边？· 火車站在銀行的哪邊？
    Huǒchēzhàn zài yínháng de nǎbiān?

    _____

79. 书店在哪里？· 書店在哪裏？
    Shūdiàn zài nǎli?

    _____

80. 电影院在医院的哪边？· 電影院在醫院的哪邊？
    Diànyǐngyuàn zài yīyuàn de nǎbian?

    _____

81. 学生在公园里做什么？· 學生在公園裏做甚麼？
    Xuésheng zài gōngyuán lǐ zuò shénme?

    _____

82. 学校的东边有什么？· 學校的東邊有甚麼？

    Xuéxiào de dōngbian yǒu shénme?

    _____

83. Write a complete Mandarin sentence, asking if it is far from the train station to the bookstore.

    _____

84. Write a Mandarin sentence, putting the following phrases in the correct order to match the English sentence.

    只 – 医院 – 路 – 学校 – 一里 – 离 – 有 ·
    只 – 醫院 – 路 – 學校 – 一里 – 離 – 有
    zhǐ – yīyuàn – lù – xuéxiào – yī lǐ – lí – yǒu
    The school is only one mile away from the hospital.

    _____

85. Write the time of day indicated by the following phrase, using Arabic numerals.

    十二点〇五分·十二點〇五分 shí'èr diǎn líng wǔ fēn

    _____

86. Translate the following Mandarin sentence into English.

    下个月是十一月。· 下個月是十一月。
    Xià gè yuè shì shíyīyuè.

    _____

87. Write the following date in Chinese, using 日 rì for the date of the month.

    September 29, 2014

    _____

88. Write a time expression in Mandarin, putting the following phrases in the correct order to match the English phrase.

    八点 – 晚上 – 钟 – 明天 – 半 ·
    八點 – 晚上 – 鐘 – 明天 – 半
    bādiǎn – wǎnshang – zhōng – míngtiān – bàn
    8:30 tomorrow night

    _____

89. Rewrite the following sentence, adding the phrase in parentheses to match the English sentence.

    我的同屋唱歌。(很好)
    Wǒ de tóngwū chàng gē. (hěn hǎo)
    My roommate sings very well.

    _____

90. Rewrite the following sentence, adding the phrase in parentheses to match the English sentence.

    别开车。· 別開車。(太快)
    Bié kāi chē. (tài kuài)
    Don't drive too fast.

    _____

91. Reply to the following compliment, saying that you do not have that quality.

    你写汉字写得非常好。· 你寫漢字寫得非常好。
    Nǐ xiě Hànzì xiě de fēicháng hǎo.

    _____

92. Write a question asking your new roommate if he sleeps a lot. Use the phrase 睡觉·睡覺 shuì jiào.

    _____

93. Write a Mandarin sentence, putting the following phrases in the correct order to match the English sentence.

    我 – 我 – 的 – 拿了 – 同屋 – 无意地 – 课本 ·
    我 – 我 – 的 – 拿了 – 同屋 – 無意地 – 課本
    wǒ – wǒ – de – ná le – tóngwū – wúyì dì – kèběn
    I accidentally took my roommate's textbook.

    _____

94. Using the following phrases, write a comparison sentence in Mandarin to match the English sentence.

    唱歌 · 唱歌   chàng gē   *sing*
    跳舞   tiào wǔ   *dance*
    好   hǎo   *well*
    They sing and dance equally well.

    _____

95. Using the following phrases, write a comparison sentence in Mandarin to match the English sentence.

    喝可乐 · 喝可樂   hē kělè   *drink cola*
    喝水   hē shuǐ   *drink water*
    多   duō   *a lot, much*
    She drinks as much cola as water.

    _____

96. Rewrite the following sentence, adding the phrase in parentheses to match the English sentence.

    小白比我考试考得好。(一点) · 小白比我考試考得好。(一點)
    Xiǎo Bái bǐ wǒ kǎo shì kǎo de hǎo. (yīdiǎn)
    Little Bai does a little bit better than I do on tests.

    _____

97. Rewrite the following sentence, adding the phrase in parentheses to match the English sentence.

    我没有他用电脑用得多。(那么) · 我沒有他用電腦用得多。(那麼)
    Wǒ méi yǒu tā yòng diànnǎo yòng de duō. (nàme)
    I do not use a computer as much as he does.

    _____

98. Write a Mandarin sentence, putting the following phrases in the correct order to match the English sentence.

    没有 – 你 – 小白 – 吃饺子 – 那么多 – 吃得 ·
    沒有 – 你 – 小白 – 吃餃子 – 那麼多 – 吃得
    méi yǒu – nǐ – Xiǎo Bái – chī jiǎozi – nàme duō – chī de
    You do not eat as many dumplings as Little Bai.

    _____

99. Write a Mandarin sentence, putting the following phrases in the correct order to match the English sentence.

    跳得 – 比 – 她 – 得多 – 她弟弟 – 跳舞 – 好

    tiào de – bǐ – tā – de duō – tā dìdi – tiào wǔ – hǎo

    She dances a lot better than her younger brother.

---

100. Write a Mandarin sentence, putting the following phrases in the correct order to match the English sentence.

    这么 – 做饭 – 没有 – 她 – 做得 – 好吃 – 我 .
    這麼 – 做飯 – 沒有 – 她 – 做得 – 好吃 – 我

    zhème – zuò fàn – méi yǒu – tā – zuò de – hǎo chī – wǒ

    I do not cook as well as she does.

ANSWER KEY

CHAPTER 1

Written Practice 1-1

1. bù
2. qǐng
3. máng
4. shì
5. chū

Written Practice 1-2

1. two
2. two
3. four
4. three
5. six
6. nine
7. five
8. six
9. eight
10. six

QUIZ

	Character	Pronunciation	Meaning
1.	用	yòng	to use
2.	豆	dòu	bean
3.	小	xiǎo	small
4.	水	shuǐ	water
5.	日	rì	sun
6.	月	yuè	moon
7.	土	tǔ	earth
8.	大	dà	big
9.	火	huǒ	fire
10.	方	fāng	square, direction, way

CHAPTER 2

Written Practice 2-1

1. 买·買 mǎi to buy
2. 喜欢·喜歡 xǐhuan to like
3. 贵·貴 guì expensive
4. 学·學 xué to study

Written Practice 2-2

1. 一个电影·一個電影 yī gè diànyǐng a movie
2. 晚饭·晚飯 wǎnfàn dinner
3. 那本书·那本書 nà běn shū that book
4. 筷子 kuàizi chopsticks

Written Practice 2-3

1. 他们每天晚上在饭馆吃饭。·他們每天晚上在飯館吃飯。

   Tāmen měitiān wǎnshang zài fànguǎn chī fàn.

   They eat at a restaurant every evening.

2. 他现在在宿舍睡觉。·他現在在宿舍睡覺。

   Tā xiànzài zài sùshè shuì jiào.

   He is sleeping at the dormitory right now.

3. 我们明天在公园打球吧。·我們明天在公園打球吧。

   Wǒmen míngtiān zài gōngyuán dǎ qiú ba.

   Let's play ball tomorrow at the park.

4. 他们十点钟喝了咖啡。·他們十點鐘喝了咖啡。

   Tāmen shídiǎn zhōng hē le kāfēi.

   They drank coffee at 10 o'clock.

QUIZ

1. 我 wǒ I
2. 那个书店·那個書店 nàge shūdiàn that bookstore
3. 那个电脑·那個電腦 nàge diànnǎo that computer
4. 我的奶奶每天下午在公园走路。·我的奶奶每天下午在公園走路。

   Wǒ de nǎinai měitiān xiàwǔ zài gōngyuán zǒu lù.

5. 我们明天晚上在饭馆吃饭。·我們明天晚上在飯館吃飯。

   Wǒmen míngtiān wǎnshang zài fànguǎn chī fàn.

6. 我妹妹昨天晚上九点钟在图书馆做了作业。·

   我妹妹昨天晚上九點鐘在圖書館做了作業。

   Wǒ mèimei zuótiān wǎnshang jiǔdiǎn zhōng zài túshūguǎn zuò le zuòyè.

7. 她今天晚上在家看电视。·她今天晚上在家看電視。

   Tā jīntiān wǎnshang zài jiā kàn diànshì.

8. 外国电影 · 外國電影 wàiguó diànyǐng foreign movies
9. 两本书 · 兩本書 liǎng běn shū two books
10. 三瓶可乐 · 三瓶可樂 sān píng kělè three bottles of cola

CHAPTER 3

Written Practice 3-1

1. Wáng Péngfēi
2. Táng Xīnhuā
3. Xú Huìkāng
4. Zhāng Píng
5. Lín Dàoyú
6. Zhōu Lì
7. Ráo Xìngróng
8. Mǎ Wěiqīng

Written Practice 3-2

1. Wáng yīshēng
2. Táng lǎoshī
3. Xú jīnglǐ
4. Zhāng tàitai
5. Lín xiānsheng
6. Zhōu xiǎojie
7. Ráo xiàozhǎng
8. Mǎ sījī

Written Practice 3-3

1. yéye OR wàigōng
2. āyí
3. nǎinai
4. yéye

QUIZ

1. a. 哥哥 gēge
   b. 弟弟 dìdi
2. a. 妹妹 mèimei
   b. 哥哥 gēge
3. a. 姐姐 jiějie
   b. 弟弟 dìdi
   c. 姐姐 jiějie
4. a. 唐 Táng
   b. 高 Gāo
5. a. Ma Zhizhen Dr. (医生 · 醫生 yīshēng)
   b. Liu Yongping Mr. (先生 xiānsheng)
6. a. 林美玲医生 · 林美玲醫生 Lín Měilíng yīshēng
   b. 孙爱民老师 · 孫愛民老師 Sūn Àimín lǎoshī
7. (b) AND (e)

8. two
9. a. three
   b. one
10. two

CHAPTER 4

Written Practice 4-1

1. 二十八　èrshíbā
2. 五十四　wǔshísì
3. 七十七　qīshíqī
4. 八十三　bāshísān
5. 九十一　jiǔshíyī

Written Practice 4-2

1. 三百八十五　sān bǎi bāshíwǔ
2. 两百一十八・兩百一十八　liǎng bǎi yīshíbā OR 二百一十八　èr bǎi yīshíbā
3. 六百八十四　liù bǎi bāshísì
4. 三百三十三　sān bǎi sānshísān
5. 七百九十二　qī bǎi jiǔshí'èr

QUIZ

1. wǔ sān yī liù èr sān èr sān OR wǔ sān yāo liù èr sān èr sān
2. bā sì líng liù bā bā bā bā
3. èr èr liù èr yī qī bā jiǔ OR èr èr liù èr yāo qī bā jiǔ
4. 六百七十九　liù bǎi qīshíjiǔ
5. 两千三百四十五・兩千三百四十五　liǎng qiān sān bǎi sìshíwǔ
6. 两万八千六百五十六・兩萬八千六百五十六
   liǎng wàn bā qiān liù bǎi wǔshíliù
7. 十三万五千八百九十・十三萬五千八百九十
   shí sānwàn wǔ qiān bā bǎi jiǔshí
8. 3,106
9. 40,270
10. 5,902

CHAPTER 5

Written Practice 5-1

1. 他们·他們 tāmen
2. 我们·我們 wǒmen
3. 你们·你們 nǐmen
4. 她们·她們 tāmen

Written Practice 5-2

1. 他们喜欢你。·他們喜歡你。 **Tāmen** xǐhuan **nǐ**.
2. 我们是学生。·我們是學生。 **Wǒmen** shì xuésheng.
3. 我要自己做。 Wǒ yào **zìjǐ** zuò.

Written Practice 5-3

1. 男孩子和女孩子喜欢吃饺子。·男孩子和女孩子喜歡吃餃子。
   Nán háizi hé nǚ háizi xǐhuan chī jiǎozi.
2. 历史跟文学很有意思。·歷史跟文學很有意思。
   Lìshǐ gēn wénxué hěn yǒu yìsi.
3. 美国人和英国人说英文。·美國人和英國人說英文。
   Měiguórén hé Yīngguórén shuō Yīngwén.
4. 我的弟弟跟我的妹妹很高。 Wǒ de dìdi gēn wǒ de mèimei hěn gāo.

Written Practice 5-4

1. 我们都是学生。·我們都是學生。 Wǒmen dōu shì xuésheng.
2. 他们都姓陈。·他們都姓陳。 Tāmen dōu xìng Chén.
3. 他们都学中文。·他們都學中文。 Tāmen dōu xué Zhōngwén.
4. 我们都上大学。·我們都上大學。 Wǒmen dōu shàng dàxué.
5. 他们都是美国人。·他們都是美國人。 Tāmen dōu shì Měiguórén.

Written Practice 5-5

1. 三个问题·三個問題 sān gè wèntí
2. 一些问题·一些問題 yī xiē wèntí
3. 一杯水 yī bēi shuǐ
4. 一碗饭·一碗飯 yī wǎn fàn
5. 一块糖·一塊 糖 yī kuài táng

Written Practice 5-6

1. 这两支笔·這兩枝筆 zhè liǎng zhī bǐ
2. 那五双鞋子·那五雙鞋子 nà wǔ shuāng xiézi
3. 这六本书·這六本書 zhè liù běn shū
4. 这七张纸·這七張紙 zhè qī zhāng zhǐ
5. 那九杯水 nà jiǔ bēi shuǐ

QUIZ

1. 我跟她是朋友。 Wǒ gēn tā shì péngyou.

2. 三个。 Sān gè.

3. 我要买那本书。· 我要買那本書。 Wǒ yào mǎi nà **běn** shū.

4. 学生和老师都喜欢那个电影。· 學生和老師都喜歡那個電影。
   Xuésheng hé lǎoshī dōu xǐhuan nàge diànyǐng.

5. 我们都是朋友。· 我們都是朋友。 Wǒmen dōu shì péngyou.

6. 十二个人·十二個人 shí'èr gè rén

7. 两碗·兩碗 liǎng wǎn

8. (c)

9. 那两个老师·那兩個老師 nà liǎng gè lǎoshī

10. 五个问题·五個問題 wǔ gè wèntí

CHAPTER 6

Written Practice 6-1

1. 他不是我哥哥。 Tā bù shì wǒ gēge.

2. 我妈妈不是老师。· 我媽媽不是老師。 Wǒ māma bù shì lǎoshī.

3. 那不是字典。 Nà bù shì zìdiǎn.

4. 我的朋友不是大学生。· 我的朋友不是大學生。
   Wǒ de péngyou bù shì dàxuéshēng.

Written Practice 6-2

1. 王美玲的朋友都是中国人。· 王美玲的朋友都是中國人。
   Wáng Měilíng de péngyou dōu shì Zhōngguó rén.

2. 王美玲的朋友都是老师。· 王美玲的朋友都是老師。
   Wáng Měilíng de péngyou dōu shì lǎoshī.

3. 王美玲的朋友都是母亲。· 王美玲的朋友都是母親。
   Wáng Měilíng de péngyou dōu shì mǔqīn.

4. 王美玲的朋友都是很好的人。
   Wáng Měilíng de péngyou dōu shì hěn hǎo de rén.

Written Practice 6-3

1. 他们不都是学生。· 他們不都是學生。 Tāmen bù dōu shì xuésheng.

2. 我们都不是老师。· 我們都不是老師。 Wǒmen dōu bù shì lǎoshī.

3. 那都不是我的钱。· 那都不是我的錢。 Nà dōu bù shì wǒ de qián.

4. 他们不都是我的朋友。· 他們不都是我的朋友。
   Tāmen bù dōu shì wǒ de péngyou.

Written Practice 6-4

1. 王老师是不是美国人？· 王老師是不是美國人？
   Wáng lǎoshī shì bù shì Měiguó rén?
2. 他是不是你的老师？· 他是不是你的老師？ Tā shì bù shì nǐ de lǎoshī?
3. 他们是不是学生？· 他們是不是學生？ Tāmen shì bù shì xuésheng?
4. 那本书是不是你的？· 那本書是不是你的？ Nà běn shū shì bù shì nǐ de?
5. 她是不是你的朋友？ Tā shì bù shì nǐ de péngyou?

Written Practice 6-5

1. 我不姓刘。· 我不姓劉。 Wǒ bù xìng Liú.
2. 我不姓何。 Wǒ bù xìng Hé.
3. 我不姓周。 Wǒ bù xìng Zhōu.
4. 我不姓马。· 我不姓馬。 Wǒ bù xìng Mǎ.

Written Practice 6-6

1. Q: 你叫什么名字？· 你叫甚麼名字？ Nǐ jiào shénme míngzi?
   A: 我叫李丽。· 我叫李麗。 Wǒ jiào Lǐ Lì.
2. Q: 你叫什么名字？· 你叫甚麼名字？ Nǐ jiào shénme míngzi?
   A: 我叫陈爱平。· 我叫陳愛平。 Wǒ jiào Chén Àipíng.
3. Q: 你叫什么名字？· 你叫甚麼名字？ Nǐ jiào shénme míngzi?
   A: 我叫王惠娜。 Wǒ jiào Wáng Huìnà.
4. Q: 你叫什么名字？· 你叫甚麼名字？ Nǐ jiào shénme míngzi?
   A: 我叫周萍。 Wǒ jiào Zhōu Píng.

QUIZ

1. a. 这是马老师。· 這是馬老師。 Zhè shì Mǎ lǎoshī.
   b. 这是白小春。· 這是白小春。 Zhè shì Bái Xiǎochūn.
2. a. 那个人是医生。· 那個人是醫生。 Nàge rén shì yīshēng.
   b. 这是书。· 這是書。 Zhè shì shū.
3. a. 他姓唐。 Tā xìng Táng.
   b. 他姓周。 Tā xìng Zhōu.
   c. 他姓马。· 他姓馬。 Tā xìng Mǎ.
4. a. 他姓张。· 他姓張。 Tā xìng Zhāng.
   b. 他叫周明德。 Tā jiào Zhōu Míngdé.
5. (c)
6. (c)
7. 他**姓**周，**叫**周明德。 Tā **xìng** Zhōu, **jiào** Zhōu Míngdé.
8. 他**叫**王平。我**叫**他小王。 Tā **jiào** Wáng Píng. Wǒ **jiào** tā Xiǎo Wáng.
9. 她叫白美玲。 Tā jiào Bái Měilíng.
10. 中文老师不都是中国人。· 中文老師不都是中國人。
    Zhōngwén lǎoshī bù dōu shì Zhōngguó rén.

CHAPTER 7

Written Practice 7-1

1. 有一点矮 · 有一點矮 yǒu yīdiǎn ǎi a little short
2. 相当慢 · 相當慢 xiāngdāng màn rather slow
3. 比较难 · 比較難 bǐjiào nán relatively difficult
4. 非常聪明 · 非常聰明 fēicháng cōngming extremely smart
5. 真笨 zhēn bèn really stupid

Written Practice 7-2

1. His father's car is extremely big.
2. That article of clothing is too expensive.
3. Our schoolwork is getting harder and harder.
4. That movie is really interesting.

Written Practice 7-3

1. 我弟弟不用功。 Wǒ dìdi bù yònggōng.
2. 我弟弟没有本事。 Wǒ dìdi méi yǒu běnshi.
3. 我的弟弟不高。 Wǒ de dìdi bù gāo.
4. 我弟弟的衣服不贵。 · 我弟弟的衣服不貴。 Wǒ dìdi de yīfu bù guì.

Written Practice 7-4

1. Older sister has a lot of friends. (*lit.*, Older sister's friends are many.)
2. The library has quite a few books. (*lit.*, The library's books are not few in number.)
3. He has a lot of problems. (*lit.*, His problems are numerous.)
4. He doesn't have much experience. (*lit.*, His experience is too little.)

Written Practice 7-5

1. I very much want to dance with him.
   OR I want to dance with him very much.
2. I like to sing very much.
3. She loves her puppy a lot. OR She really loves her puppy.

Written Practice 7-6

1. 我不怕狗。 Wǒ bù pà gǒu.
2. 我不要一本字典。 Wǒ bù yào yī běn zìdiǎn.
3. 我不想请他们吃饭。 · 我不想請他們吃飯。
   Wǒ bù xiǎng qǐng tāmen chī fàn.

Written Practice 7-7

1. 我小的时候喜欢看电视。· 我小的時候喜歡看電視。

   Wǒ xiǎo de shíhou xǐhuan kàn diànshì.

2. 我以前不懂中文。

   Wǒ yǐqián bù dǒng Zhōngwén.

3. 他以前很喜欢吃甜的东西。· 他以前很喜歡吃甜的東西。

   Tā yǐqián hěn xǐhuan chī tián de dōngxi.

Written Practice 7-8

1. (a) OR (c)
2. (b)
3. (c)
4. (b)

QUIZ

1. 我的哥哥相当懒。· 我的哥哥相當懶。Wǒ de gēgē xiāngdāng lǎn.
2. 中文不太难。· 中文不太難。Zhōngwén bù tài nán.
3. 我的新的电脑非常快。· 我的新的電腦非常快。

   Wǒ de xīn de diànnǎo fēicháng kuài.

4. 我的女儿不很高。· 我的女兒不很高。Wǒ de nǚ'ér bù hěn gāo.
5. 那个学生聪明极了。· 那個學生聰明極了。

   Nàge xuésheng **cōngmingjíle**.

   That student is **extremely intelligent**.

6. 我很想看那个电影。· 我很想看那個電影。

   Wǒ hěn xiǎng kàn nàge diànyǐng.

7. 他不信我。Tā bù xìn wǒ.
8. (a) OR (c)
9. (b)
10. (a) OR (c)

CHAPTER 8

Written Practice 8-1

1. 我明天考中文。Wǒ míngtiān kǎo Zhōngwén.
2. 她喜欢画山水。· 她喜歡畫山水。Tā xǐhuan huà shānshuǐ.
3. 他们在图书馆看报。· 他們在圖書館看報。Tāmen zài túshūguǎn kàn bào.
4. 他跟朋友说法文。· 他跟朋友說法文。Tā gēn péngyou shuō Fǎwén.

Written Practice 8-2

1. 我经常跟朋友打球。· 我經常跟朋友打球。
   Wǒ jīngcháng gēn péngyou dǎ qiú.
2. 我经常看电影。· 我經常看電影。 Wǒ jīngcháng kàn diànyǐng.
3. 我每天都吃早饭。· 我每天都吃早飯。 Wǒ měitiān dōu chī zǎofàn.
4. 我每天都洗澡。 Wǒ měitiān dōu xǐ zǎo.

Written Practice 8-3

1. 我不跳舞。 Wǒ bù tiào wǔ.
2. 我不唱歌。 Wǒ bù chàng gē.
3. 我不画画儿。· 我不畫畫兒。 Wǒ bù huà huàr.
4. 我不学法国话。· 我不學法國話。
   Wǒ bù xué Fǎguó huà.
   OR 我不学法语。· 我不學法語。
   Wǒ bù xué Fǎyǔ.

Written Practice 8-4

1. 我想明天晚上去看电影。· 我想明天晚上去看電影。
   Wǒ xiǎng míngtiān wǎnshang qù kàn diànyǐng.
2. 我们下个星期放假。· 我們下個星期放假。
   Wǒmen xià gè xīngqī fàng jià.
3. 我将来会登上长城。· 我將來會登上長城。
   Wǒ jiānglái huì dēngshàng chángchéng.
4. 我九月去中国学习。· 我九月去中國學習。
   Wǒ jiǔyuè qù Zhōngguó xuéxí.

Written Practice 8-5

1. 我明天不去公园。· 我明天不去公園。
   Wǒ míngtiān bù qù gōngyuán.
2. 我这个周末不要回家。· 我這個週末不要回家。
   Wǒ zhège zhōumò bù yào huí jiā.
3. 我今年夏天不去中国。· 我今年夏天不去中國。
   Wǒ jīnnián xiàtiān bù qù Zhōngguó.
4. 我今天晚上不去图书馆学习。· 我今天晚上不去圖書館學習。
   Wǒ jīntiān wǎnshang bù qù túshūguǎn xuéxí.

Written Practice 8-6

1. 他们正在唱歌呢。· 他們正在唱歌呢。 Tāmen zhèngzài chàng gē ne.
2. 他们在吃晚饭呢。· 他們在吃晚飯呢。 Tāmen zài chī wǎnfàn ne.
3. 他们在做作业。· 他們在做作業。 Tāmen zài zuò zuòyè.

QUIZ

1. 他会写日文。· 他會寫日文。Tā huì xiě Rìwén. He can write Japanese.
2. 我们现在不要说英文。· 我們現在不要說英文。
   Wǒmen xiànzài bù yào shuō Yīngwén.
   We shouldn't speak English now.
3. 中国人喜欢打篮球吗？· 中國人喜歡打籃球嗎？
   Zhōngguórén xǐhuan dǎ lánqiú ma?
   Do Chinese people like to play basketball?
4. 我们每个星期都考试。· 我們每個星期都考試。
   Wǒmen měi gè xīngqī dōu kǎoshì.
5. 他每天晚上都看电视。· 他每天晚上都看電視。
   Tā měitiān wǎnshang dōu kàn diànshì.
6. 我夏天经常跟父亲母亲去旅游。· 我夏天經常跟父親母親去旅遊。
   Wǒ xiàtiān jīngcháng gēn fùqin mǔqin qù lǚyóu.
7. 我以后不喝咖啡了。· 我以後不喝咖啡了。Wǒ yǐhòu bù hē kāfēi le.
8. 学生在考试呢。· 學生在考試呢。Xuésheng zài kǎoshì ne.
9. 白老师正在画画儿。· 白老師正在畫畫兒。Bái lǎoshī zhèngzài huà huàr.
10. 他正在洗澡。Tā zhèngzài xǐ zǎo.

CHAPTER 9

Written Practice 9-1

1. 我已经看了那个电影。· 我已經看了那個電影。
   Wǒ yǐjing kàn le nàge diànyǐng.
2. 我已经买字典了。· 我已經買字典了。Wǒ yǐjing mǎi zìdiǎn le.
3. 我已经下课了。· 我已經下課了。Wǒ yǐjing xià kè le.
4. 我已经做作业了。· 我已經做作業了。Wǒ yǐjing zuò zuòyè le.

Written Practice 9-2

1. 我没看那个电影。· 我没看那個電影。Wǒ méi kàn nàge diànyǐng.
2. 我没买字典。· 我没買字典。Wǒ méi mǎi zìdiǎn.
3. 我没下课。· 我没下課。Wǒ méi xià kè.
4. 我没做作业。· 我没做作業。Wǒ méi zuò zuòyè.

Written Practice 9-3

1. 我还没看电视。· 我還没看電視。Wǒ hái méi kàn diànshì.
2. 我还没做作业。· 我還没做作業。Wǒ hái méi zuò zuòyè.
3. 我还没吃晚饭。· 我還没吃晚飯。Wǒ hái méi chī wǎnfàn.
4. 我还没睡觉。· 我還没睡覺。Wǒ hái méi shuì jiào.

Written Practice 9-4

1. 我吃过法国饭。· 我吃過法國飯。Wǒ chīguo Fǎguó fàn.
2. 我坐过飞机。· 我坐過飛機。Wǒ zuòguo fēijī.
3. 我唱过卡拉OK。· 我唱過卡拉OK。Wǒ chàngguo kǎlāOK.
4. 我用过筷子。· 我用過筷子。Wǒ yòngguo kuàizi.

Written Practice 9-5

1. 我没吃过法国饭。· 我没吃過法國飯。Wǒ méi chīguo Fǎguó fàn.
2. 我没坐过飞机。· 我没坐過飛機。Wǒ méi zuòguo fēijī.
3. 我没唱过卡拉OK。· 我没唱過卡拉OK。Wǒ méi chàngguo kǎlāOK.
4. 我没用过筷子。· 我没用過筷子。Wǒ méi yòngguo kuàizi.

QUIZ

1. 我弟弟吃了两碗饭。· 我弟弟吃了兩碗飯。
   Wǒ dìdi chī le liǎng wǎn fàn.
2. 王老师画画儿了。· 王老師畫畫兒了。Wáng lǎoshī huà huàr le.
3. 他的朋友买飞机票了。· 他的朋友買飛機票了。
   Tā de péngyou mǎi fēijī piào le.
4. 我还没做作业。· 我還没做作業。Wǒ hái méi zuò zuòyè.
5. 我已经洗澡了。· 我已經洗澡了。Wǒ yǐjing xǐ zǎo le.
6. 我已经考试了。· 我已經考試了。Wǒ yǐjing kǎo shì le.
7. 我已经坐过飞机。· 我已經坐過飛機。Wǒ yǐjing zuòguo fēijī.
8. 我已经吃过中国饭。· 我已經吃過中國飯。
   Wǒ yǐjing chīguo Zhōngguó fàn.
9. 我还没坐过飞机。· 我還没坐過飛機。Wǒ hái méi zuòguo fēijī.
10. 我还没吃过中国饭。· 我還没吃過中國飯。
    Wǒ hái méi chīguo Zhōngguó fàn.

CHAPTER 10

Written Practice 10-1

1. 不会。· 不會。Bù huì.
2. 不能。Bù néng.
3. 不可以。Bù kéyǐ.

Written Practice 10-2

1. (a)
2. (b)
3. (a) preferred. However, if the focus is on the physical challenges of speaking a foreign language, then 能 néng is possible.

Written Practice 10-3

1. 你不可以在图书馆说话。· 你不可以在圖書館說話。
   Nǐ bù kéyǐ zài túshūguǎn shuō huà.
2. 你不能在饭馆抽烟。· 你不能在飯館抽煙。
   Nǐ bù néng zài fànguǎn chōu yān.
3. 你不可以在宿舍做饭。· 你不可以在宿舍做飯。
   Nǐ bù kéyǐ zài sùshè zuò fàn.

QUIZ

1. (a) OR (b)
2. (c)
3. (a) if the focus is on knowing the lyrics and music OR (b) if the focus is on the physical skills involved in performing Beijing opera
4. (c)
5. (a)
6. 你不可以抽烟。· 你不可以抽煙。 Nǐ bù kéyǐ chōu yān.
7. 你不可以在图书馆吃饭。· 你不可以在圖書館吃飯。
   Nǐ bù kéyǐ zài túshūguǎn chī fàn.
8. 不可以。Bù kéyǐ.
9. 不会。· 不會。Bù huì.
10. 不能。Bù néng.

CHAPTER 11

Written Practice 11-1

1. 你应该每天写字。· 你應該每天寫字。Nǐ yīnggāi měitiān xiě zì.
2. 你应该注意发音。· 你應該注意發音。Nǐ yīnggāi zhùyì fāyīn.
3. 你应该练习生词。· 你應該練習生詞。Nǐ yīnggāi liànxí shēngcí.
4. 你应该跟你的朋友说中国话。· 你應該跟你的朋友說中國話。
   Nǐ yīnggāi gēn nǐ de péngyou shuō Zhōngguó huà.

Written Practice 11-2

The answers below use the word 得 *děi. However, any of the four expressions for* must, have to *that are listed on page 167 of the text, is acceptable in these answers.*

1. 你们得复习生词。· 你們得復習生詞。 Nǐmen děi fùxí shēngcí.
2. 你们得练习汉字。· 你們得練習漢字。 Nǐmen děi liànxí Hànzì.
3. 你们得做作业。· 你們得做作業。 Nǐmen děi zuò zuòyè.
4. 你们得听录音。· 你們得聽錄音。 Nǐmen děi tīng lùyīn.

Written Practice 11-3

1. 我们今天晚上听音乐，怎么样？· 我們今天晚上聽音樂，怎麼樣？
   Wǒmen jīntiān wǎnshang tīng yīnyuè, zěnmeyàng?
2. 你最好坐公共汽车。· 你最好坐公共汽車。
   Nǐ zuì hǎo zuò gōnggòngqìchē.
3. 我们去喝咖啡，好不好？· 我們去喝咖啡，好不好？
   Wǒmen qù hē kāfēi, hǎo bù hǎo?
4. 我们看电视，行不行？· 我們看電視，行不行？
   Wǒmen kàn diànshì, xíng bù xíng?
5. 你给我们唱歌，好吗？· 你給我們唱歌，好嗎？
   Nǐ gěi wǒmen chàng gē, hǎo ma?

Written Practice 11-4

1. 你不应该听音乐。· 你不應該聽音樂。 Nǐ bù yīnggāi tīng yīnyuè.
2. 你不应该看电视。· 你不應該看電視。 Nǐ bù yīnggāi kàn diànshì.
3. 你不应该跟朋友说话。· 你不應該跟朋友說話。
   Nǐ bù yīnggāi gēn péngyou shuō huà.

Written Practice 11-5

1. 不准在宿舍喝酒。 Bù zhǔn zài sùshè hē jiǔ.
2. 不要在教室睡觉。· 不要在教室睡覺。 Bù yào zài jiàoshì shuì jiào.
3. 别在图书馆用手机。· 別在圖書館用手機。 Bié zài túshūguǎn yòng shǒujī.

QUIZ

1. (c) 你不应该在宿舍抽烟。· 你不應該在宿舍抽煙。
   Nǐ bù yīnggāi zài sùshè chōu yān.
2. (d) 你不必请你的老师吃晚饭。· 你不必請你的老師吃晚飯。
   Nǐ bù bì qǐng nǐde lǎoshī chī wǎnfàn.
3. (b) 你得每天交作业。· 你得每天交作業。
   Nǐ děi měitiān jiāo zuòyè.

4. (f) 请你的老师吃晚饭吧。· 請你的老師吃晚飯吧。

Qǐng nǐ de lǎoshī chī wǎnfàn ba.

5. (e) 别在宿舍抽烟。· 別在宿舍抽煙。

Bié zài sùshè chōu yān.

6. (a) 你应该帮助你的弟弟做作业。· 你應該幫助你的弟弟做作業。

Nǐ yīnggāi bāngzhù nǐ de dìdi zuò zuòyè.

7. (b)

8. (c)

9. (a)

10. (b)

CHAPTER 12

Written Practice 12-1

1. 小李有电脑。· 小李有電腦。Xiǎo Lǐ yǒu diànnǎo.

2. 小李有手机。· 小李有手機。Xiǎo Lǐ yǒu shǒujī.

3. 小李有电视机。· 小李有電視機。Xiǎo Lǐ yǒu diànshìjī.

4. 小李有自行车。· 小李有自行車。Xiǎo Lǐ yǒu zìxíngchē.

Written Practice 12-2

1. 小李没有哥哥。Xiǎo Lǐ méi yǒu gēgē.

2. 小李没有车。· 小李没有車。Xiǎo Lǐ méi yǒu chē.

3. 小李没有钱。· 小李没有錢。Xiǎo Lǐ méi yǒu qián.

4. 小李没有朋友。Xiǎo Lǐ méi yǒu péngyou.

Written Practice 12-3

1. 我们的朋友·我們的朋友 wǒmen de péngyou

2. 你们的爸爸·你們的爸爸 nǐmen de bàba

3. 他们的宿舍·他們的宿舍 tāmen de sùshè

4. 小李的自行车·小李的自行車 Xiǎo Lǐ de zìxíngchē

Written Practice 12-4

1. 她的 tā de

2. 你的 nǐ de

3. 我妹妹的 wǒ mèimei de

4. 我们的·我們的 wǒmen de

QUIZ

1. a. their/theirs
   b. your/yours
   c. my father's
2. (c)
3. (a)
4. 他们的字典 · 他們的字典 tāmen de zìdiǎn
5. 哥哥的妹妹 gēgē de mèimei
6. 爸爸的女儿 · 爸爸的女兒 bàba de nǚ'ér
7. 我的老师有四十个学生。· 我的老師有四十個學生。
   Wǒ de lǎoshī yǒu sìshí gè xuésheng.
8. 张阿姨没有妹妹。· 張阿姨没有妹妹。Zhāng āyí méi yǒu mèimei.
9. 姐姐的笔 · 姐姐的筆 jiějie de bǐ
10. 老师的弟弟 · 老師的弟弟 lǎoshī de dìdi

CHAPTER 13

Written Practice 13-1

1. (c)
2. (a)
3. (d)
4. (b)

Written Practice 13-2

1. 非常贵的衣服 · 非常貴的衣服 fēicháng guì de yīfu
2. 很用功的学生 · 很用功的學生 hěn yònggōng de xuésheng OR
   挺用功的学生 · 挺用功的學生 tǐng yònggōng de xuésheng
3. 相当便宜的字典 · 相當便宜的字典 xiāngdāng piányi de zìdiǎn
4. 比较好的电影 · 比較好的電影 bǐjiào hǎo de diànyǐng

Written Practice 13-3

1. The interesting books are his. The uninteresting ones are mine.
   书 · 書 shū book
2. The smartest person is Little Bai. The dumbest one is me.
   人 rén person
3. The fastest car is his. The slowest one is mine.
   车 · 車 chē car

Written Practice 13-4

1. [we sang] 的 de songs
2. [I need] 的 de book
3. [he respects] 的 de person
4. [I fear] 的 de things
5. [we cooked] 的 de food

Written Practice 13-5

1. 我们唱的歌 · 我們唱的歌　wǒmen chàng de gē
2. 我需要的书 · 我需要的書　wǒ xūyào de shū
3. 他尊敬的人　tā zūnjìng de rén
4. 我怕的事情　wǒ pà de shìqing
5. 我们做的饭 · 我們做的飯　wǒmen zuò de fàn

Written Practice 13-6

1. 你买的飞机票 · 你買的飛機票　nǐ mǎi de fēijī piào
2. 我妹妹吃的糖　wǒ mèimei chī de táng
3. 我们喝的茶 · 我們喝的茶　wǒmen hē de chá
4. 你写的信 · 你寫的信　nǐ xiě de xìn
5. 你画的画儿 · 你畫的畫兒　nǐ huà de huàr

Written Practice 13-7

1. [I borrow] dictionary/dictionaries
2. [I buy] shoes
3. [he sings] song(s)
4. [she raises] cat(s)
5. [you listen to] music

Written Practice 13-8

1. two descriptions: [我妹妹的] [三个] 老师 · [我妹妹的] [三個] 老師
   [wǒ mèimei de] [sān gè] lǎoshī
2. two descriptions: [这两本] [很有意思的] 书 · [這兩本] [很有意思的] 書
   [zhè liǎng běn] [hěn yǒu yìsi de] shū
3. two descriptions: [他的] [新的] 电脑 · [他的] [新的] 電腦
   [tā de] [xīn de] diànnǎo
4. two descriptions: [张老师的] [很好的] 朋友 · [張老師的] [很好的] 朋友
   [Zhāng lǎoshī de] [hěn hǎo de] péngyou

QUIZ

1. 非常聪明的人 · 非常聰明的人 fēicháng cōngming de rén
   an extremely intelligent person
2. 非常贵的车 · 非常貴的車 fēicháng guì de chē
3. 挺容易的考试 · 挺容易的考試 tǐng róngyì de kǎoshì
4. 书 · 書 shū book
   This book is very interesting. That one is not interesting.
5. 不很贵的电影票 · 不很貴的電影票 bù hěn guì de diànyǐng piào
6. a. I like <u>teacher</u>
   b. we saw <u>movie</u>
   c. you bought <u>computer</u>
   d. you ate <u>Japanese food</u>
7. a. 我喜欢的老师 · 我喜歡的老師 wǒ xǐhuan de lǎoshī
   b. 我们看的电影 · 我們看的電影 wǒmen kàn de diànyǐng
   c. 你买的电脑 · 你買的電腦 nǐ mǎi de diànnǎo
   d. 你吃的日本菜 nǐ chī de Rìběn cài
8. a. 电脑 · 電腦 diànnǎo computer — the computer that you use
   b. 人 rén person — the person whom we know OR the person whom
      we met
   c. 故事 gùshi story — the story that you didn't understand
   d. 车 · 車 chē car — the car that you bought
9. 我借的书 · 我借的書 wǒ jiè de shū
10. 手机 · 手機 shǒujī cell phone — The cell phone that he bought is very
    expensive. (The one) that I bought is cheap.

CHAPTER 14

Written Practice 14-1

1. 你去过中国吗？· 你去過中國嗎？
   Nǐ qùguo Zhōngguó ma?
2. 你喜欢中国电影吗？· 你喜歡中國電影嗎？
   Nǐ xǐhuan Zhōngguó diànyǐng ma?
3. 你会用筷子吃饭吗？· 你會用筷子吃飯嗎？
   Nǐ huì yòng kuàizi chī fàn ma?
4. 你有一本中文字典吗？· 你有一本中文字典嗎？
   Nǐ yǒu yī běn Zhōngwén zìdiǎn ma?

Written Practice 14-2

1. 你要不要吃中国饭？ · 你要不要吃中國飯？
   Nǐ yào bù yào chī Zhōngguó fàn?
2. 你想不想看电影？ Nǐ xiǎng bù xiǎng kàn diànyǐng?
3. 飞机票贵不贵？ · 飛機票貴不貴？ Fēijī piào guì bù guì?
4. 你信不信他？ Nǐ xìn bù xìn tā?

Written Practice 14-3

1. 你喝不喝咖啡？ Nǐ hē bù hē kāfēi?
2. 你看不看电视？ · 你看不看電視？ Nǐ kàn bù kàn diànshì?
3. 你听不听音乐？ · 你聽不聽音樂？ Nǐ tīng bù tīng yīnyuè?
4. 你打不打篮球？ · 你打不打籃球？ Nǐ dǎ bù dǎ lánqiú?

Written Practice 14-4

1. 你 (昨天晚上) 做了作业没有？ · 你 (昨天晚上) 做了作業沒有？
   Nǐ (zuótiān wǎnshang) zuò le zuòyè méi yǒu?
2. 你 (昨天晚上) 看了电影没有？ · 你 (昨天晚上) 看了電影沒有？
   Nǐ (zuótiān wǎnshang) kàn le diànyǐng méi yǒu?
3. 你 (昨天晚上) 写信了没有？ · 你 (昨天晚上) 寫信了沒有？
   Nǐ (zuótiān wǎnshang) xiě xìn le méi yǒu?
4. 你 (昨天晚上) 用了电脑没有？ · 你 (昨天晚上) 用了電腦沒有？
   Nǐ (zuótiān wǎnshang) yòng le diànnǎo méi yǒu?

Written Practice 14-5

1. 不学。· 不學。Bù xué.
2. 不会。· 不會。Bù huì.
3. 不喜欢。· 不喜歡。Bù xǐhuan.
4. 没有。Méi yǒu. OR 没去过。· 沒去過。Méi qùguo.

Written Practice 14-6

1. 我不学中文。· 我不學中文。Wǒ bù xué Zhōngwén.
2. 我不会做中国饭。· 我不會做中國飯。Wǒ bù huì zuò Zhōngguó fàn.
3. 我不喜欢听音乐。· 我不喜歡聽音樂。Wǒ bù xǐhuan tīng yīnyuè.
4. 我没去过日本。· 我没去過日本。Wǒ méi qùguo Rìběn.

Written Practice 14-7

1. 我是学生。· 我是學生。Wǒ shì xuésheng.
2. 我认识那个老师。· 我認識那個老師。Wǒ rènshi nàge lǎoshī.
3. 你可以在这儿抽烟。· 你可以在這兒抽煙。Nǐ kěyǐ zài zhèr chōu yān.
4. 我喜欢跳舞。· 我喜歡跳舞。Wǒ xǐhuan tiào wǔ.
5. 我很忙。Wǒ hěn máng.

Written Practice 14-8

1. 你呢？ Nǐ ne?
2. 公共汽车票呢？ · 公共汽車票呢？ Gōnggòng qìchē piào ne?
3. 中国电影呢？ · 中國電影呢？ Zhōngguó diànyǐng ne?

QUIZ

1. 你喝不喝咖啡？ Nǐ hē bù hē kāfēi?
2. 你想不想看电影？ · 你想不想看電影？ Nǐ xiǎng bù xiǎng kàn diànyǐng?
3. 你看过那个电影没有？ · 你看過那個電影沒有？
   Nǐ kànguo nàge diànyǐng méi yǒu?
4. 你昨天看电视了吗？ · 你昨天看電視了嗎？ Nǐ zuótiān kàn diànshì le ma?
5. 你们已经考试了吗？ · 你們已經考試了嗎？ Nǐmen yǐjing kǎoshì le ma?
6. 你喜欢坐飞机吗？ · 你喜歡坐飛機嗎？ Nǐ xǐhuan zuò fēijī ma?
7. 没有。 Méi yǒu.
8. 喜欢。 · 喜歡。 Xǐhuan.
9. 历史呢？ · 歷史呢？ Lìshǐ ne?
10. 小张呢？ · 小張呢？ Xiǎo Zhāng ne?

CHAPTER 15

Written Practice 15-1

1. 我会说德国话。· 我會說德國話。 Wǒ huì shuō Déguó huà.
2. 那个人是我的老师。· 那個人是我的老師。 Nàge rén shì wǒ de lǎoshī.
3. 我喜欢吃日本菜。· 我喜歡吃日本菜。 Wǒ xǐhuan chī Rìběn cài.
4. 他跟他的女朋友说话。· 他跟他的女朋友說話。
   Tā gēn tā de nǚ péngyou shuō huà.
5. 他给我一张地图。· 他給我一張地圖。 Tā gěi wǒ yī zhāng dìtú.

Written Practice 15-2

1. 你在什么地方用电脑？ · 你在甚麼地方用電腦？
   Nǐ zài shénme dìfang yòng diànnǎo?
2. 你在哪儿看电视？ · 你在哪兒看電視？
   Nǐ zài nǎr kàn diànshì?
3. 你在哪里打球？ · 你在哪裏打球？
   Nǐ zài nǎli dǎ qiú?
4. 你在哪儿读书？ · 你在哪兒讀書？
   Nǐ zài nǎr dú shū?
5. 你在什么地方吃午饭？ · 你在甚麼地方吃午飯？
   Nǐ zài shénme dìfang chī wǔfàn?

Written Practice 15-3

1. 你有多少钱？· 你有多少錢？Nǐ yǒu duōshao qián?

2. 你昨天看了几个电影？· 你昨天看了幾個電影？
   Nǐ zuótiān kàn le jǐ gè diànyǐng?

3. 你买了几本书？· 你買了幾本書？Nǐ mǎi le jǐ běn shū?

4. 你想请几个朋友吃饭？· 你想請幾個朋友吃飯？
   Nǐ xiǎng qǐng jǐ gè péngyou chī fàn?

5. 你吃了多少饺子？· 你吃了多少餃子？Nǐ chī le duōshao jiǎozi?

QUIZ

1. 我们什么时候吃晚饭？· 我們甚麼時候吃晚飯？
   Wǒmen shénme shíhou chī wǎnfàn?
   OR 我们几点钟吃晚饭？· 我們幾點鐘吃晚飯？
   Wǒmen jǐdiǎn zhōng chī wǎnfàn?

2. 我们在哪儿吃晚饭？OR 我们在什么地方吃晚饭？·
   我們在哪兒吃晚飯？OR 我們在甚麼地方吃晚飯？
   Wǒmen zài nǎr chī wǎnfàn? OR Wǒmen zài shénme dìfang chī wǎnfàn?

3. 我们跟谁吃晚饭？· 我們跟誰吃晚飯？Wǒmen gēn shéi chī wǎnfàn?

4. 谁请我们吃晚饭？· 誰請我們吃晚飯？Shéi qǐng wǒmen chī wǎnfàn?

5. 电影什么时候开始？OR 电影几点钟开始？·
   電影甚麼時候開始？OR 電影幾點鐘開始？
   Diànyǐng shénme shíhou kāishǐ? OR Diànyǐng jǐdiǎn zhōng kāishǐ?

6. 电影院在哪儿？· 電影院在哪兒？Diànyǐngyuàn zài nǎr?

7. 电影票多少钱？· 電影票多少錢？Diànyǐng piào duōshao qián?

8. 怎么写？· 怎麼寫？Zěnme xiě?

9. 怎么做？· 怎麼做？Zěnme zuò?

10. 怎么念？· 怎麼念？Zěnme niàn?

CHAPTER 16

Written Practice 16-1

1. 那些人我都认识。· 那些人我都認識。
   Nàxiē rén wǒ dōu rènshi.

2. 那两本书我都已经看过了。· 那兩本書我都已經看過了。
   Nà liǎng běn shū wǒ dōu yǐjīng kànguo le.

3. 法国和西班牙我都去过。· 法國和西班牙我都去過。
   Fǎguó hé Xībānyá wǒ dōu qùguo.

4. 飞机跟船我都坐过。· 飛機跟船我都坐過。
   Fēijī gēn chuán wǒ dōu zuòguo.

Written Practice 16-2

1. 所有的学生都考试了。· 所有的學生都考試了。

   Suóyǒu de xuésheng dōu kǎo shì le.

2. 所有的学生都病了。· 所有的學生都病了。

   Suóyǒu de xuésheng dōu bìng le.

3. 所有的学生都学中文吗？· 所有的學生都學中文嗎？

   Suóyǒu de xuésheng dōu xué Zhōngwén ma?

4. 所有的孩子都喜欢看电视。· 所有的孩子都喜歡看電視。

   Suóyǒu de háizi dōu xǐhuan kàn diànshì.

Written Practice 16-3

1. 学生都不喜欢考试。· 學生都不喜歡考試。

   Xuésheng dōu bù xǐhuan kǎoshì.

2. 孩子都不喜欢睡觉。· 孩子都不喜歡睡覺。Háizi dōu bù xǐhuan shuì jiào.

3. 我们都没坐过飞机。· 我們都没坐過飛機。Wǒmen dōu méi zuòguo fēijī.

4. 他们都不怕狗。· 他們都不怕狗。Tāmen dōu bù pà gǒu.

Written Practice 16-4

1. 他一点咖啡都不喝。· 他一點咖啡都不喝。Tā yìdiǎn kāfēi dōu bù hē.

2. 他一点鱼都不吃。· 他一點魚都不吃。Tā yìdiǎn yú dōu bù chī.

3. 我一点电视都不看。· 我一點電視都不看。Wǒ yìdiǎn diànshì dōu bù kàn.

4. 她一点作业都没做。· 她一點作業都没做。Tā yìdiǎn zuòyè dōu méi zuò.

Written Practice 16-5

1. 学生不都喜欢考试。· 學生不都喜歡考試。

   Xuésheng bù dōu xǐhuan kǎoshì.

2. 孩子不都喜欢睡觉。· 孩子不都喜歡睡覺。Háizi bù dōu xǐhuan shuì jiào.

3. 我们不都学中文。· 我們不都學中文。Wǒmen bù dōu xué Zhōngwén.

4. 他们不都怕狗。· 他們不都怕狗。Tāmen bù dōu pà gǒu.

QUIZ

1. 车都太贵。· 車都太貴。Chē dōu tài guì.

2. 王老师的考试都不很难。· 王老師的考試都不很難。

   Wáng lǎoshī de kǎoshì dōu bù hěn nán.

3. 中国饭我不都喜欢。· 中國飯我不都喜歡。

   Zhōngguó fàn wǒ bù dōu xǐhuan.

4. 他写的书我都看过。· 他寫的書我都看過。Tā xiě de shū wǒ dōu kànguo.

5. 他写的书我都没看过。· 他寫的書我都没看過。

   Tā xiě de shū wǒ dōu méi kànguo.

6. 车不都太贵。· 車不都太貴。Chē bù dōu tài guì.

7. 我的朋友都会开车。· 我的朋友都會開車。

   Wǒ de péngyou dōu huì kāi chē.

8. 所有的菜都太辣。Suóyǒu de cài dōu tài là.

9. 所有的电影我都看过。· 所有的電影我都看過。

   Suóyǒu de diànyǐng wǒ dōu kànguo.

10. 所有的学生都去过长城。· 所有的學生都去過長城。

    Suóyǒu de xuésheng dōu qùguo chángchéng.

CHAPTER 17

Written Practice 17-1

1. 我的朋友都喜欢看电影。我也喜欢看电影。·

   我的朋友都喜歡看電影。我也喜歡看電影。

   Wǒ de péngyou dōu xǐhuan kàn diànyǐng. Wǒ yě xǐhuan kàn diànyǐng.

2. 我的朋友都有手机。我也有手机。· 我的朋友都有手機。我也有手機。

   Wǒ de péngyou dōu yǒu shǒujī. Wǒ yě yǒu shǒujī.

3. 我喜欢唱歌。我也喜欢跳舞。· 我喜歡唱歌。我也喜歡跳舞。

   Wǒ xǐhuan chàng gē. Wǒ yě xǐhuan tiào wǔ.

4. 我去过中国。我也去过日本。· 我去過中國。我也去過日本。

   Wǒ qùguo Zhōngguó. Wǒ yě qùguo Rìběn.

Written Practice 17-2

1. 我们吃了豆腐，还吃了青菜。· 我們吃了豆腐，還吃了青菜。

   Wǒmen chī le dòufu, hái chī le qīngcài.

2. 我想买鞋，还想买大衣。· 我想買鞋，還想買大衣。

   Wǒ xiǎng mǎi xié, hái xiǎng mǎi dàyī.

3. 我昨天晚上看了书还做了作业。· 我昨天晚上看了書還做了作業。

   Wǒ zuótiān wǎnshang kàn le shū hái zuò le zuòyè.

4. 他学中文。他还学日文。· 他學中文。他還學日文。

   Tā xué Zhōngwén. Tā hái xué Rìwén.

Written Practice 17-3

1. 这件衣服又便宜又好。· 這件衣服又便宜又好。

   Zhè jiàn yīfu yòu piányi yòu hǎo.

   This article of clothing is both cheap and good.

2. 今天的天气又冷又湿。· 今天的天氣又冷又濕。

   Jīntiān de tiānqì yòu lěng yòu shī.

   Today's weather is both cold and damp.

3. 你的鞋又脏又臭。· 你的鞋又髒又臭。

   Nǐ de xié yòu zāng yòu chòu.

   Your shoes are both dirty and smelly.

4. 那个人又聪明又用功。· 那個人又聰明又用功。

   Nàge rén yòu cōngming yòu yònggōng.

   That person is both smart and hardworking.

Written Practice 17-4

1. 他只喜欢打球。· 他只喜歡打球。Tā zhǐ xǐhuan dǎ qiú.

2. 他们就是小学生。· 他們就是小學生。Tāmen jiù shì xiǎoxuéshēng.

3. 我只会做美国饭。· 我只會做美國飯。Wǒ zhǐ huì zuò Měiguó fàn.

4. 我们就可以在家看电视。· 我們就可以在家看電視。

   Wǒmen jiù kéyǐ zài jiā kàn diànshì.

Written Practice 17-5

1. 我才吃一口。Wǒ cái chī yī kǒu.

2. 我才做一个菜。· 我才做一個菜。Wǒ cái zuò yī gè cài.

3. 我才看半个电影。· 我才看半個電影。Wǒ cái kàn bàn gè diànyǐng.

4. 我才写一个字。· 我才寫一個字。Wǒ cái xiě yī gè zì.

QUIZ

1. 她的男朋友又高又大。Tā de nán péngyou yòu gāo yòu dà.

2. 台北的地铁也很方便也很干净。· 臺北的地鐵也很方便也很乾淨。

   Táiběi de dìtiě yě hěn fāngbiàn yě hěn gānjìng.

3. 他们喜欢吃中餐，还喜欢吃西餐。· 他們喜歡吃中餐，還喜歡吃西餐。

   Tāmen xǐhuan chī Zhōngcān, hái xǐhuan chī xīcān.

4. 我的汽车又旧又破。· 我的汽車又舊又破。Wǒ de qìchē yòu jiù yòu pò.

5. 我喜欢喝红茶，也喜欢喝绿茶。· 我喜歡喝紅茶，也喜歡喝綠茶。

   Wǒ xǐhuan hē hóngchá, yě xǐhuan hē lǜchá.

6. 小王就看了四个电影。· 小王就看了四個電影。

   Xiǎo Wáng jiù kàn le sì gè diànyǐng.

7. 小王只买了六本书。· 小王只買了六本書。Xiǎo Wáng zhǐ mǎi le liù běn shū.

8. 小王才吃九个饺子。· 小王才吃九個餃子。Xiǎo Wáng cái chī jiǔ gè jiǎozi.

9. 只有小白能吃辣的。Zhǐ yǒu Xiǎo Bái néng chī là de.

   Only Little Bai is able to eat hot and spicy food.

10. 只有小白没睡觉。· 只有小白沒睡覺。Zhǐ yǒu Xiǎo Bái méi shuì jiào.

    Only Little Bai did not sleep.

CHAPTER 18

Written Practice 18-1

1. 图书馆在南边。· 圖書館在南邊。
   Túshūguǎn zài nánbian.
2. 我的宿舍在前头。· 我的宿舍在前頭。
   Wǒ de sùshè zài qiántou.
3. 加拿大在北边。· 加拿大在北邊。
   Jiānádà zài běibian.
4. 我的狗在外边。· 我的狗在外邊。
   Wǒ de gǒu zài wàibian.
5. 我的妹妹在里边。· 我的妹妹在裏邊。
   Wǒ de mèimei zài lǐbian.
6. 公园在西边。· 公園在西邊。
   Gōngyuán zài xībian.

Written Practice 18-2

1. 图书馆的里边 · 圖書館的裏邊
   túshūguǎn de lǐbian
2. 餐厅的旁边 · 餐廳的旁邊
   cāntīng de pángbiān
3. 公园的北边 · 公園的北邊
   gōngyuán de běibian
4. 书店的前边 · 書店的前邊
   shūdiàn de qiánbian
5. 学校的对面 · 學校的對面
   xuéxiào de duìmiàn
6. 你的右边 · 你的右邊
   nǐ de yòubian

Written Practice 18-3

1. 我的猫在房子的上头。· 我的猫在房子的上頭。
   Wǒ de māo zài fángzi de shàngtou.
2. 你的车在图书馆的后面。· 你的車在圖書館的後面。
   Nǐ de chē zài túshūguǎn de hòumian.
3. 图书馆在书店的南边。· 圖書館在書店的南邊。
   Túshūguǎn zài shūdiàn de nánbian.
4. 书店在宿舍的对面。· 書店在宿舍的對面。
   Shūdiàn zài sùshè de duìmiàn.
5. 我的电脑在宿舍的里头。· 我的電腦在宿舍的裏頭。
   Wǒ de diànnǎo zài sùshè de lǐtou.

Written Practice 18-4

1. 他们在门外。· 他們在門外。

   Tāmen zài mén wài.

2. 学生在图书馆里。· 學生在圖書館裏。

   Xuésheng zài túshūguǎn lǐ.

3. 你的猫在房子上。· 你的貓在房子上。

   Nǐ de māo zài fángzi shàng.

4. 他的书包在桌子下。· 他的書包在桌子下。

   Tā de shūbāo zài zhuōzi xià.

Written Practice 18-5

1. 在窗户的下边有一个床。· 在窗戶的下邊有一個床。

   Zài chuānghu de xiàbian yǒu yī gè chuáng.

2. 在床的前头有一张小桌子。· 在床的前頭有一張小桌子。

   Zài chuáng de qiántou yǒu yī zhāng xiǎo zhuōzi.

3. 在桌子的右边有两把椅子。· 在桌子的右邊有兩把椅子。

   Zài zhuōzi de yòubiān yǒu liǎng bǎ yǐzi.

4. 在桌子上有电话机。· 在桌子上有電話機。

   Zài zhuōzi shàng yǒu diànhuàjī.

5. 在椅子的中间有一个电视机。· 在椅子的中間有一個電視機。

   Zài yǐzi de zhōngjiān yǒu yī gè diànshìjī.

Written Practice 18-6

1. 我的朋友在公园打球。· 我的朋友在公園打球。

   Wǒ de péngyou zài gōngyuán dǎ qiú.

   My friends play ball in the park.

2. 他们在宿舍的前头唱歌。· 他們在宿舍的前頭唱歌。

   Tāmen zài sùshè de qiántou chàng gē.

   They sing in front of the dormitory.

3. 我们在书店的后边上课了。· 我們在書店的後邊上課了。

   Wǒmen zài shūdiàn de hòubian shàng kè le.

   We went to / had class behind the bookstore.

4. 他们在桌子上跳舞了。· 他們在桌子上跳舞了。

   Tāmen zài zhuōzi shàng tiào wǔ le.

   They danced on the table.

5. 他们在火车站的北边卖衣服。· 他們在火車站的北邊賣衣服。

   Tāmen zài huǒchēzhàn de běibiān mài yīfu.

   They sell clothing north of the train station.

Written Practice 18-7

1. the fruit on the table
2. the bicycle outside the library
3. the restaurant behind the bookstore
4. the university north of Beijing
5. the people inside the restaurant

Written Practice 18-8

1. 公园离大学有十公里。· 公園離大學有十公里。
   Gōngyuán lí dàxué yǒu shí gōnglǐ.
2. 飞机场离火车站有五英里。· 飛機場離火車站有五英里。
   Fēijīchǎng lí huǒchēzhàn yǒu wǔ yīnglǐ.
3. 宿舍离图书馆有一百米。· 宿舍離圖書館有一百米。
   Sùshè lí túshūguǎn yǒu yībǎi mǐ.
4. 书店离公共汽车站有三里路。· 書店離公共汽車站有三里路。
   Shūdiàn lí gōnggòng qìchēzhàn yǒu sān lǐlù.
5. 大学离书店有两公里。· 大學離書店有兩公里。
   Dàxué lí shūdiàn yǒu liǎng gōnglǐ.

Written Practice 18-9

1. 中国饭馆离这儿很近。· 中國飯館離這兒很近。
   Zhōngguó fànguǎn lí zhèr hěn jìn.
   The Chinese restaurant is very near here.
2. 大学离我家很远。· 大學離我家很遠。
   Dàxué lí wǒ jiā hěn yuǎn.
   The university is very far from my home.
3. 公园离大学很近。· 公園離大學很近。
   Gōngyuán lí dàxué hěn jìn.
   The park is very close to the university.
4. 公园离这里很远。· 公園離這裏很遠。
   Gōngyuán lí zhèli hěn yuǎn.
   The park is very far from here.
5. 宿舍离餐厅很近。· 宿舍離餐廳很近。
   Sùshè lí cāntīng hěn jìn.
   The dormitory is very close to the dining room.

Written Practice 18-10

1. 学生中心离图书馆有多远？·學生中心離圖書館有多遠？

   Xuésheng zhōngxīn lí túshūguǎn yǒu duō yuǎn?

2. 你家离大学有几英里？·你家離大學有幾英里？

   Nǐ jiā lí dàxué yǒu jǐ yīnglǐ?

3. 飞机场离这儿有多远？·飛機場離這兒有多遠？

   Fēijīchǎng lí zhèr yǒu duō yuǎn?

4. 公园离学校有几里路？·公園離學校有幾里路？

   Gōngyuán lí xuéxiào yǒu jǐ lǐ lù?

5. 餐厅离宿舍有多远？·餐廳離宿舍有多遠？

   Cāntīng lí sùshè yǒu duō yuǎn?

QUIZ

1. 我哥哥在图书馆的前头吃午饭。·我哥哥在圖書館的前頭吃午飯。

   Wǒ gēgē zài túshūguǎn de qiántou chī wǔfàn.

2. 他们在宿舍的北边打球。·他們在宿舍的北邊打球。

   Tāmen zài sùshè de běibiān dǎ qiú.

3. 我的宿舍在图书馆的旁边。·我的宿舍在圖書館的旁邊。

   Wǒ de sùshè zài túshūguǎn de pángbiān.

4. 公园在大学的西南边。·公園在大學的西南邊。

   Gōngyuán zài dàxué de xīnánbian.

5. 在大学的西边有一个好饭馆。·在大學的西邊有一個好飯館。

   Zài dàxué de xībian yǒu yī gè hǎo fànguǎn.

6. 在书店里有餐厅。·在書店裏有餐廳。

   Zài shūdiàn lǐ yǒu cāntīng.

7. a. 餐厅离学生中心远不远？·餐廳離學生中心遠不遠？

   Cāntīng lí xuésheng zhōngxīn yuǎn bù yuǎn?

   b. 书店离宿舍远不远？·書店離宿舍遠不遠？

   Shūdiàn lí sùshè yuǎn bù yuǎn?

   c. 宿舍离图书馆远吗？·宿舍離圖書館遠嗎？

   Sùshè lí túshūguǎn yuǎn ma?

8. a. 餐厅离学生中心有多远？·餐廳離學生中心有多遠？

   Cāntīng lí xuésheng zhōngxīn yǒu duō yuǎn?

   b. 书店离宿舍有几里路？·書店離宿舍有幾里路？

   Shūdiàn lí sùshè yǒu jǐ lǐ lù?

   c. 宿舍离图书馆有几公里？·宿舍離圖書館有幾公里？

   Sùshè lí túshūguǎn yǒu jǐ gōnglǐ?

9. a. 餐厅离学生中心很远。· 餐廳離學生中心很遠。
      Cāntīng lí xuésheng zhōngxīn hěn yuǎn.
   b. 书店离宿舍很远。· 書店離宿舍很遠。
      Shūdiàn lí sùshè hěn yuǎn.
   c. 宿舍离图书馆很远。· 宿舍離圖書館很遠。
      Sùshè lí túshūguǎn hěn yuǎn.
10. a. 餐厅离学生中心有四十五米。· 餐廳離學生中心有四十五米。
      Cāntīng lí xuésheng zhōngxīn yǒu sìshí wǔ mǐ.
   b. 书店离宿舍有一里路。· 書店離宿舍有一里路。
      Shūdiàn lí sùshè yǒu yī lǐ lù.
   c. 宿舍离图书馆有两公里。· 宿舍離圖書館有兩公里。
      Sùshè lí túshūguǎn yǒu liǎng gōnglǐ.

CHAPTER 19

Written Practice 19-1
   1. 2 hours
   2. 10 hours
   3. 1 minute
   4. 59 minutes

Written Practice 19-2
   1. 11:07
   2. 4:40
   3. 1:59
   4. 5:34

Written Practice 19-3
   1. 一点过二十五分·一點過二十五分 yī diǎn guò èrshí wǔ fēn
   2. 八点过十七分·八點過十七分 bā diǎn guò shíqī fēn
   3. 九点一刻·九點一刻 jiǔ diǎn yī kè
   4. 两点半·兩點半 liǎng diǎn bàn

Written Practice 19-4
   1. 八点差十分·八點差十分 bā diǎn chà shí fēn
   2. 三点差一刻·三點差一刻 sān diǎn chà yī kè
   3. 九点差二十五分·九點差二十五分 jiǔ diǎn chà èrshí wǔ fēn

Written Practice 19-5

1. 晚上六点三刻·晚上六點三刻 wǎnshang liù diǎn sān kè
2. 早晨八点钟·早晨八點鐘 zǎochen bā diǎn zhōng
3. 下午三点二十分·下午三點二十分 xiàwǔ sān diǎn èrshí fēn
4. 上午十点一刻·上午十點一刻 shàngwǔ shí diǎn yī kè

Written Practice 19-6

1. 这个·這個 zhège
2. 下个·下個 xià gè
3. 上个·上個 shàng gè
4. 星期天 xīngqītiān OR 星期日 xīngqīrì OR 礼拜天·禮拜天 lǐbàitiān
   OR 礼拜日·禮拜日 lǐbàirì

Written Practice 19-7

1. five months
2. May
3. 六个月·六個月 liù gè yuè
4. 七月 qīyuè
5. 九月 jiǔyuè
6. nine months

Written Practice 19-8

1. October 25
2. July 4
3. April 14
4. January 1
5. 十二月二十五号·十二月二十五號 shí'èryuè èrshí wǔ hào

Written Practice 19-9

1. This year is 2000.
2. 去年是一九九九年。Qùnián shì yī jiǔ jiǔ jiǔ nián.
3. 后年是二○○二年。·後年是二○○二年。 Hòunián shì èr líng líng èr nián.
4. 明年是二○○一年。Míngnián shì èr líng líng yī nián.
5. 前年是一九九八年。Qiánnián shì yī jiǔ jiǔ bā nián.

Written Practice 19-10

1. 一九五二年二月十六日 yī jiǔ wǔ èr nián èryuè shíliù rì
2. 一九六一年四月十四日 yī jiǔ liù yī nián sìyuè shísì rì
3. 二○○八年六月三十日 èr líng líng bā nián liùyuè sānshí rì

QUIZ

1. 五点过十八分 · 五點過十八分 wǔ diǎn guò shíbā fēn
2. 九点差二十分 · 九點差二十分 jiǔ diǎn chà èrshí fēn
   OR 差二十分九点 · 差二十分九點 chà èrshí fēn jiǔ diǎn
3. 十点半 · 十點半 shídiǎn bàn
4. 三十五个小时 · 三十五個小時 sānshíwǔ gè xiǎoshí 35 hours
5. 两个小时 · 兩個小時 liǎng gè xiǎoshí 2 hours
6. 今年是二〇〇八年。Jīnnián shì èr líng líng bā nián.
7. 二月有五个星期。 · 二月有五個星期。Éryuè yǒu wǔ gè xīngqī.
8. 前天是星期三。Qiántiān shì xīngqīsān.
9. 上个礼拜二是二月五号。 · 上個禮拜二是二月五號。
   Shàng gè lǐbài èr shi èryuè wǔ hào.
10. 下个月是三月。 · 下個月是三月。Xià gè yuè shì sānyuè.

CHAPTER 20

Written Practice 20-1

1. 小白说得很慢。 · 小白說得很慢。Xiǎo Bái shuō de hěn màn.
2. 小白吃得很快。Xiǎo Bái chī de hěn kuài.
3. 小白写得很清楚。 · 小白寫得很清楚。Xiǎo Bái xiě de hěn qīngchu.
4. 小白画得很好。 · 小白畫得很好。Xiǎo Bái huà de hěn hǎo.
5. 小白睡得很多。Xiǎo Bái shuì de hěn duō.

Written Practice 20-2

1. 小陈跑步跑得很慢。 · 小陳跑步跑得很慢。
   Xiǎo Chén pǎo bù pǎo de hěn màn.
2. 小陈唱歌唱得很好听。 · 小陳唱歌唱得很好聽。
   Xiǎo Chén chàng gē chàng de hěn hǎotīng.
3. 小陈跳舞跳得很好。 · 小陳跳舞跳得很好。
   Xiǎo Chén tiào wǔ tiào de hěn hǎo.
4. 小陈写汉字写得很快。 · 小陳寫漢字寫得很快。
   Xiǎo Chén xiě Hànzì xiě de hěn kuài.
5. 小陈打球打得很多。 · 小陳打球打得很多。
   Xiǎo Chén dǎ qiú dǎ de hěn duō.

Written Practice 20-3

1. 他开车开得慢吗？·他開車開得慢嗎？
   Tā kāi chē kāi de màn ma?
2. 你考试考得好吗？·你考試考得好嗎？
   Nǐ kǎo shì kǎo de hǎo ma?
3. 她喝咖啡喝得多不多？
   Tā hē kāfēi hē de duō bù duō?
4. 她睡觉睡得少吗？·她睡覺睡得少嗎？
   Tā shuì jiào shuì de shǎo ma?
5. 你跑步跑得快不快？
   Nǐ pǎo bù pǎo de kuài bù kuài?

Written Practice 20-4

1. 小张不停地听音乐。·小張不停地聽音樂。
   Xiǎo Zhāng bùtíng de tīng yīnyuè.
2. 小张认真地准备功课了。·小張認真地準備功課了。
   Xiǎo Zhāng rènzhēn de zhǔnbèi gōngkè le.
3. 小张偷偷地喝酒了。·小張偷偷地喝酒了。
   Xiǎo Zhāng tōutōu de hē jiǔ le.
4. 小张好好地做作业了。·小張好好地做作業了。
   Xiǎo Zhāng hǎohāo de zuò zuòyè le.
5. 小张不知不觉地睡觉了。·小張不知不覺地睡覺了。
   Xiǎo Zhāng bùzhī bùjué de shuì jiào le.

QUIZ

1. 她写汉字写得很美。·她寫漢字寫得很美。
   Tā xiě Hànzì xiě de hěn měi.
2. 他开车开得很慢。·他開車開得很慢。
   Tā kāi chē kāi de hěn màn.
3. 我弟弟吃饭吃得太快。·我弟弟吃飯吃得太快。
   Wǒ dìdi chī fàn chī de tài kuài.
4. 我做饭做得不好。·我做飯做得不好。
   Wǒ zuò fàn zuò de bù hǎo.
5. 我跑步跑得不快。 OR 我跑得很慢。
   Wǒ pǎo bù pǎo de bù kuài. OR Wǒ pǎo de hěn màn.
6. 我唱歌唱得不好听。·我唱歌唱得不好聽。
   Wǒ chàng gē chàng de bù hǎotīng.
7. 孩子快快地跑到公园去了。·孩子快快地跑到公園去了。
   Háizi kuàikuāi de pǎo dào gōngyuán qù le.

8. 小孩子说话说得很快。· 小孩子說話說得很快。

Xiǎo háizi shuō huà shuō de hěn kuài.

9. 他偷偷地给他的女朋友写信。· 他偷偷地給他的女朋友寫信。

Tā tōutōu de gěi tā de nǚ péngyou xiě xìn.

10. 她高高兴兴地看了男朋友的信。· 她高高興興地看了男朋友的信。

Tā gāogāoxìngxìng de kàn le nán péngyou de xìn.

CHAPTER 21

Written Practice 21-1

1. 小高比小王聪明。· 小高比小王聰明。

Xiǎo Gāo bǐ Xiǎo Wáng cōngming.

2. 小高比小王用功。

Xiǎo Gāo bǐ Xiǎo Wáng yònggōng.

3. 小高比小王高兴。· 小高比小王高興。

Xiǎo Gāo bǐ Xiǎo Wáng gāoxìng.

4. 小高比小王累。

Xiǎo Gāo bǐ Xiǎo Wáng lèi.

Written Practice 21-2

1. 小王比小高高一点。· 小王比小高高一點。

Xiǎo Wáng bǐ Xiǎo Gāo gāo yīdiǎn.

2. 小王比小高快一点。· 小王比小高快一點。

Xiǎo Wáng bǐ Xiǎo Gāo kuài yīdiǎn.

3. 小王比小高高兴一点。· 小王比小高高興一點。

Xiǎo Wáng bǐ Xiǎo Gāo gāoxìng yīdiǎn.

4. 小王比小高忙一点。· 小王比小高忙一點。

Xiǎo Wáng bǐ Xiǎo Gāo máng yīdiǎn.

Written Practice 21-3

1. 小李的朋友更多。

Xiǎo Lǐ de péngyou gèng duō.

2. 张老师的考试更难。· 張老師的考試更難。

Zhāng lǎoshī de kǎoshì gèng nán.

3. 小李更漂亮。

Xiǎo Lǐ gèng piàoliang.

4. 那本书更长。· 那本書更長。

Nà běn shū gèng cháng.

Written Practice 21-4

1. 他做意大利菜做得比做中国菜做得好。·
他做意大利菜做得比做中國菜做得好。
Tā zuò Yìdàlì cài zuò de bǐ zuò Zhōngguó cài zuò de hǎo.
Objects compared:
他意大利菜比中国菜做得好。·
他意大利菜比中國菜做得好。
Tā Yìdàlì cài bǐ Zhōngguó cài zuò de hǎo.

2. 她学中文学得比学日文学得多。·
她學中文學得比學日文學得多。
Tā xué Zhōngwén xué de bǐ xué Rìwén xué de duō.
Objects compared:
她中文比日文学得多。·
她中文比日文學得多。
Tā Zhōngwén bǐ Rìwén xué de duō.

3. 他吃饺子吃得比包饺子包得快。·
他吃餃子吃得比包餃子包得快。
Tā chī jiǎozi chī de bǐ bāo jiǎozi bāo de kuài.

4. 她喝可乐喝得比喝水喝得多。·
她喝可樂喝得比喝水喝得多。
Tā hē kělè hē de bǐ hē shuǐ hē de duō.
Objects compared:
她可乐比水喝得多。··
她可樂比水喝得多。
Tā kělè bǐ shuǐ hē de duō.

5. 她写字写得比说话说得慢。··
她寫字寫得比說話說得慢。
Tā xiě zì xiě de bǐ shuō huà shuō de màn.

Written Practice 21-5

1. 小高没有小王懒。· 小高没有小王懶。
Xiǎo Gāo méi yǒu Xiǎo Wáng lǎn.

2. 小高没有小王慢。
Xiǎo Gāo méi yǒu Xiǎo Wáng màn.

3. 小王没有小高矮。
Xiǎo Wáng méi yǒu Xiǎo Gāo ǎi.

4. 小王没有小高聪明。· 小王没有小高聰明。
Xiǎo Wáng méi yǒu Xiǎo Gāo cōngming.

Written Practice 21-6

1. 自行车没有公共汽车那么快。· 自行車沒有公共汽車那麼快。

   Zìxíngchē méi yǒu gōnggòng qìchē nàme kuài.

   Bicycles are not as fast as buses.

2. 小高没有小王那么用功。· 小高沒有小王那麼用功。

   Xiǎo Gāo méi yǒu Xiǎo Wáng nàme yònggōng.

   Little Gao is not as hardworking as Little Wang.

3. 那个电影没有这个电影这么有意思。·
   那個電影沒有這個電影這麼有意思。

   Nàge diànyǐng méi yǒu zhège diànyǐng zhème yǒu yìsi.

   That movie is not as interesting as this movie.

4. 茶没有咖啡那么贵。· 茶沒有咖啡那麼貴。

   Chá méi yǒu kāfēi nàme guì.

   Tea is not as expensive as coffee.

Written Practice 21-7

1. 她看中国电影没有看美国电影看得那么多。·
   她看中國電影沒有看美國電影看得那麼多。

   Tā kàn Zhōngguó diànyǐng méi yǒu kàn Měiguó diànyǐng kàn de nàme duō.

2. 他们吃中国饭吃得没有吃美国饭吃得那么多。·
   他們吃中國飯吃得沒有吃美國飯吃得那麼多。

   Tāmen chī Zhōngguó fàn chī de méi yǒu chī Měiguó fàn chī de nàme duō.

3. 他喝茶喝得没有喝咖啡喝得那么多。·
   他喝茶喝得沒有喝咖啡喝得那麼多。

   Tā hē chá hē de méi yǒu hē kāfēi hē de nàme duō.

4. 我看电视看得没有听音乐听得那么多。·
   我看電視看得沒有聽音樂聽得那麼多。

   Wǒ kàn diànshì kàn de méi yǒu tīng yīnyuè tīng de nàme duō.

5. 他说中文说得没有说英文说得那么快。·
   他說中文說得沒有說英文說得那麼快。

   Tā shuō Zhōngwén shuō de méi yǒu shuō Yīngwén shuō de nàme kuài.

Written Practice 21-8

1. 日本饭和中国饭不一样。· 日本飯和中國飯不一樣。

   Rìběn fàn hé Zhōngguó fàn bù yīyàng.

2. 棒球跟足球不一样。· 棒球跟足球不一樣。

   Bàngqiú gēn zúqiú bù yīyàng.

3. 北京和南京不一样。· 北京和南京不一樣。

   Běijīng hé Nánjīng bù yīyàng.

Written Practice 21-9

1. 杭州跟苏州一样漂亮。· 杭州跟蘇州一樣漂亮。

   Hángzhōu gēn Sūzhōu yīyàng piàoliang.

2. 这本字典跟那本字典一样贵。· 這本字典跟那本字典一樣貴。

   Zhè běn zìdiǎn gēn nà běn zìdiǎn yīyàng guì.

3. 我的弟弟和我的哥哥一样高。· 我的弟弟和我的哥哥一樣高。

   Wǒ de dìdi hé wǒ de gēge yīyàng gāo.

Written Practice 21-10

1. 王老师跟高老师差不多一样有名。·

   王老師跟高老師差不多一樣有名。

   Wáng lǎoshī gēn Gāo lǎoshī chàbuduō yīyàng yǒu míng.

2. 我的车和他的车差不多一样慢。·

   我的車和他的車差不多一樣慢。

   Wǒ de chē hé tā de chē chàbuduō yīyàng màn.

3. 公共汽车票跟地铁票差不多一样贵。·

   公共汽車票跟地鐵票差不多一樣貴。

   Gōnggòng qìchē piào gēn dìtiě piào chàbuduō yīyàng guì.

Written Practice 21-11

1. 小白唱得跟跳得一样好。· 小白唱得跟跳得一樣好。

   Xiǎo Bái chàng de gēn tiào de yīyàng hǎo.

2. 小白走得跟说得一样快。· 小白走得跟說得一樣快。

   Xiǎo Bái zǒu de gēn shuō de yīyàng kuài.

3. 小白吃得跟喝得一样多。· 小白吃得跟喝得一樣多。

   Xiǎo Bái chī de gēn hē de yīyàng duō.

4. 小白走得跟说得一样慢。· 小白走得跟說得一樣慢。

   Xiǎo Bái zǒu de gēn shuō de yīyàng màn.

5. 小白吃得跟喝得一样快。· 小白吃得跟喝得一樣快。

   Xiǎo Bái chī de gēn hē de yīyàng kuài.

Written Practice 21-12

1. 他做中国菜做得跟做意大利菜做得一样好。·

   他做中國菜做得跟做意大利菜做得一樣好。

   Tā zuò Zhōngguó cài zuò de gēn zuò Yìdàlì cài zuò de yīyàng hǎo.

2. 她读书读得跟做事做得一样用功。·

   她讀書讀得跟做事做得一樣用功。

   Tā dú shū dú de gēn zuò shì zuò de yīyàng yònggōng.

3. 她学中文学得跟学日文学得一样多。·
   她學中文學得跟學日文學得一樣多。
   Tā xué Zhōngwén xué de gēn xué Rìwén xué de yīyàng duō.

4. 小白跟他弟弟吃饭吃得一样多。·
   小白跟他弟弟吃飯吃得一樣多。
   Xiǎo Bái gēn tā dìdi chī fàn chī de yīyàng duō.

5. 小白跟他弟弟说中国话说得一样好。·
   小白跟他弟弟說中國話說得一樣好。
   Xiǎo Bái gēn tā dìdi shuō Zhōngguó huà shuō de yīyàng hǎo.

6. 小白跟他弟弟写汉字写得一样好看。·
   小白跟他弟弟寫漢字寫得一樣好看。
   Xiǎo Bái gēn tā dìdi xiě Hànzì xiě de yīyàng hǎokàn.

Written Practice 21-13

1. 中国菜跟意大利菜，他做得一样好。··
   中國菜跟意大利菜，他做得一樣好。
   Zhōngguó cài gēn Yìdàlì cài, tā zuò de yīyàng hǎo.

2. 中文跟日文，她学得一样多。··
   中文跟日文，她學得一樣多。
   Zhōngwén gēn Rìwén, tā xué de yīyàng duō.

3. 可乐跟水，她喝得一样多。·
   可樂跟水，她喝得一樣多。
   Kělè gēn shuǐ, tā hē de yīyàng duō.

4. 牛肉跟猪肉，他们卖得一样贵。·
   牛肉跟豬肉，他們賣得一樣貴。
   Niúròu gēn zhūròu, tāmen mài de yīyàng guì.

QUIZ

1. 昨天的考试没有今天的考试这么难。·
   昨天的考試沒有今天的考試這麼難。
   Zuótiān de kǎoshì méi yǒu jīntiān de kǎoshì zhème nán.
   Object: 考试·考試 kǎoshì test

2. (c)

3. (a)

4. (b)

5. 地铁票比公共汽车票贵得多。· 地鐵票比公共汽車票貴得多。
   Dìtiě piào bǐ gōnggòng qìchē piào guì de duō.

6. 王老师的书比张老师的书更多。· 王老師的書比張老師的書更多。
   Wáng lǎoshī de shū bǐ Zhāng lǎoshī de shū gèng duō.

7. 你的哥哥比我的哥哥高一点。· 你的哥哥比我的哥哥高一點。
   Nǐ de gēge bǐ wǒ de gēge gāo yīdiǎn.
8. 小王比小高用功得多。
   Xiǎo Wáng bǐ Xiǎo Gāo yònggōng de duō.
9. 小王跟小高差不多一样快。· 小王跟小高差不多一樣快。
   Xiǎo Wáng gēn Xiǎo Gāo chàbuduō yīyàng kuài.
10. 小高比小王聪明一点。· 小高比小王聰明一點。
    Xiǎo Gāo bǐ Xiǎo Wáng cōngming yīdiǎn.

FINAL EXAM

1. Subject: 中国人 · 中國人 Zhōngguó rén
   Verb: 说 · 說 shuō
2. 我每个周末在学生中心听音乐。· 我每個週末在學生中心聽音樂。
   Wǒ měi gè zhōumò zài xuésheng zhōngxīn tīng yīnyuè.
3. 我的朋友昨天晚上给我打电话了。· 我的朋友昨天晚上給我打電話了。
   Wǒ de péngyou zuótiān wǎnshang gěi wǒ dǎ diànhuà le.
4. a. Mǎ Jiāměi xiǎojie
   b. Ráo Xìngróng lǎoshī
5. a. Lín Xiǎoyīng yīshēng
   b. Zhāng Píng lǎoshī OR Zhāng Píng jiàoshòu
6. a. no 姐姐 jiějie
   b. 2 妹妹 mèimei
7. a. 3 brothers
   b. 2 sisters
8. a. 78
   b. 956
9. a. 四百一十三 sìbǎi yīshísān
   b. 两千(〇)二十 · 兩千(〇)二十 liǎng qiān (líng) èrshí
   c. 六万四千八百八十八 · 六萬四千八百八十八 liù wàn sì qiān bā bǎi bāshíbā
10. líng yāo yāo bā liù yāo líng qī èr èr liù bā sān bā jiǔ
    OR líng yī yī bā liù yī líng qī èr èr liù bā sān bā jiǔ
11. 九十万两千三百〇五 · 九十萬兩千三百〇五
    jiǔshí wàn liǎng qiān sān bǎi líng wǔ
    OR 九十万二千三百〇五 · 九十萬二千三百〇五
    jiǔshí wàn èr qiān sān bǎi líng wǔ
12. a. 第七 dì qī
    b. 第二十 dì èrshí

13. 他们… 你 · 他們… 你　Tāmen . . . nǐ

14. 飞机票都很贵。· 飛機票都很貴。
    Fēijī piào dōu hěn guì.

15. 王老师跟白老师都会说法国话。· 王老師跟白老師都會說法國話。
    Wáng lǎoshī gēn Bái lǎoshī dōu huì shuō Fǎguó huà.

16. 这四双鞋子 · 這四雙鞋子　zhè sì shuāng xiézi

17. 五本　wǔ běn

18. a. 他是我哥哥。　Tā shì wǒ gēge.
    b. 我的朋友是大学生。· 我的朋友是大學生。
       Wǒ de péngyou shì dàxuéshēng.

19. 那个学生不是中国人。· 那個學生不是中國人。
    Nàge xuésheng bù shì Zhōngguó rén.

20. a. 他们都不是老师。· 他們都不是老師。Tāmen dōu bù shì lǎoshī.
    b. 我们不都认识他。· 我們不都認識他。Wǒmen bù dōu rènshi tā.

21. 她是不是你的妹妹？　Tā shì bù shì nǐ de mèimei?

22. a. 你叫什么名字？· 你叫甚麼名字？　Nǐ jiào shénme míngzì?
    b. 我姓 (your family name) 叫 (your given name)。
       Wǒ xìng (your family name) jiào (your given name).

23. 你的鞋子太多。　Nǐ de xiézi tài duō.

24. 我不想睡觉。· 我不想睡覺。　Wǒ bù xiǎng shuì jiào.

25. a. 我不喜欢那双鞋子。· 我不喜歡那雙鞋子。
       Wǒ bù **xǐhuan** nà shuāng xiézi.
    b. 我不想买那双鞋子。· 我不想買那雙鞋子。
       Wǒ bù **xiǎng** mǎi nà shuāng xiézi.

26. a. 这个菜特别好吃。· 這個菜特別好吃。
       Zhège cài tèbié hǎo chī.
    b. 这双鞋子有一点贵。· 這雙鞋子有一點貴。
       Zhè shuāng xiézi yǒu yīdiǎn guì.

27. 他们会唱京剧。· 他們會唱京劇。
    Tāmen huì chàng **Jīngjù**. They can sing Beijing opera.

28. 我们吃烤鸭吧！· 我們吃烤鴨吧！
    Wǒmen chī **kǎoyā** ba! Let's eat roast duck!

29. 她每天晚上看小说。· 她每天晚上看小說。
    Tā měitiān wǎnshang kàn **xiǎoshuō**. She reads novels every night.

30. 我的朋友每个周末都打球。· 我的朋友每個週末都打球。
    Wǒ de péngyou měi gè zhōumò dōu dǎ qiú.

31. 今天晚上一定会下雪。· 今天晚上一定會下雪。
    Jīntiān wǎnshang yīdìng huì xià xuě.

32. 她在写着信呢。· 她在寫着信呢。
    Tā zài xiě zhe xìn ne.

33. a. 她在书店买书了。· 她在書店買書了。
    Tā zài shūdiàn mǎi shū le.
    b. 她在书店买了三本书。· 她在書店買了三本書。
    Tā zài shūdiàn mǎi le sān běn shū.
    c. 她在餐厅吃午饭了。·她在餐廳吃午飯了。
    Tā zài cāntīng chī wǔfàn le.

34. 我的同屋已经睡觉了。· 我的同屋已經睡覺了。
    Wǒ de tóngwū yǐjing shuì jiào le.

35. 我还没买课本呢。· 我還没買課本呢。
    Wǒ hái méi mǎi kèběn ne.

36. 我还没考试呢。· 我還没考試呢。
    Wǒ hái méi kǎoshì ne.

37. 我吃过中国饭可是我还没去过中国。·
    我吃過中國飯可是我還没去過中國。
    Wǒ chīguo Zhōngguo fàn kěshì wǒ hái méi qùguo Zhōngguo.

38. 你去过中国吗？· 你去過中國嗎？ Nǐ qùguo Zhōngguo ma?
    OR 你去过中国没有？· 你去過中國没有？ Nǐ qùguo Zhōngguo méi yǒu?

39. a. 我今天晚上可以去看电影吗？· 我今天晚上可以去看電影嗎？
    Wǒ jīntiān wǎnshang kěyǐ qù kàn diànyǐng ma?
    OR
    我今天晚上可以不可以去看电影？· 我今天晚上可以不可以去看電影？
    Wǒ jīntiān wǎnshang kěyǐ bù kěyǐ qù kàn diànyǐng?
    b. 不可以。Bù kěyǐ.

40. a. 你会写这个字吗？· 你會寫這個字嗎？
    Nǐ huì xiě zhège zì ma?
    OR
    你会不会写这个字？· 你會不會寫這個字？
    Nǐ huì bù huì xiě zhège zì?
    b. 会。· 會。Huì.

41. 你在图书馆不可以(吃饭 / 说话 / 打电话)。·
    你在圖書館不可以(吃飯 / 說話 / 打電話)。
    Nǐ zài túshūguǎn bù kěyǐ (chī fàn / shuō huà / dǎ diànhuà).

42. 你能不能帮助我做作业？· 你能不能幫助我做作業？
    Nǐ néng bù néng bāngzhù wǒ zuò zuòyè?

43. 你应该每天(都)给妈妈打电话。· 你應該每天(都)給媽媽打電話。
    Nǐ yīnggāi měitiān (dōu) gěi māma dǎ diànhuà.

44. 你得每天都上课。· 你得每天都上課。
    Nǐ děi měitiān dōu shàng kè.

45. 你不必每天都洗澡。Nǐ bù bì měitiān dōu xǐzǎo.

46. 你不应该抽烟。· 你不應該抽煙。
    Nǐ bù yīnggāi chōu yān.

47. 你最好别跟同学喝啤酒。· 你最好別跟同學喝啤酒。
    Nǐ zuì hǎo bié gēn tóngxué hē píjiǔ.

48. a. 丽丽有本子和书包。· 麗麗有本子和書包。
       Lìlì yǒu běnzi hé shūbāo.
    b. 丽丽没有电脑和手机。· 麗麗沒有電腦和手機。
       Lìlì méi yǒu diànnǎo hé shǒujī.

49. This pair of shoes is my sister's.

50. 我同屋的手机 · 我同屋的手機
    wǒ tóngwū de shǒujī

51. 你哥哥是我姐姐的同学。· 你哥哥是我姐姐的同學。
    Nǐ gēge shì wǒ jiějie de tóngxué.

52. 那个书包不是我的。· 那個書包不是我的。
    Nàge shūbāo bù shì wǒ de.

53. a. 她今天穿 tā jīntiān chuān
    b. 我昨天看 wǒ zuótiān kàn

54. a. 挺有意思的书 · 挺有意思的書 tǐng yǒu yìsi de shū
       OR 很有意思的书 · 很有意思的書 hěn yǒu yìsi de shū
       a very interesting book
    b. 特别难的考试 · 特別難的考試 tèbié nán de kǎoshì
       an especially difficult test

55. 哥哥 gēge
    Your older brother is very tall. Mine is not tall.

56. 没有意思的电影 · 沒有意思的電影 méi yǒu yìsi de diànyǐng

57. 老师拍的照片 · 老師拍的照片 lǎoshī pāi de zhàopiàn

58. 你喜欢跳舞吗？· 你喜歡跳舞嗎？ Nǐ xǐhuan tiào wǔ ma?

59. 你会不会说日本话？· 你會不會說日本話？ Nǐ huì bù huì shuō Rìběn huà?

60. 我学中文，你呢？· 我學中文，你呢？ Wǒ xué Zhōngwén, nǐ ne?

61. 她有没有男朋友？ Tā yǒu méi yǒu nán péngyou?

62. 想。Xiǎng.

63. 谁跟你一起去吃晚饭？· 誰跟你一起去吃晚飯？
    Shéi gēn nǐ yīqǐ qù chī wǎnfàn?

64. 你们在哪儿看电视？· 你們在哪兒看電視？ Nǐmen zài nǎr kàn diànshì?

65. 你昨天买什么了？· 你昨天買甚麼了？ Nǐ zuótiān mǎi shénme le?

66. 你觉得哪件衣服最好看？· 你覺得哪件衣服最好看？
Nǐ juéde nǎ jiàn yīfu zuì hǎokàn?

67. 我们几点钟考试？· 我們幾點鐘考試？ Wǒmen jǐdiǎn zhōng kǎo shì?

68. 我的朋友都很喜欢唱卡拉 OK。· 我的朋友都很喜歡唱卡拉 OK.
Wǒ de péngyou dōu hěn xǐhuan chàng kǎlāOK.

69. 他每天都给他的女朋友打电话。· 他每天都給他的女朋友打電話。
Tā měitiān dōu gěi tā de nǚ péngyou dǎ diànhuà.

70. 所有的美国人都会开车吗？· 所有的美國人都會開車嗎？
Suǒyǒu de Měiguó rén dōu huì kāi chē ma?

71. 他们都不会说英文。· 他們都不會說英文。
Tāmen dōu bù huì shuō Yīngwén.

72. 她一点 (中文) 都不会 (说)。· 她一點 (中文) 都不會 (說)。
Tā yīdiǎn (Zhōngwén) dōu bù huì (shuō).

73. 我姐姐去过中国，(也 / 还) 去过越南。·
我姐姐去過中國，(也 / 還) 去過越南。
Wǒ jiějie qùguo Zhōngguó, (yě/hái) qùguo Yuènán.

74. 我弟弟 (和 / 跟) 妹妹都是高中生。
Wǒ dìdi (hé/gēn) mèimei dōu shì gāozhōng shēng.

75. 我买了一双新的鞋子，(也·还) 买了一件新的大衣。··
我買了一雙新的鞋子，(也·還) 買了一件新的大衣。
Wǒ mǎi le yī shuāng xīn de xiézi, (yě/hái) mǎi le yī jiàn xīn de dàyī.

76. 鞋子又漂亮又便宜。Xiézi yòu piàoliang yòu piányi.

77. 我弟弟只会唱中国歌。· 我弟弟只會唱中國歌。
Wǒ dìdi zhǐ huì chàng Zhōngguó gē.

78. 火车站在银行的东边。(右边) · 火車站在銀行的東邊。(右邊)
Huǒchēzhàn zài yínháng de dōngbian. (yòubian)

79. 书店在西南边。(在银行的南边) · 書店在西南邊。(在銀行的南邊)
Shūdiàn zài xīnánbian. (zài yínháng de nánbian)

80. 电影院在医院的北边。· 電影院在醫院的北邊。
Diànyǐngyuàn zài yīyuàn de běibian.

81. 学生在公园里打球。· 學生在公園裏打球。
Xuésheng zài gōngyuán lǐ dǎ qiú.

82. 学校的东边有 (一个) 饭馆。· 學校的東邊有 (一個) 飯館。
Xuéxiào de dōngbian yǒu (yī gè) fànguǎn.

83. 火车站离书店远吗？· 火車站離書店遠嗎？
Huǒchēzhàn lí shūdiàn yuǎn ma?
OR 火车站离书店远不远？· 火車站離書店遠不遠？
Huǒchēzhàn lí shūdiàn yuǎn bù yuǎn?

84. 学校离医院只有一里路。·學校離醫院只有一里路。
   Xuéxiào lí yīyuàn zhǐ yǒu yī lǐ lù.

85. 12:05

86. Next month is November.

87. 二〇一四年九月二十九日　èr líng yī sì nián jiǔyuè èrshíjiǔ rì

88. 明天晚上八点半钟·明天晚上八點半鐘
   míngtiān wǎnshang bādiǎn bàn zhōng

89. 我的同屋唱歌唱得很好。
   Wǒ de tóngwū chàng gē chàng de hěn hǎo.

90. 别开车开得太快。·別開車開得太快。
   Bié kāi chē kāi de tài kuài.

91. 我写得不好。· 我寫得不好。
   Wǒ xiě de bù hǎo.
   OR 我写汉字写得不好。·我寫漢字寫得不好。
   Wǒ xiě Hànzì xiě de bù hǎo.

92. 你睡觉睡得多不多？·你睡覺睡得多不多？ Nǐ shuì jiào shuì de duō bù duō?
   OR 你睡觉睡得多吗？·你睡覺睡得多嗎？ Nǐ shuì jiào shuì de duō ma?

93. 我无意地拿了我同屋的课本。· 我無意地拿了我同屋的課本。
   Wǒ wúyì de ná le wǒ tóngwū de kèběn.

94. 他们唱歌唱得跟跳舞跳得一样好。··
   他們唱歌唱得跟跳舞跳得一樣好。
   Tāmen chàng gē chàng de gēn tiào wǔ tiào de yīyàng hǎo.

95. 她喝可乐喝得跟喝水喝得一样多。··
   她喝可樂喝得跟喝水喝得一樣多。
   Tā hē kělè hē de gēn hē shuǐ hē de yīyàng duō.
   OR
   她可乐跟水喝得一样多。· 她可樂跟水喝得一樣多。
   Tā kělè gēn shuǐ hē de yīyàng duō.

96. 小白比我考试考得好一点。· 小白比我考試考得好一點。
   Xiǎo Bái bǐ wǒ kǎo shì kǎo de hǎo yīdiǎn.

97. 我没有他用电脑用得那么多。· 我沒有他用電腦用得那麼多。
   Wǒ méi yǒu tā yòng diànnǎo yòng de nàme duō.

98. 你没有小白吃饺子吃得那么多。· 你沒有小白吃餃子吃得那麼多。
   Nǐ méi yǒu Xiǎo Bái chī jiǎozi chī de nàme duō.

99. 她比她弟弟跳舞跳得好得多。
   Tā bǐ tā dìdi tiào wǔ tiào de hǎo de duō.

100. 我没有她做饭做得这么好吃。· 我沒有她做飯做得這麼好吃。
   Wǒ méi yǒu tā zuò fàn zuò de zhème hǎo chī.

INDEX

used to negate kéyǐ 可以, 154–55, 161, 217

used to negate modal verbs, 154–55, 217, 221

used to negate néng 能, 154–55, 161, 217

used to negate obligation verbs, 169

used to negate shì 是, 85, 88, 89–90, 133, 217

used to negate stative verbs, 115

used to negate xìng 姓, 93

used to negate yào 要, 133

used to negate yīyàng 一样·一樣, 352

Characters. *See* Mandarin Chinese, characters

Chinese (language). *See* Mandarin Chinese

Chinese names. *See* Names

Classifiers

    defined, 23

    gè 个·個, as a general classifier, 69–70

    indicating the number of nouns, 68–73

    rules of, 69

    used with specifiers, 74–75

Clauses

    defined, 25

    used to describe nouns, 199–208

Commands, 173

Comparisons, 338–59

    less than, expressed with méi yǒu 没有, 345–49

    more than, expressed with bǐ 比, 338–44

    the same as, expressed with yīyàng 一样·一樣, 350–59

    use of zhème 这么·這麼 and nàme 那么·那麼 in, 346–47

Compass direction words, 276–77, 286

Conjunctions, defined, 22. *See also* And

Connecting words, defined, 22

Consonants, 5, 8–9

Content questions. *See* Questions, content questions

Contour tones, 5–7

Dates

    complete, 319

    of the month, 313, 315

Days

    counting, 312

    parts of, 307

    of the week, 309–10

de 的

    used in description clauses, 201–2, 203–5, 206–7, 209

    used to express possession, 185–87, 188–89

    used with adjectival verbs to describe actions, 324–28, 331–34

    used with adjectival verbs to describe nouns, 194–98

Demonstratives, defined, 23. *See also* nà/nèi 那; zhè/zhèi 这·這

Description clauses, 199–209

Direct objects. *See also* Objects

    with actions that have duration, 125

    defined, 25

Distance, 289–94

    units of distance, 289

dōu 都 *all/both,* 66–67, 84, 85, 86–88, 249, 250–51

    location of, in a sentence, 248

    negated, 251–55

duō 多 *many, a lot,* 111–13

Duration

    expressed with action verbs, 124, 125

    position of duration phrases in a sentence, 31

Every, emphasized with suóyǒu de 所有的, 250–51

Family names. *See* Names, family

Future actions, 130–33

gè 个·個, as a general classifier, 69–70

gēn 跟

    linking nouns and pronouns, 63–65

    as a preposition, 64

Greetings, 98

guo 过·過

    used to express past actions, 147–48, 149

    used with le 了, 150, 225

    used with méi yǒu 没有, 219

Guoyu, 4